Karina Machado was born in Urug... her parents emigrated to Sydney. She grew up hearing stories of her mum's psychic gift, which ignited a life-long curiosity about life after death (and other mysteries). Passionate about books and writing since she taught herself to read Golden Books, Karina always knew she had to 'work with words', and after graduating from the University of New South Wales with an English major in 1994, she began her career in journalism as an editorial assistant at *TIME* magazine. Today, she's a senior editor at *WHO* magazine and the author of *Spirit Sisters* (2009), *Where Spirits Dwell* (2011), and, now, *Love Never Dies*. She lives in Sydney's Sutherland Shire with her husband and two children.

Keep in touch with Karina online at karinamachado.com or on Facebook and Twitter.

Also by Karina Machado

Spirit Sisters
Where Spirits Dwell

KARINA MACHADO

Love never dies

True Australian stories
of after-death contact

MACMILLAN
Pan Macmillan Australia

First published 2014 in Macmillan by Pan Macmillan Australia Pty Ltd
1 Market Street, Sydney, New South Wales, Australia, 2000

Cataloguing-in-Publication entry is available
from the National Library of Australia
http://catalogue.nla.gov.au

Typeset in 12/16 pt Adobe Caslon by Midland Typesetters, Australia
Printed by McPherson's Printing Group

For my husband and children
And in memory of Nicola, whose light shines on

Table of Contents

'Unable are the loved to die. For love is immortality.'
—Emily Dickinson

'Love is strong as death.'
—Song of Solomon 8:6

Author's Note

This book would not have been possible without the generosity of my interviewees, who were prepared to share their highly personal experiences of love and deepest loss. I'm honoured and grateful that they've placed their trust in me. I'm hopeful that the following accounts justify their efforts. Some names and identifying features have been changed.

Introduction

I used to be so scared of dying. My terror took hold in childhood, when I learned that the sun would one day consume the earth, and nothing could prevent it. I'd lie in my little bunk bed at night and try to imagine this world void of life, closing my eyes tight against its unknowable breadth. Only one thing gave me comfort: stories of life after death – of ghosts and wonders and mysteries all around. Buoyed by hope, I flew from fear on the wings of these stories.

All these years later, I've arrived here, to tell hope-filled stories of my own – stories of people who've sensed the spirit of a person they've loved and lost. This is a book about the indestructibility of love.

Some readers will know that it is my third book on the subject of life after death. Yet it was writing about *love* after death as part of my research for previous books that paved the way for the one you're reading today. The stories I gathered for *Spirit Sisters*, and its sequel, *Where Spirits Dwell*, changed my life. Slowly, I was awakened to mysteries that abound, in suburbia as in the bush, to the extraordinary events experienced

1

by ordinary people from every walk of life, to the mind-bending gamut of phenomena. While some stories were heart-stopping, goosebump-raising chillers, others made my pulse quicken for reasons that were the very opposite of fear.

I learned that some people are haunted by love.

And those were the stories that most haunted me.

It's always an honour and a privilege when I'm gifted a tale, but it was the mothers' profound stories of loss – and defiant hope – that would not leave me. After meeting these courageous women, I was a different person. One who held her children a little tighter, a little longer; one who found it easier to forgive trifles, to appreciate the goodness in people and to open her heart wider. These were powerful experiences, not only for the women who shared their stories – and in some cases, spirit communication was the only thing that kept a mother from wanting to join her child – but also for the reader, who could take away the bare truth at the heart of each encounter: love, as our late loved ones would have us know, never dies.

That radiant idea, as small as three words, as vast as the sky, inspired this book. Every page, I hope, is a testament to its miraculous power, and to the courage of the 60 or so people from all over Australia who shared their life-changing – sometimes lifesaving – experiences with me: strong as trees, they stand tall in the wake of deepest loss, keen to honour their cherished dead with a tale of love mightier than death. Mired in grief, they struggled to cope in a world emptied of warmth and light. For them, the earth had consumed their sun. Yet, in experiencing the presence of their loved one, each found solace and the path to healing. Children, partners, siblings, parents, friends and extended family, all reaching out to brush away the tears of those left behind with assurances of eternal love.

As you'll go on to read, these assurances arrive in many ways. A teenage boy appears to his sister on the eve of his funeral, urging her to take care of their mother; in a dream more vivid than life, a young husband returns to his widow in time to prevent another tragedy; a grandmother lovingly settles her lonely daughter's babies; with a cheeky grin, a son shows himself to his mother as she weeps in her kitchen; a gentle artist who fled life sends his sister exquisite green feathers wherever she goes; a man soothes his broken-hearted brother with an other-worldly embrace . . .

For the receivers of these gifts, these were moments to make them smile through their tears. With eyes smarting and skin tingling, I listened to their stories, marvelling time and again at the healing force of these encounters, at how often they gave way to a feeling of renewal, of darkness lifting – of hope returning.

In the chapters that follow, stories are grouped by the common message or reason for the communication. For instance, in Chapter One, 'A Time to Heal', the messages all offer solace to the bereaved. In Chapter Five, 'Watching Over Us', deceased loved ones return exactly when we need them most, each story suggesting that though they're gone from our sides, the departed who'd cared for us in life still do so in death, just as they continue to want to help out during challenging times.

Chapter Seven, 'Family is Forever', honours familial bonds, where love flows like a river through multiple generations. Over and over, I was astounded to hear of the vital role long-gone family members, even those we've never met, continue to play in our modern lives. Stories from my own family have always played a key part in my life – since childhood, they've fed my passion for the unknown and inspired my work. Many years ago, my mother told me of an experience that planted the seed of my fascination for the kinds of stories that fill this book. I'd like to share it with you here.

*

One humid and tear-streaked day in the sunset of 1973, my parents boarded a ferry from Montevideo to Buenos Aires, the first leg of their journey towards new lives in Australia. At the edge of the River Plate, my mother imprinted the city of her birth, its skyline an unfinished poem, onto her dark and solemn eyes. Armed only with one suitcase and a two-year-old me, they were on their way to a country which promised them the world.

Dizzy from the churn of the khaki waters and the mingled perfumes of the crowd who pressed kisses on her cheeks and prattled advice and blessings, my mother spotted him among the crowd, spotlit by his height. His hands were slung deep inside his pockets and a black sweater fell across his shoulders. His eyes were pinned on the turgid river, which seemed to have already begun its dirty work of separation. Excitement thrummed in the brackish air, but fear and sorrow, too. My mother will never forget my paternal grandmother squeezing me hard against her chest, howling into my hair.

My mum kept still and silent, until, as if awakening from a spell, she rushed to him, her closest cousin, Roberto, and threw her arms around his neck. *'Hasta que te vea de nuevo, Roberto!'* Until we meet again! She wore her new high-heeled sandals but still he towered over her. She leaned her head against his chest, breathed in his smell of home and wept.

Of the huge and tangled family she was leaving behind, Roberto was her shadow, closer even than her two brothers. An only child with delicate skin and the whitest teeth, he was

4

usually shy but when he laughed, adorable dimples bloomed. They grew up together, always together – my mum and Roberto, surrounded by the most expensive toys, parents who fawned over him, the best teachers their hard-earned money could buy. In turn, his cousin introduced him to her three scrawny dogs and her boundless imagination, which could turn yesterday's stale bread into the most scrumptious filet mignon. Sitting side by side in the dirt, though Roberto invariably stained his crisply ironed white shirt, Mum told him about her astral travels, and the family she'd left behind in her past life. Between them, they turned the pages of last Sunday's newspaper, as Mum taught him to read, succeeding where private school teachers could not. Afterward, as a reward, they'd pore over the obituaries, marvelling, in that morbid way of children, at any familiar names.

Sometimes they'd scamper hand in hand through their grandfather's vegetable patch scented of parsley and oregano, or naughtily trample his purple geraniums. Roberto let her drive his red 'Maserati' (he was the only kid in the whole neighbourhood with his own toy car) and invited her to his spotless home where they'd sip hot chocolate from fine china mugs and share morning tea of orange cake served upon starched napkins. In less elegant moments, my mum, Silvia, who'd long ago read the melancholy in her cousin's DNA and shielded his soft core from bullies and hardships accordingly, fearlessly defended Roberto in scraps. Then she'd dust herself off and march home, nests of her black hair lost in battle drifting like tumbleweed in her wake.

At the port, he held her tightly as they relived, wordlessly, a lifetime spent side by side. Minutes later, the ferry lifted anchor and we were gone. What my mother could not have known on that vintage December day was that in years to come, it would be Roberto's turn to say goodbye, and that when that day came, he would find his way to her.

Researching this book, I was struck for the first time by the similarities between the journey taken by spirits we've loved and lost, and the act of leaving everything behind and beginning again in an unknown place, as my family and so many others have done. 'Death is like immigration,' Ban Guo, whose story of connecting with his father's spirit appears in Chapter Three, told me during our interview. 'You move to a new home, but you don't forget the old place and the old people.' Ban's analogy shone in its simplicity. Our loved ones, he reassured me, will love us forever, and not even death can stop them from letting us know it.

Years passed, Roberto married and had children, and in our new home in Sydney, my mother gave birth to my sister, who lamented missing her home in the womb the moment she found her voice. Meanwhile, my homesick mum penned Roberto letters, which she always signed, 'Your cousin, who loves you'. In one, she described how in immigrating she'd lost much more than she'd gained, how the dreams she'd carried across the seas had never manifested, how sometimes she didn't know if she was woman or ghost.

And so time turned, arriving at last at one September morning in the mid-1990s. My mother awoke on her side of the bed, the other side long since cold, her pillow drenched in tears. She sat up, still sobbing, and recalled an extraordinarily vivid dream. In it, Roberto held her tight, and emotions – despair, the joy of a reunion and all-encompassing love – swirled around the pair, as palpable as the warm, solid and familiar figure who held her.

Once again, she'd rested her head against his chest, felt the scratchy weave of his favourite black pullover, breathed in the tang of a Montevideo summer. Once again, they were children, running amuck through the herb garden in a giggly game of chase. 'Don't leave! Don't you leave!' she pleaded with him, knowing instinctively, in that magical language of dreams, that this was a final farewell.

'No,' he replied gently. 'I have to go now.'

She looked up to offer a last kiss on his cheek, but found a black abyss where his face should have been. Then he turned and walked away, his tall form fading to nothing.

Afterward, as tears as heavy as pearls slid down her face, she reasoned she'd been neither awake nor asleep during the experience, which had left her deeply unsettled. A few hours later, feeling calmer, she phoned Uruguay and her father told her, in a whisper stinging of horror, that, no, things were not well with them at the moment, since they'd just learned that her cousin Roberto was dead. Yesterday, he'd shot himself through the mouth with his father's antique shotgun. Her father sighed and it was as if my mother could see him, his green eyes red from weeping, as if thousands of kilometres of land and ocean between them had melted. A part of her knew, too, what he would say next. The gunshot had erased Roberto's face.

But the violence of his passing played no part in the images that swam before her as she processed the news. Foremost was the child she'd so loved, the dimpled cheeks, his joyous laugh. The day he died, on his teenaged son's birthday, he was 42, the same age as his father, Americo, when he died from a heart attack, as I've described in my first book, *Spirit Sisters*. A chain of fathers and sons, linked by loss.

What type of mind-boggling and stubborn love could return Roberto to my mother's arms in a distant country after his death? How was it possible that she should see him so present, so solid and – except for the void where a beloved face should have been – so lifelike? The experience, she says, unfolded within and without her, so that everything – colours, textures, senses and emotions – were sharper and denser than in everyday life.

Roberto said goodbye in a dream, or something like a dream, but as you'll read in the following pages, our darling dead find so many other ways to send us love letters from heaven. They flutter to earth on butterfly wings, write messages of hope on Scrabble tiles, drift from the ceiling in showers of feathers, help settle our babies, save us from illness and harm, stand whole before us in the garden or at our bedside, and speak to us in voices spun from sky and clouds.

Just as immigration, with its tyranny of distance, cannot sever the bonds between people who care deeply for each other, so it seems relationships continue to grow and thrive, even after death. Roberto continues to visit my mother today, greeting her in that shadowland between the pillow and cherished memories. Her skin announces his arrival, sprouting goosebumps in waves of ice and heat. Death, Mum suggests, is not as final as immigration, because Roberto always returns.

This celebration of the ways our loved ones come back seems the right way for me to conclude the trilogy that began with *Spirit Sisters* in 2009, though my understanding of the spirit world is still evolving. My childhood fascination with spooky tales has given way to acknowledgment that a spiritual encounter can be much more than a spine-tingling treat, it can offer a lifeline to the bereaved. I've always believed in the power of storytelling and the stories in this book offer crucial lessons for us all.

Humility, and the value of keeping an open heart, are high

on the list. If a friend tells you they've awoken to their late lover's breath warming their cheek, or that they've seen their mother beaming, rosy-cheeked and restored to health, at their bedside, don't be fast to judge. Rather, rejoice that you're hearing something precious. As the American writer Willa Cather once said, 'Where there is great love, there are always miracles.'

1

A time to heal

⌒⌒

Piercing the wall of grief

*'There is a land of the living and a land of the dead,
and the bridge is love.'*
—Thornton Wilder

Late one afternoon in 2005, Margaret Marlow looked around in the quiet solitude of her Queensland home and noted all of the paraphernalia of domestic life in its place. Here, the kettle, there the toaster, the shiny kitchen appliances. Everything looked just as it did yesterday, and the day before that. Yet Margaret was not the same. A few months earlier, her son, John, 36, had died in a car crash, and nothing had been the same since. 'I was having a really bad day,' she recalls. 'I'd been crying all day. I was just putting a pot of water on the hotplate and I just felt . . .'

She pauses, searching for the right words.

11

'It was a really strange feeling, like there was some presence there, like I could hear a very faint rustling sound in the corner of the room. I jumped before I saw it. Like I really jumped because I knew there was something there! I saw my son's face, he was only appearing from the waist up and he looked younger. He had the half-grin on his face that he always had. He had a creamy-coloured shirt on – I didn't recognise what he was wearing – and his skin was really, really clear, like porcelain.'

Although the vision lasted only a few seconds, the effects were profound. After recovering from her initial shock, Margaret felt blessed to have been touched by something wonderful. 'I felt so privileged, because I thought, how hard must that have been for him to place himself there like that?' Thinking back to the expression John had on his face, that signature larrikinish grin of his, Margaret believes it meant, 'Yeah, I get you Mum. I know what you're going through.'

Empathy radiates from these encounters: for the person in mourning, they offer vital acknowledgment of their pain and the understanding that their loved one, whose return proves they still love them from afar, is doing their best to assuage their sorrow. Margaret, who went on to write a book, *I Can See Clearly Now*, about her experiences sensing her son's spirit, is certain John felt her distress on that tear-streaked day, and that's why he visited: 'I believe he was there to say, "Mum, it's okay."'

Grief is universal and as old as time. The Roman statesman Marcus Cicero, who died in 43 BC, was famously crippled by grief when his daughter Tullia died. Nothing except millennia divides the experiences of Margaret and Cicero, whose sorrow survives in letters of condolence penned by his peers. Yet Tullia herself lives on in the story of the Perpetual Lamp, a potent symbol of life and love everlasting. Legend tells that in the fifteenth century, Tullia's burial place was discovered in Rome and inside her tomb was a lamp still burning after 1500 years. In 1613, the poet John Donne celebrated the flame of eternal love in 'Eclogue, 1613. Decemb. 26':

> Now, as in Tullias tombe, one lamp burnt cleare,
> Unchang'd for fifteen hundred yeare,
> May these love-lamps we here enshrine,
> In warmth, light, lasting, equall the divine

Like Tullia's lamp, John's appearance was a testament to the indestructibility of love, lighting Margaret's path to healing on one of her darkest days. His cherished face returned to her, a celestial offering in the everyday confines of her kitchen. In the knowledge that her son remains present in the daily lives of the family who miss him, Margaret could wipe her eyes and go on, refreshed, into an evening bright with new possibilities.

Spontaneous visits from deceased loved ones are known as after-death communications, or ADCs, as US researchers Bill and Judy Guggenheim first described them. Following interviews with 2000 people for their 1996 book *Hello From Heaven!*, the Guggenheims estimated that one in five Americans had experienced an ADC. These phenomena, however, cross barriers of culture, religion, age, gender, socioeconomic background and time – reports of ADCs date back 2000 years. For as long as people have grieved, they have sensed the presence of their departed loved one, and drawn solace from it.

Those we've loved and lost find myriad ways to reach out. To name a few, they'll speak out loud and clear; wrap us in a cloud of their signature scent; stand before us in broad daylight or at our bedsides, looking robust and lit with joy; imbue our spaces with their all-encompassing presence; send their love with butterflies who alight, fearlessly, on our faces and outstretched palms; or hold us tight in vibrant dream visitations that feel more real than life itself.

In 2001, the year after her father died, Jenny Gersekowski, a 58-year-old former farmer and photo-journalist from near Toowoomba, met him again in a powerful dream. Jenny recalls: 'I could feel his warmth, I could feel his arm. He was dressed in a flannelette shirt. He said to me, "I'm alright. Don't worry about me, I'm okay, so don't worry." I'll never forget that, it was just extraordinary.'

Eight years later, following the death of her husband of 33 years, Alan, Jenny experienced a different form of ADC: 'I felt him putting his arms around me in bed. I felt his breath on my neck,' she remembers. Today, it's a more subtle hint of Alan's presence that embraces her all day, every day. 'I just feel his love. I just feel the unconditional love close to me, though his presence is probably not as strong as it used to be,' she reflects. 'I think now he's actually trying to let me live my own life a bit more.'

Whether the experience is visual, auditory, olfactory, tactile, sentient, symbolic or in dreams – among the principle categories identified – the primary purpose of an ADC is to heal. 'ADCs are essentially expressions of love because they are all about helping each other,' writes leading grief counsellor Dr Louis LaGrand in his 1999 book *Messages and Miracles: Extraordinary Experiences of the Bereaved*.

Often, as Margaret's story above illustrates, an encounter occurs just as the person experiencing it is at their lowest ebb, the communication working like a pick-me-up, buoying the bereaved, giving them the strength to go on.

Sydney talent manager Deb Carr was inconsolable following the suicide of her brother, Gary, aged 34, on 2 November 1998. 'It was the most horrendous day of my life,' says Deb, her blue-grey eyes turning stormy at the memory. Three days later, she recalls, 'I was lying in bed crying, and I was wide awake, *wide awake*, and I heard him call me. I heard him yell out, "Deb, I'm okay!" I heard his voice, it was not in my mind, it was *his* voice,' she insists. 'Then I had a vision of him and I was in the vision, too, sitting on a stone bench, crying with my hands on my face, just sobbing uncontrollably, and he came up to me and put his arm around me and he looked just like Gary, scruffy, in a jumper and black jeans. He put his arm around me and he held me and he just winked at me and said, telepathically, "Everything that you believe in life after death is true. I am so happy."'

As with all the stories in this chapter, and many throughout the book, the experience heralded a turning point in Deb's healing process. 'I felt so comforted, because he and I used to talk about what happens when you die,' she says. They'd always been very close and Gary, a talented artist and cartoonist, used to phone her to chat every day.

Growing up in New Zealand, Deb, Gary and their two brothers used to spend hours scrambling over hedgerows in their huge backyard, lush with plum trees and rambling vines. Her favourite memory is playing 'clubs' with the boys, with Deb as secretary and 'poor Gary the treasurer', she remembers with a smile. But a shadow fell over their world when Gary turned ten;

his grades dropped, he became aggressive and health problems dogged him.

It later emerged that this was when a priest, a family friend, had begun to sexually abuse Gary. The rage that ensnared him and the depression that plagued him in adulthood are the poisonous outcomes of the abuse, says Deb. She tells me about a prophetic artwork of Gary's that portrays the story of his stolen childhood – and its ultimate outcome. 'There's a castle in the background, a demon crouching and a little boy running, he's got a little schoolbag and he's put his hand out and a beautiful angel is picking him up and bringing him to heaven.'

Since Gary's death, Deb receives regular signs of her brother's steadfast love, such as the meaningful appearance of feathers, and she has also met Gary in her dreams. One poignant dream visitation took place three years after he died. The setting was a funeral at a church, where five coffins were being brought in and Gary stood at the altar, jubilant. 'He was dancing and putting his arm out, saying, "Bring those coffins up here! You bring them up here, Debbie. You don't know how happy it is over here! They don't know what they're in for."' Deb believes the quintet of caskets represented the five living members of their family. 'In the dream I sat down in a pew next to Dad and he was crying. I held his hand and said, "Dad, what are you crying for? Gary is really, really, really happy." Then I woke up and my pillow was saturated, saturated with my tears.'

Sustaining Deb is her conviction that Gary is 'teaching art in heaven' and her unwavering belief that life, like love, goes on. 'I'll be with him again. There's no doubt about it. When I go, he'll be there,' she declares. Until then, the memory of their reunion on the stone bench is always with her, like a treasured photo tucked close to the heart. 'I think about it all the time –

I can still hear him and see exactly what it was like. It told me he was safe. I'd been worried that he was suffering more in the afterlife. I was worried he wasn't being cared for because of what he'd done, but I think God said to him, "No, darling, it's time to come home. You've done your stuff, it's time to come home."'

Communicating with her brother's spirit also prevented Deb, a divorced mother of two and now aged 51, from succumbing to the same despair. 'If he hadn't come to me, I don't know if I would have not done the same thing myself. It's kept me going through some tough times,' she says.

Deb's belief echoes LaGrand's assertion in his 2006 book, *Love Lives On*, that these encounters are 'major forces that . . . often change the course of one's life.' Such events, he writes, 'bring about healing and expanded consciousness for mourners'.

More than twenty years after he had a gut-wrenchingly vivid dream about his late father, Grant Hyde still looks back on it with wonder: 'I will live with it in my heart until I'm old and useless,' he says. A former Sydney Roosters rugby league player, Grant, 44, is now a novelist, personal trainer and father of two. He reveals that the standalone experience was 'uplifting' and says, 'It made me feel really good.'

It was a Sunday afternoon in 1992 and in the bowels of the Sydney Football Stadium, Grant, then 23, sat with his elbows atop his knees and his head bowed. A month earlier, his father, Ray, also a former Roosters player, had died of mesothelioma, aged 62. Though he spoke little of it, Grant was deeply grieving the loss of his 'best mate'. In minutes, he and his team-mates would take to the field against the Western Suburbs Magpies and the atmosphere crackled with anticipation, testosterone and tension. But Grant's thoughts lingered on the dream he'd had last night, *all* night, it seemed. Though 'dream' was, perhaps, too measly a word to contain what had happened, because last night, his father returned to his side.

In the dream, Grant recalls, 'I was on the field standing in the defensive line facing a giant front-rower coming at me. He was a scary-looking bloke with a shaved head. I heard a voice next to me, a young man's voice, saying, "Here he comes, give it to him for your old man, hey?"

'I looked to my side and there was my dad. Not as an old, sick man that was so fresh in my memory, but as a young powerful footballer, the likes of which I'd only seen in the scrapbooks. He had thick blond hair and his body was strong and lean. It was definitely my dad, it just felt right. I asked, "What are you doing here, I thought you were gone?" He shook his head and said, "As long as you remember me, son, I'm never gone."'

In the locker room, Grant smiled to himself and took a deep breath. Thinking about the dream, he felt invigorated, ready to take on his opponents. 'It was the best I'd felt since my dad died,' Grant says. 'I felt like I'd spent the previous night with him, playing the game we both loved.' When the siren sounded for the match to begin, Grant got to his feet and whispered to his old man, 'I'll see you out there, mate.'

Fatherly support also arrived just in time for Sunshine Coast radio presenter Mary-Lou Stephens after her 61-year-old dad, Dick, died from asthma complications in 1987. Mary-Lou was 26 and in the grip of a heroin habit and a destructive relationship. 'It was Dad's death that stopped me using. When he died, everything changed and I needed to change with it,' writes Mary-Lou in her 2013 memoir, *Sex, Drugs & Meditation*.

But what kept her recovery on track was the way their relationship flourished *after* his death. Now 52 but with a vibrant personality and girlish voice that makes her seem half that age, Mary-Lou tells me: 'After my dad died, it really was'd only time I felt him loving me.' She explains how trauma in his own upbringing made him emotionally distant. 'He was too scared to love, too scared to be himself.'

But after his death, he began again.

Mary-Lou had a benchmark dream that summed up the new way forward for her father: 'We were sitting in a church, but there was no church service and there were lots of people and we were all reading books. Some people had very small books and others had big books and I looked over to my dad and he was only a quarter of the way through a large book.' She remembers that, in the dream she sighed with relief, because she knew he wouldn't be able to leave until 'he finishes the book'. She understood he'd fulfilled only part of his mission in helping her – there was still a great deal of work to be done.

For the next eighteen months, Mary-Lou felt her dad around 'very strongly'. '*Very* strongly,' she reiterates. 'There was a dramatic feeling of him being free of all that pain – it was phenomenal! I truly felt him with me all the time.' Knowing she could finally count on her father's love gave Mary-Lou the courage to triumph over her addiction. 'I feel like crying when I say this, but he was going to stick around with me, or for me, for that amount of time because that's what I needed. You know, it probably took me that long to get the heroin out of my system. I couldn't believe the grip it had on me.'

Yet her father's love held her even tighter. Mary-Lou describes it as 'this presence of a loving dad, which I'd never experienced when he was alive, a love like a warm embrace'. She says it helped her to leave drugs behind and pour her energies into her passion for country music (she used to sing and play guitar in a band called, aptly, Chain of Hearts) and land her dream job in radio.

Today, Mary-Lou, who's found solace and spiritual nourishment in meditation, no longer senses her father's presence as powerfully, but she'll never forget how he was there when she needed him. And, many years later, he was there for her again, preventing her from having a car crash (which she describes in Chapter Eight, 'The Power of Love'). If ever she's missing him more than usual, she picks up her favourite photo of him, taken on the east coast of Tasmania, and imagines it's a snapshot of his new life: 'It's just him standing in this field with the sea behind him and the sky above and he's so happy and joyous and free, smiling at the camera.'

As transformative as these ADC experiences are, in many cases they prove to be only the first, as spirit family members and friends find new ways to continue to deliver their message of love. Eileen, a 68-year-old retired occupational therapist, lost her husband Tom to a heart attack in 1988. Tom, a doctor, was only 55 years old and his sudden death left Eileen mired in pain. But just a few days after Tom died, she received a precious love letter from the hereafter.

'I'd kept his letters to me and I found my letters to him in his drawer,' says Eileen. 'I'd read his letters, just as a way of trying to be close to him, and then something made me read my letters to him, too. On the third one, on the back of the envelope, he had written, *Stand still to hear me in thine own heart beating, pause to feel my presence in this room, know that when you call me, I am with you.*'

Eileen felt the hairs on her arms stand on end.

Decades later, as she reads the words aloud to me from her peaceful home in northern Victoria, where birds sing in the background of our conversation, it happens to us both. The stirring words, which she believes Tom authored, are an apparent testament to love after death. More than that, they are like a poetic instruction manual: the bridge is love, but you must know how to cross it. In our frantic 21st-century lives, it is easy to feel lost in the maelstrom and disconnected from ourselves – finding solitary time for reflection and spirituality is a luxury many of us feel we cannot afford. Tom's words declare love never dies, but that we must stop – 'stand still' – listen, and have faith, to know it.

Reading his words for the first time, his widow felt her loneliness lift. 'I took that as a message for me,' she says. 'I felt very, very happy. Reassured.'

There is another layer to Eileen's lovely story. Three years before Tom's death, and before they were married, Eileen, who's a Christian and a follower of the universal spiritual teachings of the late Indian healer Sathya Sai Baba, went through a time of 'feeling a lot of despair'. Then one day she opened her Bible at random to look for some sort of guidance – a ritual she hadn't done since childhood but which had felt right in that moment – and the pages fell open to Psalm 46 of the Old Testament. Eileen recalls: 'I read down the columns and there didn't seem to be anything particularly significant, then I came to a couple of lines in bold type, completely different to the other print on the page. It said, "Be still and know that I am God." I blinked and looked away and looked back again and it was just normal print.'

It's intriguing that those ancient words, which magically shouted an answer of hope to Eileen, have so much in common with the verse Tom later penned. In solemnity and profundity, in their call for calm and stillness, in the way they worked as a salve for Eileen's pain, his words echo the biblical passage. How this could be is a mystery Eileen accepts may never 'be solved, at least, not until she meets her husband again. She knows it is just a matter of time. 'Tom believed that, too. He believed our loved ones are all waiting for us when we die.'

Sydney novelist Jess Tarn, 23, takes comfort from this, too. Her brother, David, was three years old when he drowned in a swimming pool in Singapore, where her family then lived. It was 1993 and Jess was four, only eighteen months older than David. But since then she has carried the burden of having been the last person who spoke to him, though she was barely more than a toddler herself. Her baby brother's last moments play on loop inside her head, a movie whose agonising ending she can never rewrite.

Clusters of ex-patriot families surround a public pool in the unrelenting humidity of mid-afternoon in Singapore.

Children squeal and laugh, splash and shout. Small hands slap the surface of the water, cool and blue and benign. Mothers chit-chat.

'I was holding my mum's hand and she was talking to someone,' says Jess. 'David came up to me and asked me if he could go for a swim. Me being a naïve four-year-old, I said, "Yeah."'

A tiny boy. Light-brown hair. Eyes like an Australian sky. Ever resourceful, he pulls and tugs at his puffy orange floaties until he is free. The water, so cool and blue, calls him. He jumps.

By the time a passer-by noticed 'a shadow at the bottom of the pool' it was too late for David. Jess recalls, 'One of my mum's friends dove into the pool, picked him up and they attempted CPR', but being so young herself at the time, Jess doesn't remember much. She knows her family, numb with loss, took David home to be buried near his grandfather, in Port Macquarie, New South Wales. She knows Eric Clapton's 'Tears in Heaven' played at his funeral.

For the next ten years, she'd cry whenever she heard that song; yet these were the moments when David seemed closest. Clapton's lament for his own little boy was vast and deep enough to speak for Jessica, too. The lyrics carried David's smile, the melody brought his blue-sky eyes within reach. 'I honestly believe he was around me whenever I was listening to that song or whenever I was upset.'

Few memories remain to fill the David-sized space at her side but all brim with love. 'He was always cheeky, absolutely beautiful and gorgeous. Mum used to tell me that whenever he was in trouble, he'd always run to me, so I was his second mother,' says Jess. She laughs as she remembers one of his cutest quirks: 'Whenever he was taking his pants or undies off, instead of stepping out of them and then picking them up, he'd take one foot out and then kick his little foot up to grab it so he didn't have to bend down.'

But David was barely more than a baby, so the sweet memories must end almost as soon as they start. For years, Jess struggled with the disparity between the years he lived and the future he was denied – the future they were all denied. 'He missed out on so much, because he was so little,' she says with tears in her voice. 'He is never going to get that first kiss or have a partner, those are the things that I think about. The boy he was. The man he would have been.'

In early 2008, following the death of a beloved great-aunt, Jess had an experience which proved a breakthrough in her healing. 'I am Catholic, but I hadn't been to church for ages,' she explains. 'I was really upset this day and I went out for a walk. I passed a chapel and went inside. I think I just let everything out, like I just cried over everything, and then it felt like someone was turning my head to the left. There was a picture in stained glass of a little boy who was standing up and an old woman who was kneeling down: Aunty Mary and David.'

The sensation of her head being physically guided towards the image – so representative of her loved ones – was undeniable, Jess stresses. Most important, though, was the instantaneous relief it brought. 'I felt like the whole weight was lifted off. I knew that they were together and that they were there with me,' she says, laughing and crying at the same time. 'And that made me feel so much better. Together, they turned my head.'

David is also a frequent visitor in Jess's dreams, usually appearing as the toddler he was, with one unforgettable exception: 'I was dancing in the rain and I was wearing a reddish-purplish dress and, I don't know, I just felt free,' reflects Jess. 'Then all of a sudden, this faceless man comes along and we just start dancing. I think that was David, you know? I felt so happy. I wanted the dream to come true. There was no music, just the sound of the rain . . .'

Joyous as a sun-shower, reassuring as a smile, beguiling as a poem – such is the love that imbues the following stories, too: a soulmate and a husband, no longer by their loved ones' sides, yet ever a soothing presence in their lives, eager to help mend their broken hearts.

A hand to hold

'She's opened up the door for me to find out where she is.'

The first time Vikki saw a photograph of Kelsey, though she'd never met her before, it was like a reunion. Her skin and muscles, her heart and head, all floated, as if magnetised, towards the picture of the statuesque woman with blue eyes and red hair. The newspaper article was about a breeding farm for stallions where Kelsey worked. The photo showed her walking a mare and not even the hosed-down hues of the flimsy newspaper could dim her grace and presence. Or maybe she just shone for Vikki. 'I don't really read the newspaper,' Vikki, now 38, tells me, 'but for some reason, that day I did.'

Not long afterwards, the pair came face to face. Vikki, a horse trainer, had been working at a horse farm in rural Victoria for three years; she'd taken a couple of months off and when she returned to the farm, in October 2002, her stomach flipped at the sight of her new colleague, Kelsey. But love didn't bloom straightaway. 'We didn't exactly hit it off as friends at first, in fact we didn't like each other,' says Vikki, chuckling. Though they soon thawed out – 'we started to realise we both liked the same things, we were the same person, pretty much' – and on Kelsey's birthday in December, they had their first kiss.

Bonded by their love of horses and tastes in music – Melissa Etheridge and the Baby Animals were on high rotation – theirs was a serene and happy partnership built on their mutual appreciation of the simple things: just being together, dreaming big, living life. 'Kelsey was one of those people that you could always tell when she walked into a room, everyone would look at her,' Vikki says. 'She was very bubbly and outgoing, easy to talk to. She used to draw a lot of people to her because she was so easygoing. She would try her hand at absolutely anything. She'd say no to nothing and nothing would frighten her.'

Kelsey wore that fearlessness like armour until two days before her death from ovarian cancer in 2011, aged 33.

Her diagnosis in 2009, Vikki recalls, winded the couple who'd pledged to be together until long after Kelsey's autumnal hair turned silver. 'We all thought she was going to pull through,' says Vikki. 'We had plans. The minute she got better, we were getting out of Dodge. We were going to bum it for a year or two, no more horses, no more anything.'

Fiercely private, Kelsey eschewed fuss and pity. 'Her attitude was, "I'll get over it, so don't worry about it." And she fought it for two and a half years,' says Vikki. 'She never stopped working. She worked through chemo, feeling sick, radiation therapy. She worked through everything.'

On the morning of Wednesday 7 December 2011, Vikki woke up and ran the bath water for Kelsey, as was their routine. By this stage, Kelsey was receiving palliative care at home and Vikki tended to her with exquisite tenderness, climbing into the tub with her partner every day and sponging her skin, half-blinded by unshed tears. Today Kelsey surprised Vikki by saying she didn't want her bath, she was too tired, but almost immediately changed her mind and began to get in, even as the bath was still filling.

'Are you okay?' asked Vikki, unsettled by Kelsey's urgency.

'Yeah, I'm alright.'

'Well, you didn't bring your pyjamas in, I'll just go out and get them.' Vikki turned to walk towards the bedroom.

'No, no, get in,' said Kelsey. 'This could possibly be our last time we're going to spend together.'

Vikki obeyed, but after two minutes, Kelsey had had enough. She couldn't sit up anymore. Vikki lifted her gently out of the bath, dried her and was helping her back to the bedroom when Kelsey stopped and looked into her eyes, a mirror of her own – sea and sky, impossible to know where one ended and the other began.

'You know you're my hero for doing all of this,' said Kelsey. 'You're just my hero.'

Sharing this, Vikki's strong and clear voice trembles and I'm awed by their love.

Kelsey died that evening at 9 pm. In her final hours, she'd slipped in and out of consciousness, with her mum and Vikki by her side, planting gentle kisses on her palms.

Kelsey's first dream visitation to Vikki had all the hallmarks of their quiet, low-key love. Vikki recounts: 'In the dream, I remember walking into our bedroom and she was asleep in our bed, facing the other way on her side of the bed. I remember, as vivid as anything, just hopping into bed and touching her on the shoulder and saying, "I love you, honey." And she rolled over and said, "I love you too."'

Another ADC seemed less subtle: around five days after Kelsey's death, Vikki was jolted from a deep sleep by the sudden blaring of one of their favourite songs, 'Love Takes Over' by David Guetta, which had played at her funeral. 'The music was coming from outside of me, from somewhere in the house,' remembers Vikki, but she could not locate its source. Her mum, who'd been watching the cricket in the lounge room, didn't hear a sound.

Sometimes, it's Kelsey's voice that wakes Vikki, calling her from the corner of the bedroom where Vikki piles up the gifts she buys for Kelsey – anniversary and birthday presents, a card for Valentine's Day, 'stuff like that'. Vikki will respond – 'Yeah honey?' – even though she's just woken up from a deep sleep. 'I know it's her because it's her voice and it's in the room and the voice is talking to me,' Vikki explains, then pauses. 'She says my name.'

Just over a week after Kelsey's death, her brother took Vikki to Noosa for a weekend away, a kind gesture 'to get me out of the house', says Vikki. 'Her family are now my family.' Walking with him at dusk along the beachfront, Vikki noticed the many couples holding hands as they strolled by. 'I remember saying to Kelsey in my head, "Well, honey, you and I would have loved to be walking along here, holding hands." And I felt something touch the inside of my left hand and it made me close my hand as if to say, "We *are* holding hands." It was the feeling that she had actually just put her hand in mine.'

Vikki held her hand shut until they arrived at the restaurant and she took her seat at the table.

That's not the only time Kelsey has laid healing hands on her partner. 'Once, I was pretty much incapacitated with grief in the middle of a paddock, feeding some horses, and I was hunched over, bawling my eyes out. It had been a very emotional day and I just couldn't take it anymore. There was no one to hear me out in the middle of 250 acres so I thought I would let it all out, and I swear, I just felt her put her hands on my back and say, "It's okay." It just made me feel better straightaway, like that,' says Vicki, snapping her fingers. 'The feeling was, it's going to be okay, and then I stopped crying and said, "Okay, I got it."'

During the most searing times, when Vikki, who wears around her neck a love heart pendant with Kelsey's ashes inside, struggles to accept a future which doesn't include the chance to hold her lover again, to draw a washcloth across her fragrant skin one last time, the only way forward is through Kelsey's communications: 'She's opened up the door for me to find out where she is and what's going on,' says Vikki. 'I look to the sky and the stars but I think she's right beside me. She's in the truck next to me when I go to work – we used to go everywhere together. She's still sitting in the seat sleeping away while I drive somewhere. She's still there. She's not getting away that easy.'

Letting in the light

'I said, "Am I dreaming or am I awake?" He said, "You're awake. I'm with you."'

Natasha Ponente stood at the altar of St Dominic's Church in Melbourne and stared out at 350 faces. Her trembling hand held the eulogy but her throat was as closed as her heart, shut tight against a world that could inflict so much pain. The words she'd written tilted and swayed, became just so many black markings on a page. The quiet roared. She took a breath and turned her head to the right, towards the coffin, counting the roses on its lid in an attempt to calm down. When she looked up again, the pews were empty and she stood alone with the casket full of her future, a beam of sunlight painting it gold and amber.

To Natasha, it was now just the two of them. The doors were shut against the sweltering heat, but a breeze, as gentle as murmurs of love at midnight, found its way to her side, delivering the strength she needed. Natasha found her voice and began to read to her husband, Leigh, who'd exchanged vows with her in this very spot just two years ago. Tenderly, she read him her eulogy, her final love letter.

Exactly two weeks earlier, on 14 December 2012, Leigh had turned 31. Before leaving for her government job, Natasha pounced onto their bed at their Melbourne home and belted out 'It's Your Birthday' in the tinny voice of schoolgirl Lisa, from Leigh's favourite TV show, *The Simpsons*.

'Bubby, you sound like a strangled cat,' said Leigh, groaning.

Natasha laughed and whacked him with a pillow. 'Well, here's hoping I get better over the next 50 years.'

There was much to look forward to in the young couple's lives. Summer days were long, hot and pulsing with Christmas, and 2013 loomed, with its promise of huge changes ahead for the high-school sweethearts, who planned to buy a house and start a family in the new year. Those dreams, the languid heat and the holiday vibe, the houses strung with lights and baubles – all helped to anchor Natasha when the dread that had been gnawing at her since early November threatened to consume her.

Natasha, now 33, recalls, 'There were some nights when I would go to bed and say to my husband, "If I'm not up by the time you get up, you have to check on me, and check on me through the night as well."'

Leigh, who could not stomach the thought of harm coming to his wife, would frown, and reach for her: 'What's the matter, Natasha?'

She would just shrug and shake her head, telling him, 'I've just got this bad feeling.'

Before the bottom fell out of Natasha's world, Leigh, too, had a premonition. One night, his howl of fear speared the black quiet of 3 am. Shuddering and weeping, he reached for Natasha, pulling her close then closer still. To Natasha, her heart racing with fatigue and confusion, it felt as if he wanted to unzip his skin and enfold her safe within. 'Oh my God, come here,' he said, his voice small and unfamiliar. His body shook as Natasha asked 'What's the matter?' again and again. In reply, he squeezed her tighter.

Eventually he was able to explain: 'I just had a dream you died and there was nothing I could do to save you and you left me.' He was panting with fear. 'Please, promise me you'll never die.'

Natasha hushed and soothed him, like a child. 'I said, "Okay. It's okay. I'm here." But he was terrified, like the fear of God was in him, and he said, "There's nothing I could do. I found you. *I found you*. I just found you in bed."'

A week later, Natasha stood at the bathroom mirror, applying makeup and getting ready for work. From the doorway, Leigh chattered away about the day ahead, when suddenly a morbid scene played in her mind. 'I had this flash of people giving me condolences and me pushing them away,' she says. It was over in seconds. Baffled, she put it down to subconscious ramblings, her mind revisiting something she'd seen on TV. But she couldn't help wondering, 'What was happening to them?' First, there was her feeling of dread, then Leigh's dream and now the hint of heartbreak she glimpsed in the bathroom mirror – the sense of foreboding was growing and steering Natasha towards the conviction that her life was in peril.

But today was Leigh's birthday, and Natasha was determined to peel off the dread she'd been wearing since the last days of spring. Today, she would focus on Leigh and the celebrations planned for the evening. Ostensibly, it was to be a Christmas party thrown by Natasha's uncle, but it was also a surprise party for Leigh, who, despite his youth and slight physique, would dress up as Santa for the children at the bash.

It was a lively night. Leigh, handsome in the G-Star Raw jeans and T-shirt his wife had bought him for his birthday, was in his element; chatting to everyone, making sure guests were fed and watered, and walking them out with a heartfelt thankyou at the end of the night. By the time he and Natasha got home, it was 2.45 am. Though they were yawning, they perked up when they saw that one of their favourite Christmas movies, *The Ref*, was about to start on TV. They cuddled up on the couch to watch it and afterwards, dragged themselves to bed. It was almost 7 am before they finally fell asleep.

Before shutting his eyes, Leigh turned to Natasha. 'Listen, don't let me sleep too long,' he said. 'We've got to finish the Christmas shopping.' Natasha promised not to let him sleep past 2 pm: 'The last thing I heard was him snoring very, very heavily, then I drifted off to sleep.'

Natasha and Leigh met on 9 October 1995. It was the first day of the last school term and as Natasha waited for the bus, she spotted 'this little boy with long blond hair just staring at me'. In his slim fingers, the sixteen-year-old future jeweller was buffing a granite rock. 'He flashed me a big smile and the first thing that came to mind was, "What a weirdo! Who polishes rocks?"' remembers Natasha. Eventually, he summoned the courage to talk to the striking and confident brunette who was two years his senior and, as tends to happen with a couple who grow up together, the pair forged a loyal and passionate relationship that was not without its volatile moments.

'Look, we would bicker – our friends gave us the nicknames Ike and Tina Turner – but then five minutes later, it would be over and done with,' says Natasha. But their love defined them. 'I once said to him that I felt like when we weren't together, my heart didn't beat, and he always said if I died, he wouldn't live.'

Leigh was Australian, 'but he was more Italian than I was', says Natasha. 'He was what we call "the Albino Gino".' The fun-loving prankster struck up an instant rapport with her grandparents, who'd unwaveringly side with Leigh if he went to them with sob stories of how his wife had wronged him. Leigh's closeness to her family seemed older than it could be, like a remnant from some other time. It was a quality of Natasha and Leigh's relationship, too. Little things – his relatives had once sold a house to her relatives – linked them, as well as calamities. When Natasha was fifteen, a vivid nightmare that had haunted her for six weeks came true when her brother had a near-fatal car accident and was rushed to hospital. The same night, as it later emerged, Leigh's family were also there, facing their own heartbreak of a loved one's life in peril. Two families, then strangers to each other, faced life-changing events together. Says Natasha, 'It's like we really were one person split in two.'

The day after the Christmas/birthday party, 15 December, Natasha opened her eyes to the late morning light. The day was mild, she noted with relief, it would be nowhere near as hot as the previous Saturday, when the temperature had soared to 37 degrees. The time on her iPhone said 10.50 am and she wanted to get started on all the things she had to tick off her to-do list. Closing the bedroom door carefully behind her, she poured herself a glass of orange juice before dumping in a load of laundry. Lunch came and went in a blur of housekeeping and chores. Every time Natasha was about to walk into the room to wake her husband, something would draw her away from the door – her mobile would beep, the washing machine would trill, or her home phone would ring. Looking back, she wonders if the chain of distractions served as warnings, or tactics orchestrated by a higher power to delay the inevitable.

Just after 2.30 pm Natasha realised she'd let Leigh sleep in too long. She bustled into the room and raised the blind, letting afternoon light flood the space. Her mirrored wardrobe doors and dressing table mirror both reflect her bed in the centre of the room and Leigh was facing the mirrors. 'Come on, wakey wakey,' she teased his reflection, but then, it was as if her heart was freefalling out of her chest, to land with a thud at her feet.

'I thought, "Why are you looking at me like that?"' With a wail she registered he wasn't breathing. 'Leigh, Leigh, Leigh,' she pleaded, bawling, as she began CPR and called the ambulance. 'It was like slow motion. How I didn't drop dead, I don't know. The shock of it . . .'

Leigh's heart had stopped in his sleep. Though the paramedics restarted it, he'd been deprived of oxygen too long and Natasha held her husband in her arms at the hospital as he slipped away. Only 24 hours earlier, they'd been celebrating his birthday and looking forward to what the dawning year would bring – now, Natasha was left to process this cataclysmic loss.

The pain of it was like nothing she'd known, like being eaten alive from the inside out, but there was Leigh's funeral to organise and she was determined to see it through with her usual thoroughness and attention to detail. On Monday 17 December, two days after his death, Natasha was searching through his clothes for the suit and tie – his special wedding tie – she wanted him dressed in. She found the garments, as well as her gift of the G-Star T-shirt he'd worn at the party in his final hours. 'I'm putting this in the laundry,' she remarked to an aunt who was helping her. 'I have to wash it because it's all sweaty. Then I'm going to put this in the coffin with him.'

Four days later, on the Friday, Natasha took the suit to the funeral directors' premises, where close friends and family lovingly dressed Leigh. In her fog of grief, she'd forgotten the T-shirt she'd wanted to place in the casket. The next day, Natasha returned to her husband's side. Her hands hungered for the everyday tasks of fixing his collar, taming his hair, adjusting his tie, tugging at a lapel. They sought him out, force of habit, force of love. 'I was smoothing down his suit and making sure he was all okay, then what do you think I found sitting at his feet?'

It was Leigh's birthday T-shirt, the one she'd washed to put in his coffin but forgotten about. 'I got such a fright I squealed,' says Natasha.

She knew there was no logical explanation for how that T-shirt appeared in the coffin. She certainly hadn't delivered it to the funeral director since yesterday, and neither had anyone in their family. She rang each of the men who'd dressed Leigh and all confirmed there was no T-shirt. Frantic enquiries then revealed it was listed in the receipt of items that had accompanied Leigh's body from the hospital to the coroner on Sunday 16 December. But Natasha knew that was impossible. 'I had that T-shirt with me at home on Monday,' she says – and her aunt had seen her put it in the laundry that day.

'It was a sign no one could ignore. That T-shirt was in *my* possession,' says Natasha. 'I took that as a sign that Leigh was with me, a very cheeky sign, as if to say, "You just bought me this. Do you think I'm going to leave it behind?" It was absolutely amazing.'

Welcome though it was, the mind-bending event wasn't enough to draw Natasha out of her misery. She was alone in a foreign landscape where every signpost had been wrenched out. The successful and vivacious woman was struggling more than she would ever reveal to her friends and family. Rent with grief, incapable of facing a future without her soulmate, she began to plan her own death. She went as far as writing a pros/cons list, and letters – to her parents, her brother – and notice of resignation to her boss. On Friday 2 February 2013, Natasha says, 'I went to bed and I knew that weekend, it was going to happen. When I set a rule for myself I don't break it.'

At 4.45 am the next morning, Natasha opened her eyes. As usual, she savoured a few moments' respite before reality presented itself, mountainous and rude, into the forefront of her mind. This time, though, it was tempered by a jolt of relief that she would soon be joining her love. She fell back asleep and dreamt she was in a large function room filled with computers resembling poker machines. She received an email on her phone, but could not access it, so she tried one of the computers. 'All of a sudden, Leigh was beside me and he was wearing the G-Star Raw T-shirt and jeans and he looked exactly like he always did. He had his hair the way he always wore it. I could smell his Chanel Egoiste. He was just Leigh, in every way. I turned to him and said, "Am I dreaming or am I awake?" He said, "You're awake. I'm with you."'

Natasha now realises those words, Leigh's words, marked the turning point in her healing – they were the first signpost in her alien world. She recalls their conversation: 'I said to him,

"Do you know how sad and hurt I am?" He said, "Yes, bubby, I know, and I'm so sorry but I'm never far away from you." I was crying and he was crying and we were just holding one another. I could actually feel his touch on me! I could smell him. We had a full conversation. He said, "I was with you. I know you tried to save me." I said to him, "What am I going to do?" And he told me that one day we'd be together again, that there are too many things I need to do first, but then he would come and get me. I said, "But when? Just do it now." He said, "No, I can't take you yet. You'll be okay. I'll never be away from you."'

Natasha woke up, her pillow 'absolutely saturated' in tears and the unmistakable scent of Leigh's signature aftershave thick in the air. She could feel him brushing her hair with his fingers, as he'd always done when he was drifting off to sleep; it was a physical sensation. 'I knew in my heart that he was there.'

She is certain the timing of the visitation was no accident. 'When he came to me that night, I believe he knew what I was planning to do. He was my saviour because no one else would have gotten through to me, and I thank him for that. I honestly do believe that he saved me that night.'

Leigh's return empowered her to set aside self-destructive thoughts and embrace hope. Now, she's learning to remember the good times with a smile on her face: the frequent overseas trips, their open affection and deep conversations, their once-in-a-lifetime love. 'I believe in my heart that a love lost is better than no love at all,' says Natasha, who senses Leigh around her every day – from smelling his scent in her office to feeling him brush her hair at night and playfully hog the blanket, as he'd always done. 'I had him for sixteen years and the truth is, if I'd been given a crystal ball to know what was going to happen, I wouldn't have traded it for anything.'

Memories of the bond they shared prop her up during the hardest times. On the day of Leigh's funeral, after he'd helped her find a way to deliver her eulogy written in tears, an exquisite moment from their wedding day bloomed in her mind. As Leigh's coffin was carried out of the church, and the soaring strains of 'The Prayer', by Andrea Bocelli and Celine Dion, filled the cavernous space, Natasha remembered how the song had played during their first wedding dance.

Just as they'd found a way to be alone at the funeral, even as hundreds of mourners wept before them, so it had been at their wedding reception, when they wrapped their arms around each other, murmuring in private, as they slow-danced together, oblivious to their guests. Natasha recalls, 'When we were dancing, I was crying and he wiped my tears away and said, "I never want you to forget this moment in time, bubby. If anything ever happens to me, just remember that I'm always going to be holding you like I am now."'

*

Experiences like these are the proverbial gifts that keep on giving. For the people who have shared their stories in this chapter, not only did they draw solace and strength to take that all-important baby step forward in their healing, but in tear-stained moments to come they can always cast their minds back to seek sanctuary in their memories of the day their loved one reached out with an offering of hope.

Margaret's experience of seeing her son's smiling face lasted only seconds, but it changed her day, her outlook and her future. Life, like love, goes on and acknowledging this shines a ray of hope onto a grey tomorrow. Intercession from the spirit world steered Mary-Lou off a dangerous path, unburdened Jess, rebooted Gary, and gave Vikki and Natasha respite at times when longing for their soulmates threatened to become too much to live with.

We, too, can learn so much from each encounter. Hold your partner long and tight, thank your parents for their guidance and treasure your child's smile, while you can. David Tweddle, whose 23-year-old son, Gary, died after losing his way in the Blue Mountains of New South Wales in 2013, reminded us all of an often-overlooked truth in a raw and haunting tribute that he posted on Facebook – as widely reported in the media – when it became clear there was no hope of his son's safe return: 'Money, possessions and material becomes irrelevant now . . . cherish every second you are fortunate enough to have with the people you love. Waste not one moment, be available and show love at every opportunity . . .'

2

A Safe Arrival

Assurances of wellbeing

'Death – the last sleep? No, it is the final awakening.'
—Sir Walter Scott

Six months after her grandmother died of a heart attack, Karen Davis woke to see her standing at the end of her bed, looking alive and as beautifully groomed as she'd always been, in a pressed skirt and blouse, with her hair blow-waved and set and her face perfectly made up. 'I opened my eyes and I sat up and she was still there. I remember thinking, *Am I awake? Am I awake?*' says Karen, 45, a novelist and former police officer from Sydney's Sutherland Shire. 'She smiled and said nothing, but without speaking, I knew she was telling me she was okay.'

'I'm okay' – two tiny words at the heart of so many of the stories told to me by the people I've met. Only two words, yet they can mean the universe to the person left behind, agonising over where their loved one is following a traumatic or sudden death, if they've had a safe crossing, if they're accompanied, if they're finally free from illness and suffering. For the bereaved, they are two tiny words laden with the promise of a more peaceful tomorrow.

For Karen, who'd been extremely close to her 'Nanna', the experience was also the fulfilment of a pact they'd made just days before her grandmother's death. Then 22 and still on a high from a recent Hawaiian holiday, Karen was feeling a little guilty about how her schedule was keeping her from spending time with her nan, so she popped over one Saturday. At the kitchen table the pair spoke for hours about career, romance and the possibility of life after death. Karen recalls: 'I said, "You come back and tell me what happens. And she said, "Don't worry. If there's any way I can do it, I will." It was in a joking way and that was that. She passed away about ten days later.' And six months after that, Karen's grandmother kept her promise.

Six months also happens to be the time elapsed between the death of Karen's mum, author Lynne Wilding, in 2007, and her robust return in a dream visitation that was more like an alternative truth, or an untravelled path. After battling ovarian cancer for three years, Lynne, 65, had looked frail at the end, but in Karen's dream, 'she just looked normal and really healthy'. Lynne was leaning against the kitchen counter to chat as she'd often done in the evening after helping Karen with her two daughters while she and her husband worked. Karen recalls her mother said, 'I don't feel sick anymore. I'm really good.' Then, keen to demonstrate her recovered health, she said, 'Look what I can do,' before walking through the wall and standing out in the backyard. She walked back into the kitchen through the wall and said to Karen, 'How clever am I?' Then she repeated, 'I'm not sick anymore, I feel really good.'

Karen woke up sobbing with happiness and relief and was drawn to go downstairs, where, inexplicably, a delicious aroma filled the rooms. 'The house smelt like cookies!' marvels Karen, whose Mum had never been a keen baker. 'It didn't make sense to me at the time but it was a really strong smell.' Was Lynne speaking in the language of scents, letting her grieving daughter know that everything is sweet – that she's home? One thing is certain: 'I felt a lot lighter after that,' says Karen. 'I thought that was probably her way of telling me that she's good, that she's okay.'

Rachel Larkins, a 42-year-old writer and mother of two from Melbourne's East, also had the gift of seeing a parent restored to health and happiness after a drawn-out death: her father, Bob, who was 61 when pancreatic cancer claimed him in 1999. A week after the memorial service, Rachel was housesitting for a friend in a beautiful home at the base of Mount Wellington in Tasmania. Embraced by trees, rocks and river, it was the ideal setting for Rachel to walk in nature, to dwell in treasured memories and grieve the loss of her dad, a radio announcer and actor whose 'wonderful' voice echoes in Rachel's heart and mind. On the second night, 'I was asleep and I woke up and Dad was sitting on the end of my bed,' says Rachel. 'He looked healthy, he looked like how I always thought of my dad. He wasn't emaciated, he had his usual chubby cheeks. I could see through him, he wasn't solid. He was different to the rest of the room. I can't say there was a light around him but there was light that was a part of him. I thought, "Oh, it's Dad!"'

There was no fear, Rachel says, only a sense of guardianship. 'I saw him completely clearly, he was turned so that he was looking over me, he didn't do anything, but I had a really strong sense that he was just watching over me, that he was there, that he was close by. I didn't try to talk to him or anything, it was just this feeling of, "Oh, that's alright then, I can let things go," and I just went back to sleep. The next morning, I thought, "Wow, that was just what I needed."'

His return was 'in keeping with what he would do', says Rachel. 'He always thought of my sister and I as his little girls, he always wanted to protect us and look after us and that was some of the stuff we'd talked about at the end. It just felt like Dad came back to say, "It's okay," and let me know he was still watching over me.'

Naomi Kalogiros's mother-in-law found a novel way to let her family know she was well and happy in spirit following a long illness. 'Only my husband witnessed this 3 am apparition in early 2012,' tells Naomi, whose plentiful contacts with the spirit world I first related in *Spirit Sisters*. 'Our new dog, Midori, sleeps in the hallway opposite our bedroom door. One night my husband awoke to find the dog sitting up as if someone was feeding her. As his vision focused a little more, he noticed his mother standing there feeding the dog what he describes as "invisible food". Midori seemed happy and was actually eating the food being given to her. After this he saw his mother stand straight, turn and look at him with a loving smile. The dog let out a huge burp (which is something she does after eating her dinner each night!) and with this, his mother vanished.'

Naomi's home is a hub for visits from spirit loved ones, as all of her immediate family members share the increased aware-ness (commonly known as psychic ability) that makes such an encounter all the more likely. 'We don't feel awkward talking about what we see, feel, sense or smell,' says Naomi, who's 42 and the mother of two sons, Alex and Thomas. 'We feel honoured to be able to see the deceased and to feel their presence.'

When she was eight years old, Bridgett Bassett, who lives in the US, was also honoured by a visit from a loved one – her grandmother, who died after being sick with cancer for many months. 'When she passed it was a sad time,' recalls Bridgett, now aged 36. 'Every day after school I would be dropped off at her house to spend the afternoon with my grandfather until my parents were done with work. After Grandma died the house was silent and lost its glow. I could still smell her there, but could no longer see her.

'I didn't go upstairs very often, but for some reason, on this particular day, I chose to take a nap in one of the rooms at the top of the stairs. I waited for sleep to find me. When it did, I slept rather well, and found it difficult to open my eyes because I was so comfortable, but I heard my grandmother call out my name. When I opened my eyes, she was standing beside me. I could see her smile, and feel her hand brush my cheek. She was in full form. I couldn't see through her or anything like that. It was as if she really was there with me in the physical sense.

'I smiled back up at her, and then she was gone. I don't recall her walking out the door, or away from me, she just disappeared,' says Bridgett, who felt comforted, not afraid. 'I stayed there in bed for a while, trying to comprehend what just happened. I never told anyone afterwards. I just felt special, and was glad for the chance to see her again. I no longer felt so sad and alone, like I knew somehow she would always be watching over me.'

Sharon Tierney also had firsthand experience of a spirit who cared. The 44-year-old author from Newcastle, New South Wales, has a lifetime's worth of spiritual experiences to relate, including one magical moment more than a decade ago when she was given the chance to offer closure to her then-boyfriend, who'd long mourned the death of his sister in a car accident. Arriving at his parents' home for a weekend away, she was shown three spare rooms and invited to pick one for the night. Sharon made her choice and tucked herself in, her boyfriend settled into the room across the hall. Suddenly she was awoken unapologetically from a deep slumber. 'There was this tremendous energy,' says Sharon, who opened her eyes to see a woman 'lying right on top of me, like her face was right above my face'.

She had seen enough photos of her boyfriend's late sister to recognise her. 'I could only see the top half of her body; she was just floating, translucent. I could see the details of her face and the dark hair but the bottom half was like a fog. She was just floating above me. Obviously, I was taken aback! She just said to me, "Let my brother know I'm okay."'

Once the young woman had 'faded away', Sharon, still trembling with the shock and awe of the midnight meeting, rushed to wake her boyfriend and ask him whose bedroom she'd picked. When he confirmed it had been his sister's, she told him she knew, because she'd just seen her. His eyes grew round. 'She came to me,' said Sharon. 'She just wanted to let you know that she's okay.' They hugged and even now Sharon recalls, 'I could feel his relief.'

Sharon felt privileged to have been the conduit for what proved to be a life-changing gift from beyond. 'He was really comforted by that. He was changed from that day on, just to know she was okay. Just to hear those two words . . .'

It wasn't the only time Sharon would be woken in the night by a spirit visitor. She and her husband, Mike, spent three years living in the UK where Mike's mum, in the grip of illness, hadn't left her house for a decade. The couple decided to move back to Australia, reconciled to the sad reality that they would be unlikely to ever see her again. Three weeks later, Mike's mother passed away.

The next night, Sharon and Mike were asleep when an all-encompassing wave of ecstatic joy washed over them. 'I was straight up in bed like a bolt of lightning had hit me and Mike woke up at exactly the same time. He was like, "My God, this bolt of energy!" It just hit us,' says Sharon.

But for Sharon the experience went a step further: 'I saw his mum at the end of the bed and she was doing a little dance! Just jumping up and down. She was so happy. She was out of the house! Mike felt the energy, whereas I saw her at the end of the bed doing this little jig. Just happiness, absolute happiness! I grabbed the phone and rang his dad straightaway and described the little dance, because I'd never seen her active, and he said, "That is her. That is what she would do if she was happy – she'd do that little jig." Now we knew that she was fine, out of the house and not trapped in this illness anymore. She's free.'

Nic Hume knows that the same is true of her sister-in-law, Fiona, who was 32 and mum to three young children when she died of bowel cancer in 2009 after a year-long struggle with the disease. 'We sat with her during her final days and, as she waded in and out of consciousness, listened to her talk with people we could not see and have what appeared to be conversations with her children in the future,' remembers Nic. The 38-year-old candidly states that she and her sister-in-law hadn't been the best of friends, but their relationship progressed as the severity of Fiona's illness became clear. As the end neared, Nic reassured Fiona that she'd always be there for her family.

A founder of the Australian Paranormal Phenomenon Investigators, Nic's search for 'concrete evidence that the other side exists' was sparked in childhood, when she watched the full-bodied apparition of a butler stride across the hall of a historic home in Nowra, on the New South Wales south coast. During one of her vigils at her sister-in-law's bedside, she asked Fiona if she could give her a sign when she reached the other side. Nic recalls, 'She gave me this weird look and said, "Oh well, I can't make any promises."'

Three days after Fiona passed away, Nic was parking her car in her garage. 'All the windows were up and the fan and air-conditioner were off,' she explains. 'The car came to a stop and I turned to take off my seatbelt and as I glanced towards the passenger seat, there was a thick mist that dissipated before my eyes. I had to do a double-take to understand what I was seeing. Then it hit me – it was Fiona, giving me the sign we spoke of. I thanked her.'

Perhaps Fiona would have done so anyway, even without being asked – much in the same way you'd phone a parent, partner or friend to let them know you've arrived safe and well at the end of a long journey. To let them know you're okay.

So it is in the next two stories, which tell of a group of friends who rejoiced to witness, en masse, the return to health and vitality of their mate after he succumbed to asthma; and a young man who returned, beaming with joy and vitality, to help lift his brother from the depths of sorrow.

Last drinks

'He looked straight at me. He had the bluest, bluest eyes.'

Get-togethers were common enough at Phil Bowen's Sydney home. People would gather there to share beers, listen to music and chat. One night in 2007, four friends were over: Phil's girl-friend, his flatmate, and a colleague with his girlfriend. They were getting ready to sit down to dinner when Phil looked up and saw his best mate Ian walk down the hallway and into the bathroom. Ian wore his usual downtime gear: faded cut-off jeans, slippers and a white T-shirt. At any other point in the past five years Phil would not have looked twice, but not this night. Barely a week before, Phil had attended Ian's funeral.

'I thought, *Shit! Shit! What the fuck is he doing here?*' Phil recalls. 'I watched him fade away in hospital. I watched him go from a person to a shell. It was like, "Whoa, hang on mate. I said goodbye to you."' Phil says that the person was definitely Ian, he'd know him anywhere but 'you could see through him'.

Then Phil's girlfriend tugged at his sleeve, hissing, 'Did you see that?'

Not trusting his own eyes, he bluffed: 'No, what did you see?'

She said, 'I just saw Ian,' and described the same image that Phil had seen, right down to 'the Hush Puppy brown slippers we bought him,' as she told Phil.

Phil, whose sharp recall for details and dates belies his larrikinish persona, describes himself as 'a welder, machinist, postie, librarian, bloody everything'. The colourful character thought he'd experienced all life could throw at him in his 49 years; nothing, however, had come close to this. Yet rather than scream, panic, investigate or run for the door, Phil and his girlfriend merely got on with the business of dinner, never imagining what would come next.

Phil and Ian had been mates for years, ever since Phil heard Ted Nugent blaring over the back fence and, approvingly, went around to introduce himself to the thin and lanky German with piercing blue eyes and a wry sense of humour. They 'became great friends, better than brothers', eventually working together at a local engineering factory and becoming housemates, too. Arguments never came between them, rather they used to 'cry laughing all the time'.

'Ian had a heart of gold,' says Phil. 'He was a softie. I remember one day the neighbour's kid was running around at six in the morning with no shoes on and he woke me up, going off his head. He made the kid stand on a bit of A4 paper and drew a shape around his foot so that he could buy him a pair of shoes.'

Though it never slowed him down, Ian suffered from severe asthma and Phil learned what to do when his friend needed help. 'There were many times when I'd wake up in the middle of the night and he'd be yelling out. I'd go into his room, turn the light on, get him dressed, put some money in his pocket then ring a cab. Then I'd go and pick him up from the hospital.'

It was a severe asthma attack that killed Ian at the age of 47. Phil admits to 'blubbering like a baby' the last time he saw his friend, who was in a coma in hospital; Ian died fifteen minutes after Phil left the room.

Ian was one of those people who got along with everyone, as shown by the packed funeral service at Woronora Cemetery. And he was much loved by his mates. Phil recalls that when he placed Ian's welding helmet on top of his coffin, a whole row of burly blokes 'looked down on the ground and buckled'.

Yet there he was, wandering down the hallway of Phil's house, just like any other night when they got together with friends . . .

Minutes after Phil and his girlfriend saw Ian, the group of five sat down to eat at the dining table inside a sunroom which faced the backyard through a wall of glass windows. Phil's gaze was drawn up, away from his plate, and what he saw dismantled everything he knew about life, death and the bonds of mateship.

'Here he is again! This time walking around the side passage and round the back, like he's just come home from work,' says Phil. 'Then, when he walked past the back windows – they're massive windows – he stopped and looked straight at me, and I thought, "Those bloody eyes." He had the bluest, bluest eyes. The look on his face was like, "I've forgotten something" or "I was going to tell you something", but then he turned around and walked off at his normal pace.'

It seemed so commonplace, so 'like his old self', that Phil felt no fear, only 'wonder'. He reflects, 'You know, you hear about this sort of stuff and you wonder about what happens to us after we die. After this, I started to ask questions, thought maybe I should have listened in school, in all those religion classes.' And, according to Phil, everyone at the table saw Ian.

Seeing his mate in full colour, restored to health and vitality, has left its mark on Phil. 'It's made me a little more tolerant, like, understanding of people. I was quick with the temper before and now I'm not. It's made me think a lot more.'

Although Phil no longer lives at that house, on certain spring nights he casts his mind back to that evening when only a glass window stood between life and what follows. With each year that passes, the details sharpen, not blur, and the colours grow brighter. Every second, every scene, gleams in his memory. And every year, on Ian's birthday, Phil lifts a glass to his departed friend who found a way to tell him what he was incapable of saying in his last moments.

Goodbye for now, his blue eyes said. Look after yourself. All is well.

A brother's gift

'He was floating towards me with the biggest smile on his face.'

Two days after he died from an epileptic seizure, Theo came back to his brother, Emmanuel, who lay on his bed like a shell of a person. Whatever had been inside him – all the pieces that joined together to form 'Emmanuel' – were gone, vanished into the well of grief that had also devoured every other normal aspect of life. It was Saturday night, but it may as well have been Monday, or Wednesday – to Manny, as he is known, the days of the week meant nothing; eating and drinking were artefacts from his former life and the only true, tangible thing in his world was pain. So Theo arrived to help. But he didn't come alone.

Manny is telling me about his experiences while we're in a café in Sydney's Queen Victoria Building. The café bustles and clatters loudly around us, yet I am oblivious to the noise as Manny, a 35-year-old social worker and counsellor, relates his story in a measured and formal but softly spoken way.

On 28 June 2007, Theo, aged 27, made lasagne for dinner and was hanging out washing in the backyard of the home where he lived with his parents and two brothers, when he collapsed. He'd been diagnosed with epilepsy eight years before, so his family knew what to expect. Usually, Theo's seizures would last about five minutes, and it would take a further twenty minutes for him to regain consciousness. 'This time, he just didn't,' says Manny.

He remembers everything about that night in forensic detail, including the 'little things' that offered clues, in retrospect, that this time was not like the others. 'Every time Theo would have a seizure, our dog would freak out and run away, but on this particular night, she literally sat on him the whole time and wouldn't leave his side. She sandwiched herself between his legs and wouldn't budge. That was strange to me,' Manny recalls.

And rather than the 'hysterical' behaviour she'd typically display during Theo's seizures, their mum 'was very calm and very normal about the whole situation', he adds, 'which I found interesting because it was so inconsistent with her previous pattern'.

When Theo collapsed, his family rushed outside and followed their usual first-aid procedure: making sure he wasn't bleeding or injured, and placing him in the recovery position. After sitting with him a few moments, his parents went back inside and Manny remained, holding his brother's hand and speaking soothing words. By now it was 8 pm and rain had started to fall. A blanket was fetched for Theo, who lay on the back verandah of the house. The clothes he'd hung on the line lifted and lurched in the chill winter wind, getting slowly drenched.

At some point during Manny's vigil, Theo stopped breathing. Realising this, volts of dread, disbelief and adrenalin shot through Manny. 'I know now that was the moment he died, but at the time, I thought that couldn't possibly be true, so I dismissed it from my mind and ran inside to call emergency.' Within minutes, the family home swarmed with ambulance officers. For half an hour, Manny shone a flashlight into his brother's face while paramedics battled to revive him, their job hindered by the darkness and rain.

Soon after Theo's transfer to a nearby hospital, Manny was directed to a waiting room. There, a doctor coldly announced from the doorway that Theo had been declared dead on arrival.

It now fell to Manny to tell his mother, stepfather and youngest brother. Like a bomb aimed at their tightly woven family unit, the news shattered their beliefs, their dreams, the future they'd imagined for Theo and each other. The fragments of the family reassembled in a private room in the hospital where their son and brother now lay. From there, they phoned the rest of their large extended clan – aunts, uncles, cousins, who arrived over the next three to four hours to say their own farewells.

As the days unfolded, a revised reality rearranged itself around Manny. Time crawled by in a haze of cigarettes and bitter coffee. Grief sharpened his hearing and sense of smell. Life continued, but it had become a loud, smelly and crowded gathering Manny had no desire to join.

Saturday night at around 11 pm – Theo had been gone for 48 hours and Manny was a ghost of himself, floating aimlessly between kitchen, bedroom and couch, haunting the home where the presence of his dead brother was more alive than anyone living there. 'I had gone to my room to lie down, not to sleep because, you know, we couldn't really sleep in those days,' he says. 'I remember very clearly lying on my bed, staring out my window and yet even though I was awake and conscious of what was going on, I felt like I had actually left my body, and there was like . . .'

Manny pauses, searching for earthly words to describe something otherworldly. 'It sounds corny but it's God's honest truth,' he blurts, surprising me with a burst of boyish laughter. Returned to that moment, he sheds the sombre demeanour he wears like a uniform and joy shines from his dark eyes. 'There was a white light, circular in shape, and this white light was coming towards me. As it was getting closer, there were very distinct figures that had manifested themselves and immediately, I knew that it was my brother. He was floating towards me with the biggest smile on his face – I felt he was completely happy and at peace, and that feeling was very strong in me and very strong in him, he was showing me that.'

Yet Theo wasn't alone. 'There was someone else standing behind him, and I have no doubt that was my dad.'

Manny takes a sip of his coffee before explaining that his and Theo's father, house painter Anthony, died in a workplace accident when Theo was just a year old. Like Theo, Anthony was 27 when he died and their deaths were 27 years apart. Manny was three when his father died and 30 when Theo died, to name just a handful of the 'similarities and connections' Manny has drawn between the two losses. Now, as Manny's out-of-body experience showed, the years of separation melted away, and father and son revelled in their reunion.

'Theo's aura and everything around him was white and my dad was almost in a shadow, in complete contrast. While my brother was radiant, our dad was the exact opposite, almost as if to not take the spotlight away,' recalls Manny. 'In that image, it was very clear to me that it was my dad and my brother, and then it was the sense that my brother wanted to stay longer but he was told to go back. Then I remember my dad putting his hand out and Theo holding his hand and then walking away.'

The communication left him 'reassured', says Manny, whose Greek orthodox religion teaches that spirits linger for 40 days to say their goodbyes before ascending to the spirit realm. 'I feel like my dad made that happen for me to find some comfort in knowing they were together, and my brother made that happen to let me know he was with my dad.'

Though Manny never doubted what he saw, he received further validation when he met with Theo's best friend a few months later. As they chatted, Manny sensed the young woman was keen to share something, but wasn't sure how to begin. 'Your brother came to me after he died,' she finally said. 'I was in the living room watching TV and all of a sudden I felt myself detaching from my body while I was still awake. Then I saw this light, a white light came floating towards me and I saw your brother's face and he was happy and smiling. He hugged me and then he left.'

Manny was stunned. 'It totally freaked me out because it was so similar to my experience.'

Theo's blissful return on that cold Saturday night was his first attempt at repairing his brother's gouged-out heart, but it wouldn't be the last. Next came the dreams: 'They'd be a variation on Theo telling me, "I'm okay, I'm happy, I'm at peace, don't be sad, try to be happy, try to move on,"' recalls Manny, whose brother's loving entreaties showed him a path out of despair, though he is still a pilgrim on it. He remains haunted, for instance, by the sequence of events on the night of Theo's death, about whether enough was done to save him – though Theo has made clear he finds him blameless. Manny remembers a dream he had when Theo said to him, 'You have to stop beating yourself up because there's nothing you could have done. It was my time to go.'

But he's never far. In Chapter Four, Manny tells of the astonishing ways Theo communicates using butterflies as signs; and since taking up meditation, Manny has discovered a new way to connect with his adored middle brother, now flourishing in spirit in a way ill health never permitted him in life.

Theo was a hemiplegic, the right side of his body was paralysed (a consequence of having brain surgery for meningitis as an infant), so he 'always walked with a slight limp, and his fingers were somewhat contracted' says Manny, adding that Theo was balding and heavy in life, the latter a side effect of steroid medication. But during meditation, Theo appears strong and trim in white trousers and a white shirt – and with a full head of hair. 'In every visitation, all of his health problems are gone; it's almost as if he's his true self, the person he was meant to be, which is kind of sad that he couldn't be that on earth. But wherever he's gone he's reached that potential.'

The visitations are evolving, notes Manny. At first, it was only Theo he'd see, standing on the edge of a glittering stream, hills undulating in the distance, but lately 'he's bringing other people through, too'. Now their father, Anthony, grandparents and even the family's first dog, a red setter called Lucy, are joining Theo. There are also new faces, but Manny can't identify them yet.

In life, too, Theo was a beacon for people. A gifted cook (he could whip up multiple salads and professional-standard party platters in minutes), he was beloved for his kindness, generosity and 'heart as big as a mountain, as deep as the sea', as Manny remembered him in his eulogy. Those words could also describe Manny's suffering in the wake of Theo's death, suffering for which the only panacea was Theo himself, beginning with the wondrous night when he wrapped Manny up in the light of his love.

'The reality is that if I didn't believe there was something else after this life, I wouldn't be sitting here now, because I would have done something. My overwhelming grief . . .' Manny trails off, his eyes round and brown and infinitely sad.

'It's been the longest five years of my life,' he reflects, 'but the more these things happen to me, the more peace that I come to, knowing he's okay and in a better place, with people that love him and care about him.'

*

Seeing a precious person endure a drawn-out illness, only to lose the battle, can have a devastating impact, as the stories in this chapter have shown, but an assurance of 'safe arrival' can help repair a shredded heart. All the more so if these assurances take the form of visual encounters, as a new 'updated' picture of the departed loved one remains as a healing souvenir for the person left behind.

Karen's darling grandmother stood at her bedside, looking as real and beautiful as life, to let her know 'I'm okay' six months after her death from a heart attack. Rachel drew comfort and a sense of being looked after when she saw her dad sitting on the end of her bed following his death from pancreatic cancer. The visit 'was just what I needed', said Rachel.

Phil's best friend Ian came home after his funeral to look him in the eye, as no-nonsense as ever, and show him that death was not the end.

For Manny, who was a shell of himself after the death of his brother, seeing him glowing with health and bursting with happiness in the care of their father was the boost he needed to stay afloat in the murky ocean of grief he'd fallen into. Theo's message – 'I'm okay' – was the lifesaver he grasped to keep from sinking below tsunami waves of sorrow. To this day, should big seas loom, the memory of Theo's message is a lighthouse to guide him safely through.

3

Celestial Wisdom

❧

Words of advice from the afterlife

'The most beautiful thing we can experience is the mysterious.'
—ALBERT EINSTEIN

It was a brilliant October day in 1989 and, with the sun warming her back, 68-year-old Eileen set about planting potatoes in the garden of her home in rural Victoria. In a fortnight, it would be the first anniversary of her husband's death, but Eileen was feeling fine; for the first time in many months, she wasn't thinking about Tom, who'd died of a heart attack the previous spring.

But Tom must have had Eileen on his mind.

'All of a sudden, he was standing there in front of me,' says Eileen of her tall, slim and grey-haired husband. 'I couldn't see him with my eyes, I saw him from somewhere in my chest

– it seemed to come from *there*, and I could hear his message to me. Again, I couldn't hear it with my ears, but I knew what he was conveying to me and I could see the sweater he was wearing – it was his favourite, fawn-coloured with a cable pattern down the front.'

Tom's message – 'Look after yourself' and 'You can't do all this by yourself' – was a simple plea from a husband concerned for his wife. Not even death could unpick the threads in the tightly woven tapestry of their conjoined lives. 'I was trying to look after two acres and all the rest, trees and grass and everything else, and his message was very warm and loving.'

Afterwards, Eileen found herself 'lying on the ground sobbing', but she wiped away the tears with a smile on her face. 'I felt very happy, very reassured and very grateful,' says the mother of two who eventually took heed and moved into a smaller, more manageable home. 'Receiving Tom's message was just the most wonderful experience of my life.'

From simple and heartfelt pleas like Tom's, to specific instructions and words of wisdom about making the most of life, messages are often carried in after-death communications. Indeed, they are the *purpose* of many such communications. Though their content varies greatly, all highlight a common sentiment: our late loved ones do not stop caring about the progress of our day-to-day lives.

Kim Hammond found that out on a wintry night in 1998, when his late mum dropped by to cheer him up. It was the first time Kim had ever sensed her spirit, or any for that matter, and he felt bathed in abundant euphoria. 'I was feeling a bit down at the time. I hadn't had a partner for three years or more,' says Kim, 55, a glazier and divorced father of two who lives a tranquil, rustic and solitary life on the south coast of New South Wales. 'I had a lady friend who said she was coming around for tea, but then she rang up and said she couldn't make it, so I just said to myself, "Ah well, I'll put some music on." I was feeling a bit low.'

Kim put on Metallica's *Reload* album and was 'dancing around a bit' in the living room, wondering if he should go to his mate's house to watch the State of Origin instead, when something happened which he finds difficult to convey. 'It was the feeling of happiness,' says Kim, who knew as surely as he'd ever known anything that his mum had joined him. 'It was like she was there, with my eyes closed, I could see her. It's hard to explain how the room was filled with happiness . . . It was like . . . you know when you're in a room full of smoke? It has a big effect on you. Well, this was a room full of happiness. There was nothing to see but the whole room was full of happiness, you know? It was really overwhelming joy. It felt like I was a foot off the ground.'

Enmeshed in the joy was a message from his mother. Kim explains that he didn't hear these words spoken out loud, more like the idea was planted in his mind, but her message was clear: 'Do whatever you want and never let anybody tell you that it's the wrong thing to do. If you want to walk backwards to Africa, go ahead and do it. As long as you're happy doing it . . ."'

Kim seems to have followed the advice of his free-spirited mum, who used to listen to his records – from David Bowie to Black Sabbath – while he was at school and later offer her opinions on them. He's now living quietly in his little house on the coast, with four pianos but no electricity and an expertly crafted homemade pyramid in the backyard. 'I'm pretty free and easygoing,' he agrees in his articulate and gentle voice. 'I don't work full-time, I still go surfing, motorbike- and trail-riding and I drove to Ayers Rock [Uluru] in 2011.'

From time to time he still ponders the mystery of that distant winter's night. 'It sort of gives you this feeling that there is something else out there,' he says. 'Life isn't just cut and shut.'

Sydneysider Gordon Lowe also received a liberating message from his mother, Peggy, who had died of a heart attack at the age of 68. Gordon himself was recovering from a heart attack at St Vincent's Hospital in 2012 and was resting in bed when he heard the subtle 'droning' sound he'd come to recognise as the first sign of a loved one's spirit trying to get in touch with him. While he'd usually 'try to resist', Gordon says this time he felt no trepidation: 'I thought, "Well, I've got nothing to lose now. They might be able to help me.'

Gordon, a 63-year-old building manager, then fell into a 'very, very peaceful sleep' in which he dreamt of his simple and carefree childhood with his nine siblings in Bathurst, New South Wales.' When he woke, it was with the certainty that his mother had come to tell him, 'You're going to be alright, don't worry' and 'Speak your mind and have no fear'.

The message to speak his mind and have no fear has given Gordon the courage to become more assertive in his work and personal life. Gordon, who's also received messages of reassurance from the spirit of his brother, Kerry, never doubts the steadfast presence of the people he's loved and lost: 'Have you ever walked down the street and felt tingly? Like you brush someone? Or you stop and look and think, "Gee, that's a lovely flower," just as your mother might have said? Then you think, "I wonder why I did that?" Well, I think they walk with us,' says Gordon. 'They keep us safe and well.'

And our loved ones in spirit care about the smallest details, too, as primary school teacher and mother of three Michelle found in December 2012. It was four weeks before Christmas when her 65-year-old former neighbour, turned dear family friend, Lois, died five months after being diagnosed with cancer. To add another layer of gloom to what was supposedly the festive season, this would be the last Christmas celebrated in Michelle's family home, in a leafy suburb in Sydney's south, as her parents were downsizing and moving out.

In the lead-up to it, something was 'really bugging' Michelle – the matter of a Christmas tree. Her father had thrown out their old one and a replacement had been ordered online but it still hadn't arrived, so Michelle dispatched her husband to pick up whatever he could find at the supermarket. At that late stage all he could get was 'one really tiny, measly tree', says Michelle, 35, who concedes she was fixated on finding something special to commemorate their last Christmas at home. 'I wasn't comfortable with it at all.'

Meanwhile, at Lois's home, there was another Christmas tree saga unfolding. Unbeknown to Michelle and her family, Lois's husband wanted to dispose of their oversized tree but his daughter, Kate, was urging him to reconsider as her mum had adored it. The solution to both families' dilemmas was there for the taking, and it seems Lois – a strong person who'd always loved helping others – got to work pointing it out.

The evening after she'd delivered the unsatisfactory tree to her mum, Michelle went to bed and fell asleep. 'All of a sudden, I find myself standing up in Lois's lounge room and she's pacing the room, frustrated. There was a table with a small tree on one side and her big tree on the other and she was pacing in front of the table. I said – but I didn't use words – "What's the matter, Lois?" She stopped and she stood next to a miniature Christmas tree; it was just like Mum's new one, and Lois made it glow purple, because my mum has purple decorations, and she was showing me it was Mum's tree. And then she paced over to the other side, past her big tree, and just wandered off through the doorway into the kitchen.'

Michelle woke up with her heart hammering. She shook her husband awake. 'I said, "Oh my God, Lois has just communicated with me! She showed me Mum's small crappy tree and she wasn't happy about it.'

Later Michelle told Kate about her dream, and Kate 'put it all together'. Lois's husband was thrilled to find the perfect new home for his outgoing Christmas tree – which he delivered the next day, along with a pudding Lois had made before she died for her cherished friends. Laughing, Michelle says that in life, 'Lois organised everyone around her and she's still the same – she hasn't changed.'

It wasn't the first time Michelle had received a message from the spirit of a loved one. When she was 22, she had her first communication from her grandfather, who'd died of cancer when Michelle was eight. 'He came to me in a time of trouble and he gave me a solid message and direction of steps I needed to take,' remembers Michelle. She describes the experiences with him and Lois as dream visitations that occur 'when I'm not asleep and not awake'. They are never frightening, she points out: 'I don't have fear when it's someone who loves you and they're there to help you.'

In her first dream visitation, she saw herself in her grandfather's office, though he'd never had one in life. 'He was important. He had an office with a desk and two chairs. He was sitting behind his desk. He was wearing a suit and he looked like a fitter version of himself. I held my arms up in the air to cuddle him and it was like every emotion in one. It was joy, sorrow, laughter, sadness – it was really intense.'

The pair exchanged thoughts through their minds. 'When I put my arms out to hug my grandfather, his response was, "I can't communicate with you like that – *this* is the only way I can communicate." I think he was referring to telepathic communication,' says Michelle. 'He said, "Just don't walk out, do not walk out," and it made sense when I thought about the difficulties I was facing. I followed his advice and things worked out.'

Kate, Lois's daughter, has received her own messages from her mum via dreams. It makes perfect sense – in life their closeness was something rare and marvellous; death may have stretched their bond of love but it couldn't sever it. 'I'm an only child and my relationship with my mum was more than just mother and child,' the 44-year-old, who works in publishing, tells me. 'Not taking anything away from my husband, but my mum was not only my mum, but my best friend, my sister, my everything, my rock, and I was her everything. We were very dependent on one another.'

Soon after Lois's death on 1 December 2012, she explained her departure to her grief-torn daughter in a dream as a way of helping her cope. Kate recalls the dream:

Mum and I were on a road trip. We stopped at a service station and she came out of the station in her dressing gown and slippers and said to me that she was sorry but she couldn't go on any further as she was tired and just wanted to go home. At that stage I was still very angry with her for leaving me and would yell at her constantly. I felt this was her way of telling me that she was sorry she had to go so soon but she just couldn't keep up the fight any longer.

Beau McKnight, a 35-year-old mother of six from Queensland, shared a story with me that suggests not only does love
never die; sometimes, it is not even born, yet it takes its place –
impactfully – in the trajectory of our lives. A few months before
she gave birth to her stillborn daughter, Rhiannon, in 1997,
Beau received a visit from a being whose message smoothed the
way for what was to come. She recalls: 'I dreamt of a tall angel
surrounded by the most beautiful, all-encompassing blue light
– I was immersed in it. It was the bluest blue you'd ever seen.

'The being spoke to me for a long time, telling me things and
getting me ready for a major event about to happen in my life.
When I awoke, I didn't remember anything of what he or she
said and haven't since. Was it a guide? An angel? I don't know.'

What's indisputable, says Beau, is the solace it gave her after
the heart-splitting shock of her perfect daughter being stillborn
at full-term. The memory of the dream, which overflowed with
love and the secrets of the universe – though they weren't hers
to remember – was like a soft blanket being draped around
her shoulders. 'The experience taught me there are higher powers,'
says Beau, who tells of subsequent meaningful connections with
Rhiannon's spirit in later chapters. 'We aren't in control.'

It's what Shakespeare hinted at when he wrote, 'There are
more things in heaven and earth . . . than are dreamt of in your
philosophy.' Mysteries beyond our perception are at the heart
of the next trio of stories, too: a woman heals, physically and
emotionally, thanks to sage words from her long-dead mother;
a teenaged boy's concern for his mother shines through when he
returns on the eve of his funeral; and a dying father's instructions to his overwrought son prevent family disintegration.

Nestled in each encounter, a potent message – propelled
by love.

A mother's mantra

'I'd fall back into the absolute warmth of this golden light as my mother just floated above me, smiling.'

Denise Mack's mother, Valentine, died at the age of 74 in 1984, but she remains 'a constant presence' in Denise's life. An author who lives in Victoria, 66-year-old Denise says, 'Sometimes I'll see her standing at the edge of the bed at night, but it's more commonly a sense of her presence, a total calmness,' which is in keeping with the 'calm and gentle' nature she possessed in life. In 2011, during a tumultuous time in Denise's life, Valentine's love and warmth enveloped her daughter when she needed it most.

Not only did her mother's smiling face and 'otherworldly' voice hasten Denise's recovery from serious abdominal surgery, the message Valentine shared helped put the pieces of her broken life back together, as she tells below:

It was in 2011 and I was at a huge crossroads in life. I had sold my house but the future looked blank and I didn't know where I was going to move, didn't know what I was going to do. All the furniture was packed up, all my belongings were in boxes and the removalists were coming the next morning at eight o'clock. I had arranged temporary accommodation but I didn't want to go there.

So from ten o'clock the next morning, for me, life was just a total blank. And during the weeks leading up to this – this is probably the most important point – it occurred to me that I might die because I couldn't see anything ahead. I had always seen my life and then set about creating what I saw, and because I couldn't see anything this time, I thought, 'Well, this might be the time I die.' This occurred to me quite factually, with no emotion behind it.

The day prior to moving out of my home of fifteen years and into temporary accommodation, I went to bed with a slight pain in my abdomen. During the night I started vomiting. The next afternoon I rang one of my sons who lived fifteen minutes away and said, 'I think I need to go to hospital.' He came straightaway and we decided between us that it was probably food poisoning and to wait till the morning. At seven o'clock the next morning my son came back to help with the removing, took one look at me and called the ambulance. I was almost comatose by this stage. I was taken to hospital where they discovered, over a period of a week to ten days, a bowel obstruction.

They put me on a drip and for twelve days, I had nothing to eat or drink apart from what was coming through the drip and I was slipping in and out of consciousness. But the doctors thought it would clear itself so they just monitored me. On the twelfth day, the head surgeon burst into the ward with his entourage, took one look at me and said, 'This woman will not live another twelve hours unless she is operated on immediately.'

So up I go to the operating room. As I floated in and out of consciousness, I still thought, 'Is this the way I die? Is this how it's going to happen?' Waiting outside the operating room I could see the sun set over the eastern suburbs and it was autumn and there were lovely, soft reds and oranges, and I thought, 'Well, this might be the last thing I see on this planet, but hang on, I've got more to do yet, more to accomplish, more to give, more to create.'

What seemed like a few minutes later I awoke and the surgery nurse was beside me saying, 'It's over, you're okay. Here is a gadget for morphine – press it when the pain gets too bad and use as much as you like.'

So I closed my eyes and for the next twelve hours I went to a place that was neither asleep nor awake. And I was surrounded by and infused by gold and yellow light and the light seemed to be everywhere, in me, outside of me, it was me. I have to add that I didn't use any morphine at all during this time, so while I was in this light or was the light, I felt the presence of my mother hovering, which was not unusual, she's present a lot of the time in a peripheral way and she had a very Mona Lisa smile when she was alive and I could see or feel this smile when she was hovering. And then there was a voice, but not a voice, you know? It's hard to describe but it's more like an energy vibration. And this voice was so deep and warm, it was her voice but not her voice, it was just something otherworldly, and she said very clearly, 'Everything is well, Denise. All is well, not only are you going to continue to live but you are now living your So Hum life.'

[Author's note: 'So Hum' is a contemplation mantra used during meditation to focus on the mystery of being. It means 'I am that', with 'that' standing for all of creation – it speaks to the idea of the interconnectedness of the universe.]

Being a yoga teacher and in the health and wellbeing industry, that advice just seemed perfectly natural to me. This So Hum vibration lasted all night and was only broken when the nurse came to have a look at my vital signs and I'd surface and then fall back into that between-waking-and-sleeping space and back into the absolute warmth of this golden light as my mother just floated above me, smiling.

In the morning an Iranian doctor, who was so perceptive and I think quite a special doctor, came in and said, 'But you haven't used any of your morphine? I can't believe this, you've just had major surgery! This is amazing, no one doesn't ever use their morphine. I've never come across this in all the years I've been a doctor.'

Then I slept more and through that day the golden light, my mother's image, the voice and the mantra of the So Hum continued.

Her appearance, and the experience of the light, all of that to me really didn't have so much impact on whether I was going to survive this operation. It was absolutely to do with the rest of my life. It kind of catapulted me into another era. It was totally life-changing. I was very relieved and grateful that I could now see a future. The experience of my mother coming and the light and all of this wasn't astonishing or unusual for me because I have experienced a number of these situations, but it was more one of deep gratitude. I felt now I was living in a state of grace.

Beyond the last goodbye

'His hands were together, as if he was praying.'

Like most teenaged siblings, Bianca, fifteen, and her brother, Stephen, eighteen, occasionally argued over trivial things – an ill-judged joke, the distribution of chores, taunts shaped like arrows aimed at the heart. But beneath the bickering, the pair were bound by a closeness that informed their lives – though there was no call to ever speak of it – a sense of staunch togetherness they took for granted.

On 12 August 1988, Bianca rose early. It was a Friday but she had a reprieve from school. Her grandmother had been staying at their home in the northern Sydney suburb of Brookvale to care for Bianca and her sister, Torrie, aged nine, while their single mum juggled two jobs. Since leaving school two years earlier, Stephen, too, helped support his mother and sisters. Now their grandmother wanted to drive back to her apartment in Nelsons Bay, on the central coast of New South Wales, to attend to some things and gather more belongings, before returning to Sydney to continue looking after her grandchildren. Bianca and Torrie were going with her for the weekend. Though Bianca grumbled inwardly – she would have preferred to stay home, near her friends – she knew she had little say in the matter.

The morning was crisp and dazzling, the sky a bowl of brightest blue, but Bianca was in no mood to appreciate it. Today marked four days since she and Stephen had stopped speaking to each other. Charged silences, crossed arms and downturned mouths filled the spaces in their relationship where laughter and camaraderie usually dwelled. 'I can't really remember why we weren't talking,' says Bianca, whose calm and matter-of-fact voice cracks, to her surprise, as she recalls events from a quarter of a century ago. 'And because I was younger than him, I was full of pride. I would never talk to him first – he would have to talk to me first and apologise to me first,' she says, with a sad chuckle. 'Yeah, I was very stubborn. I would never try and repair the arguments.'

Leaving her bedroom with an overnight bag slung across her shoulder, she stopped short outside Stephen's room, neighbouring her own. His door was open but he was still in bed. 'I actually said, "Goodbye, Stephen," and that was very unusual,' Bianca says.

Looking up at his sister, Stephen's wide-set eyes mirrored her confusion. She had no idea why she'd paused here, why she'd broken her usual resolve. 'Oh! Bye, Bianca,' he said, with a glimmer of his characteristic cheekiness, before returning his gaze to the ceiling.

Their grandmother beamed, grateful the kids were getting on again. 'She said to me, "I'm so proud of you for saying goodbye to him,"' remembers Bianca, her words pitching and dipping, as if adrift in a tempest. 'That was the last time I spoke to him.'

Later that Friday night, in Nelsons Bay, Bianca and her sister were trying to connect the video recorder they'd given their grandmother for her birthday. Pressing buttons here and there, Bianca managed to set the time display. As her grandmother prepared dinner in the kitchen, Bianca found herself mesmerised by the numbers on the digital display: 6.35. 'I was just staring at the time and feeling really quite homesick for some reason, I just wanted to be home.'

The next morning, her mother and uncle arrived at her grandmother's house – unexpectedly. Drawn to the window by the thud of slamming doors, Bianca watched them approach, aware in some way that in seconds – the time it took for them to reach the door – this life would cease for her and another would take its place. Everything was about to change.

Her grandmother opened the door. Dread spilt inside Bianca, spreading like a bloodstain in waves of zinging heat that crept up her spine and across her belly. Icy, pulsing fire that told her what she'd experienced last night, tuning the VCR, was preparing her for this. Still dressed in her work clothes from the day before, her mother was like a broken doppelganger of herself. It seemed she was covered in a network of fissures, where one misstep would see her crumble into shards on the welcome mat.

Then Bianca's uncle stepped forward and 'sort of grabbed us' she recalls. He said, 'Stephen's had an accident.'

Up through the tunnel of years, his sister's hazel eyes grow red from weeping. Twenty-five winters have rushed by, Bianca is now 40 years old, a mother of two, a registered nurse who's weathered much in her life and work – but the news that her brother was dead felt like an assault. Twenty-five winters doesn't change that; the pain is frozen in time, perfectly preserved. In the same way Stephen is forever young, I think, studying a photo Bianca sends me. Tall and slim, posing astride his beloved motorbike, bought with proceeds of one of his first pay packets, the dark-haired teen has the swagger of a young George Clooney.

For Stephen, the combination of youth, inexperience and his passion for bikes proved lethal. As Bianca's uncle explained that awful Saturday morning, Stephen had been killed riding his motorbike the previous evening. His passenger, a friend he was picking up to take to a party, also died. The accident happened at 6.35 pm, the precise moment Bianca found herself hypnotised by the pulsing digital clock on the VCR.

The grieving family made the trip back to Sydney. All was the same yet nothing was. Time itself was twisted out of shape. 'For about a week after his death, I'd wake up in the mornings and hear his motorbike in the driveway, revving up to go to work,' says Bianca. 'It was quite loud in my ears, you know, and then I had to remind myself that he's dead.'

Ahead of the funeral, family came to stay and their little home was packed. To make space, Bianca and her mum moved into Stephen's room, sleeping side by side in his double bed. On the eve of the service, Bianca's mum was out cold after taking a sleeping tablet, but Bianca sat up reading, battling a gnawing unease. Something was about to happen. The knowing manifested as anxiety, as an inability to pin down the words on the page.

She set aside her book and looked towards the end of the bed.

There was Stephen, wearing his favourite black-and-grey striped dress shirt, the one his mum had given the funeral directors. The one he's wearing in the photo with his motorbike, staring down the lens of a truncated future. In the stark glare of the overhead light, as his mother slept, he was revealed. 'It was as bright as anything in that room,' marvels Bianca. There were no shadows to dart into or mould into shapes, no dreams to beg back, no dim lamplight to blur the truth. There was only Stephen.

He knelt.

'All I could see was from his abdomen up and his hands were together, as if he was praying, and he was really staring at Mum and I. He was looking straight at us.'

Bianca's fear melted away when she saw him. 'I felt scared beforehand because I knew something was going to happen, but I didn't quite know what. And then he just appeared to me, and the feeling that I got – he wasn't talking – was "Look after Mum". That's what I felt he was trying to communicate. Then I closed my eyes and he was gone.'

Bianca watched her brother for only 'seconds' but it was enough 'to really see him clearly'. His image is branded onto her heart: 'There was a transparency to him. He was grey, but I could see him as clear as anything,' she repeats. 'His eyes were wide open. He had big, dark blue eyes and he was just looking at us and he looked sad.'

Afterwards, Bianca went to sleep easily, which she concedes

was strange, but it's in keeping with many other such encounters with the spirits of loved ones. Their return is the sweetest lullaby.

In quiet moments, she still tries to decipher the message in his stance and expression. 'I don't know why he was kneeling down at the end of the bed, with his hands together in prayer,' says Bianca, whose family is Catholic but not strictly so. 'I don't know whether that was just to let me know he was going to God or whether he was taking that stance not to frighten me. I'm not sure.'

She often wonders why he appeared so troubled. 'It could have been regret and feeling sorry that he's left us. He was a bit reckless,' muses Bianca. 'I guess he was the man of the house and he was worried about leaving us.'

Stephen wore the same heartbroken look during an encounter at a cinema in Warringah Mall two weeks later, when Bianca was stunned to see his gaze locked on hers in the mirror behind the ticket counter as she paid for an ice cream. 'I saw his eyes,' she recalls. 'I don't know whether you'd say he superimposed himself on me, because I was expecting to see me. He was just staring, *really* staring at me.' This time, Bianca was very shaken and the two friends who'd suggested an outing to the movies to take her mind off things helped soothe and calm her. Stephen appeared to share her shock. 'He could see that I was frightened because he looked scared, too. And then he looked down at the ground, like in a sad way.' Then he vanished.

For two years, Stephen regularly visited Bianca in her dreams, usually just as a watchful presence on the sidelines. But some were much more powerful. The first and 'most significant' of these took place around a month after the accident. One morning, Bianca and a friend rode their pushbikes to the accident scene and talked about what had happened, trying to understand the sequence of events that had led to Stephen's death. That night, she had the dream. Stephen, and the boy who'd died with him, were standing in front of her, exactly as they'd been in life.

'Stephen said to me, "Bianca, do you want to see how we died?" like it was an everyday sort of question. And I said, "Yes, I do want to know." And so he showed me.

'It was like I was actually sitting on the motorbike, watching what they would have seen. He showed me how they hit the back of the car in front and then they flew over to the opposite side of the road.' In what was perhaps a tender gesture on Stephen's part, any disturbing details were omitted. 'He just showed me the impact with the car in front, how the motorbike tipped up and then they . . . once they came off the bike, it just went white, nothing.'

When she woke up, Bianca felt free of her desperation to know how he'd gone. Her burden lifted: 'He answered my question.'

Today Bianca, who first showed signs of having increased psychic awareness in childhood, rarely senses Stephen's spirit anymore. 'I think he's just moved on, you know. But I think he hung around us for a long while because it must have been an awful shock for him to have had the accident and to leave us. That was really sad.' Yet there is less grief now, when Bianca thinks of her big brother. Seeing him again on that distant night was a gift that continues to yield, more so with every year that drifts by. 'I just feel really privileged to have had that experience, which was so special and amazing,' she reflects. 'I feel really happy that there is another life beyond this life that we live. I think we go to a happier place, and a safer place. I feel at peace.'

She knows this is the case for Stephen, too, knows his velvet navy eyes are ablaze with light and infinite love, as he watches over her.

A place beyond

'I was so relieved to know he wasn't suffering anymore.'

After a lifetime of growing up with an emotionally distant, but loving, father, Ban Guo was overjoyed that he'd finally found a way to connect – albeit in the shadow of death. After his father suffered a severe stroke in 2000, Ban sat for hours at his bedside, encouraging him as he took tentative steps towards a recovery doctors warned would not be permanent. Time spent together, free of the pressures of work or study, proved fertile ground for their blossoming relationship, which took hold like the mythical beanstalk, growing with speed and vigour up and up, to a place beyond the clouds.

Ban was three years old when his family emigrated from Hong Kong to Sydney, where his dad, Kwong, established a bustling Chinese restaurant called The Bamboo Cave in Fairfield, in Sydney's west. From the time Ban was six, Kwong worked merciless hours there, while his wife, Leng, cared for their four children. 'In a way, I wasn't close to my father because I didn't really see him very much. He started work at 8 am, to go to the markets and get the vegetables, and the restaurant didn't close until 10 pm,' says Ban. Nonetheless the 50-year-old smiles as he recalls the steamy, scented hive of his father's kitchen, his passion for cooking and how 'even the Mayor of Fairfield used to come to dine with his councilmen'.

But the demands of the business took its toll on Kwong, whose high blood pressure and heart problems forced him to sell in 1980 in favour of a series of part-time jobs. By then, Ban was working by day and studying at night so, once again, life sent them in opposite directions. 'He would say, "You live your life the best way you want to live it and I will enjoy my life." I was on good terms with him but I wasn't particularly close to him, it was more of a formal relationship,' reflects Ban. Robberies and dealings with dishonest people had also disillusioned his generous but reserved father, reinforcing 'his philosophy that it's a tough world and you've got to be tough to survive'.

That was true for Kwong, who was dogged by health problems for the next two decades: 'Every four years he'd have a major operation but he'd always bounce back.' In 2000, however, the situation seemed dire. 'I was at home and my mum rang to tell me that Dad had collapsed and he was unconscious,' says Ban, who rushed to the emergency department at the local hospital to be told it was touch and go. 'I thought, "This is terrible, because I didn't really get to know him all that well." But following his transfer to the Royal Prince Alfred hospital, where he had keyhole surgery to dissolve a blood clot, Kwong began to slowly improve.

'Some days he felt so good he just wanted to walk out of there,' says Ban, in his gentle, slow and deep voice. 'My spirits went up. All of us were really happy.'

Four times a week, Ban would finish his government clerical job and go straight to the hospital, where he'd spend three hours by his father's side. Though a tracheotomy had compromised Kwong's speech, it made no difference to the love and appreciation flowing freely, finally, between father and son, who were content just to be together. Eventually, in the anticipation that his dad would recover and his mum may need help to look after him, Ban took a year's leave from his job, happy that he was doing everything he could for his dad. Happy that they were bonding.

After eight weeks at the Royal Prince Alfred, Kwong was transferred to a rehabilitation hospital nearby, where doctors were amazed by his recovery, though they warned he could still suffer a second stroke. Miraculously, Kwong – still tube-fed and in a wheelchair – was declared well enough to go home for Christmas, but his family's delight was short-lived. Soon after Christmas, a second stroke incapacitated the battling patriarch, who was now in a coma. 'Doctors told us it was so severe the brain stem was damaged, and slowly he'd stop breathing. Slowly, the organs would stop working and he would pass away.'

Deciding the next step to take divided the family. Ban's three sisters and his mother wished to follow the doctors' advice to withdraw treatment and let Kwong slip away peacefully at home, but Ban and his uncle wanted to pursue the shred of possibility that he might recover. 'We thought there was still a chance,' says Ban, who wanted to put his father on life support. 'There was conflict between me and my sisters. I just couldn't accept that my dad was going to die.'

Now it was Kwong's turn to put forward his point of view.

It was 8 pm and Ban, dizzy with exhaustion, stepped away from his father's hospital bedside and found a half-comfortable chair in a nearby waiting room. Amid the family turmoil, and the distress of witnessing his father's fitful breathing and the painful bedsores he was developing, Ban had not slept for two nights and began to doze off. Next thing he knew, 'I saw my dad looking young, healthy and fit, the way I knew him before his illness. There in the hospital room, he rose out of bed and

I thought, "Oh, Dad's recovering! This is so good." But my dad looked at me with a very solemn expression and said to me, "Ban, what you're doing is causing the family and me a lot of distress because, look at me . . ." and then he turned and pointed to his body on the bed. He didn't say anything to me, but it was like he was putting his thoughts into my mind. He looked at the bedsores, at his breathing slowly deteriorating, at the blood in his catheter. He looked himself up and down and I think he even showed a bit of anger,' remembers Ban. 'He put the thought into my mind, "Is that the way you want me to be? If I continue living, that's me. *That's me.* You're not in this situation and you're causing it." Then I saw images of my sisters looking very distressed and heard, "Look at what you're doing to the family, too." He was not very happy with me.'

The overall message was, Ban says, 'He was going to somewhere better and I should let him go the light.'

Ban's first thought when he woke up was 'It was just a bad dream', but after turning the event around in his mind, examining it from every angle, he reached the conclusion 'Dad was trying to tell me something'. Freed from his feeble body, the spirit of Kwong had reached out to his son, pleading for his understanding and compassion. This was not an after-death communication, as Kwong had not yet passed, but could be classified as a 'crisis apparition', where in the moments preceding death, a spirit makes contact with a loved one, often to say goodbye or prepare them for what is to come – but Kwong had a more specific purpose.

He accomplished his mission: Ban changed his mind about how to proceed with his father, and informed his uncle of his decision. 'Though I was still very sad, I understood. I reconciled with my sisters and told them about my experience. They said,

"Yes, Dad needed to tell you this, because if he didn't show himself in this way we would still be in conflict, and in the meantime, he suffers."'

The very next day, peace, tenderness and a touch of magic, not beeping machines and fear, accompanied their father out of his life. Ban recounts: 'My sister went to see my dad in hospital and as she held his hand she said, "Dad, you fought the good fight. You've been a good father and we have so many wonderful memories of you. If you want to go to a better place, you can go." Then, after being in a coma for so long, he slightly turned his head, a tear came down his face and he stopped breathing and passed away.'

Ban is grateful he was able to spend time with his father after he died. 'I felt the sadness I'd had before lift, as he was no longer in pain. He looked so peaceful. He looked at rest. I was so relieved to know he wasn't suffering anymore. I had thought I'd collapse with sadness but, no, it was just a feeling of assurance to know that he's okay now.'

Reflecting on where his dad is now, Ban says, 'It's like going from one country to another. I think there's another world out there, a world that is different. It's like being born again into a new life, but we remember our old lives. It's a new life where sickness and death is a door to something else beyond this world.'

*

Reading over the words of wisdom delivered by loved ones in spirit in the stories above, it strikes me how simple – yet profound – most are:

'Look after yourself.'
'Follow your heart.'
'Speak your mind.'

'Look after Mum.'

'Let me go.'

They remind me of a list I have laminated on my fridge. Among its tips for a 'mindful' day it tells me to: Wake with the sun, sit, let the darkness come, and sleep when tired. Just looking at it calms me when I'm worried or anxious because it's a reminder that life is actually less complicated than it appears. If we're stretched too thin, we usually have no one to blame but ourselves.

The caring messages from the hereafter in this chapter seem just as brief and a bit abrupt – like a rushed farewell on a crackly international phone line – but they're loaded with significance, offering a hidden-in-plain-sight blueprint to a more fulfilling way of life. Thanks to the willingness of those who have shared their experiences, we can all partake in that wisdom, but of course, to anyone on the receiving end of guidance from beyond, such a message is life changing in another way: it proves the people we've adored and lost are still playing a loving and active role in our lives.

4

The Butterfly Effect

✺

Signs and symbols of enduring love

*'My brother used to ask the birds to forgive him . . . for all is like
the ocean, all things flow and touch each other; a disturbance in this
place is felt at the other end of the world.'*

—FYODOR DOSTOYEVSKY

Flicking through the newspaper on a chill and gloomy
Saturday, I stopped short at a page-three photo of a peacock
warming itself by an electric heater inside a lounge room. Reading the accompanying article, in *The Daily Telegraph* (29 June
2013), I learn that the glorious creature visits the home of the
Azzopardi family in Sydney's suburban Baulkham Hills every
day between 9 am and 4.30 pm – a routine it's followed since
2009. Recently, said the report, it's even started venturing
indoors for warmth.

What really piques my interest is this: the bird first appeared
on the day Tony Azzopardi laid to rest his elderly mother. Before

she died, Tony used to take photos of the cockatoos feeding in his yard and show them to his ailing mum to lift her spirits. As Tony told the newspaper: 'Mum may have sent it to say, "If you think your white cockatoos are nice, take a look at my peacock."'

The report made me smile. Not only because, in my experience, it's an example of one of the most common types of after-death communications – the symbolic ADC – but because the article was published on the very day I was beginning work on this chapter.

Coincidence? Many believe there's no such thing, and all of my reading and research has led me to arrive at the same conclusion. Writing *Spirit Sisters*, back in 2008, I interviewed Perth resident Sheila Berry, who was forced to dismantle everything she believed about life, love and death when the perfect outline of a butterfly mysteriously imprinted itself on her glass door, seven months after the death of her daughter, Jackie. 'Everything was so clear – even the pattern on the wings!' Sheila told me. An impression of every miniscule part of the insect's anatomy had been transferred onto the glass, even the antennae, confounding Sheila and an expert at Perth Zoo.

It was only the beginning – from then on, butterflies began to flutter into Sheila's world in the most incongruous places and situations.

The same happened to Jo Struck, whose story features in *Where Spirits Dwell* (published 2011). Jo's baby, Jay, died of SIDS and his signature became the butterfly – on one occasion Jo was at midnight mass when a butterfly flew in and perched on her arm for the duration of the service.

Whether via butterflies, feathers, birds, songs, a sequence of numbers, or any of the countless other ways a symbolic connection is made, what matters is its significance – the peace and healing it carries. The 'how' is almost inconsequential, although Carl Jung's theory of synchronicity suggests everything and everyone in the universe is linked – from our physical 'reality' to the contents of our minds and souls. Studies in quantum physics support this. For anyone keen to explore this further, its concepts of non-locality (subatomic particles communicating across vast distances) and a holographic universe (every part of the universe contains all the information possessed by the whole) are good starting points.

Theories and science aside, each symbolic encounter is an emissary of hope, encompassing wonder, magic and a glimpse of love eternal. Both dreamlike and mysterious, these experiences are so wonderful and perfectly plotted, that if you were to witness such a scene in a film or in fiction, you may groan at the implausibility. These are stories within stories – the stories of our lives, which may be already written whether we like it or not, says psychologist Robert H. Hopcke in his book *There Are No Accidents*: 'At those moments we call synchronistic . . . We are faced with the question . . . if I am not the author of my story, who is?'

At the heart of each synchronistic event, noted Jung, is numinosity – a sense of being touched by the divine. From miniature motifs (typically butterflies, feathers and birds) with an uncanny knack of turning up in a bereaved person's life in response to an unvoiced need, to once-in-a-lifetime wonders that juxtapose childlike simplicity and majestic awe, these moments draw our attention inwards to what's often overlooked in the clamour of 21st-century living: the spiritual and the sacred. When such encounters take place after the loss of a loved one, they reaffirm, writes Hopcke, 'connections that we have with those around us whom we loved and with whom we have shared our lives . . . repairing and making whole what death has torn asunder'.

Valerie Brook, who lives in the UK, relates an experience on the grand end of the scale: 'I love rainbows and I always called my mum to come look, but she was never as enamoured by them as I. The day before her funeral, we were returning home from the undertakers after viewing and I was obviously feeling very sad. As we walked along the street, ahead of us, opposite our house, was the church from where we had engaged the vicar for her funeral. Behind it was the most beautiful rainbow. I'd never seen a rainbow in that part of the sky before, and haven't seen one since. I know it was her saying she was happy and alright. I smiled the rest of the walk home.'

Buddhists maintain our minds are as boundless as the sky, so perhaps it's fitting that many symbolic and synchronistic after-death communications play out on that stage. How many of us, though, can claim to have seen a heart-shaped cloud, let alone an abundance of them? American mum Kim sees them all the time, ever since her toddler, Meghan, was killed when a dresser fell on her at home. Kim has snapped many pictures of heart-shaped clouds and posted them on her public Facebook page, Meghan's Hope, established to raise awareness of the dangers of unsecured furniture. 'I am not always in a place where I can photograph them, or they dissipate before I can,' says Kim. 'I see them most often on days of significance, when I'm thinking about her, or if I "need" it.' Going through her images, so lovely in their carefree innocence, I feel my skin prickle time and again in recognition of something special at work.

Jean, who lost her husband of 49 years, Morgan, in October 2008, knows what that's like. Morgan died from bowel cancer, which, to the couple's profound shock, was diagnosed as soon as Jean had completed six months of chemotherapy in her own battle with the disease. 'I was absolutely devastated. I met him when I was twenty and we had one of those lovely marriages where we were best friends and soulmates and lovers,' Jean tells me in her kind and quiet voice. 'I know I was lucky to have him but it just makes me miss him more, if you know what I mean.'

Two months after her husband's death, Jean, who lives in Sydney, went out to play her usual round of bridge with friends in an attempt to regain some sense of normalcy, but the outing did not lift her mood. 'I came home feeling terribly down and weepy and just miserable,' she says. 'I walked into the house and sat down and had a good cry. Then I looked up at our clock, a grandfather clock that hangs on the wall. It came out from Scotland with my grandfather. Morgan loved that clock and it was his pride and joy, he kept it in perfect condition, it was always absolutely on time.'

Since her husband's death, Jean had taken over the upkeep of the clock he had so treasured and now, wiping her eyes, she thought she'd better get up and wind it. As she began to turn the key, the phone rang, making her jump. It was her daughter, Lyn. Jean took the cordless phone back to the clock to continue winding as they chatted, when the clock started to strike . . . twelve times. It was just after 2.15 in the afternoon.

Her heart beating wildly out of kilter with the loud striking of the misbehaving timepiece, Jean wondered what in the world was happening. She became very upset, saying to her daughter, 'Oh my God, something's gone wrong with the clock! It's just struck twelve. It's never done that before. It's never been wrong.'

Lyn replied, 'Mum, that's Dad letting you know he's with you. It's what you were begging him to do just a minute ago.'

Jean was still turning over her daughter's words at 3 pm, when three deep and sonorous chimes announced the antique clock's return to order.

Since then, however, the clock has occasionally repeated its unusual performance. 'It only happens when I'm very upset,' reveals Jeans. Once, when her son, Brad, came to visit, he was winding the clock at 5.30 pm and it struck twelve times. Jean is relieved that her children have witnessed the phenomenon. When it happens in their presence, it feels to her as if Morgan is making the most of the opportunity to say hello to his family: "It's just like Morgan is saying, "Don't worry, I'm here with you." To this day I believe he's here with me.'

Clocks play a key role in many reports of after-death communication. When I was in primary school, we'd sing 'My Grandfather's Clock' in assembly. It included the line, 'But it stopped, short, never to go again when the old man died,' and, true to the song, instances of clocks stopping at the moment of their owner's death are too numerous to overlook.

Jenny Gersekowski discovered this had taken place following the passing of her mum, Mavis, in 2003. 'A day after she died, my sister and I went into her house to check on a couple of things,' says Jenny. 'I looked at the kitchen clock. It was flickering and had stopped on the exact time she had died: 6.50 pm. I know the time of death because I had previously asked the nursing sister at the Toowoomba Hospice what time she had recorded. For that clock to stop on the exact time was a sure sign it was her. When I put the battery back in it, it started again.'

For Amelia, a bookseller from Melbourne, the twinkling notes of a child's toy helped lift the veil of gloom that hung thick over her household following a tragic accident. Amelia explains: 'When I was sixteen my nearly two-year-old sister Felicity drowned in our backyard pool. One of my other sisters, Mary, had this doll – it was a sweet, pretty, wind-up thing with a big face that played music; Felicity was always trying to play with it and Mary used to get cross with her. After Felicity died, when Mary was feeling a bit down, it would just start playing for no reason. We swear to God it was Felicity.'

Timing always plays a vital part in these encounters. In her book, *Closer Than You Think*, Deborah Heneghan, who maintains a close friendship with her sister, Kathy, despite her death when they were teens, tells stories of powerful moments of connection between departed loved ones and their living friends and family. One interviewee is Boston pathologist Deborah Morosini, whose sister, Dana Reeve, wife of the late actor Christopher Reeve, died of lung cancer in 2006. 'When our bond is strong with a loved one, that relationship continues,' Morosini said. 'Dana sends me messages all the time. She answers every question I have, leads me to the people I need to meet, and makes me laugh every day. For me, it mostly takes the form of symbols and songs, always just at the right moment in the most perfect of ways.'

Songs as signs pop up time and again in my interviews and in literature about after-death communications. Margaret Marlow, who earlier described seeing the smiling face of her deceased son, John, in her kitchen, associates music with her son's presence, which is fitting, as the 36-year-old had been a talented musician. It first occurred a month after he died in 2005, Margaret says: 'I'd woken up and heard this most beautiful music. It was a flute playing and it was the clearest sound I'd ever heard. I thought, "I'm not dreaming, I'm awake." I got out of bed and went to the window to see if I could hear anything, but I couldn't. It stopped then and I thought, "No, that music, it came from somewhere else."'

Margaret knew the enchanting melody; it was from the 1952 hit song, 'The Ballad of High Noon'. She thought, 'Gee, that's a weird song, I haven't heard that song for years and years,' so she researched the lyrics and immediately recognised their relevance to her son's partner of twenty years, Tracey. 'I rang her and told her and she said, "Today would have been the twentieth anniversary of our meeting." Things added up, and I'll never forget that music,' Margaret says.

Another musical sign arrived in response to Margaret's plea to the universe. Sitting by the dam on her five-acre Hervey Bay property, she threw her request for a sign to the wind, to the sky and the waters at her feet. 'Give me something,' she urged. She waited, but there was nothing. Saddened, she began to walk back to the house. Then something 'glittering like the sun' caught her eye.

'There was a CD stuck in a bush,' she says with a laugh. 'It was the CD that was shining. It was just drawing me to it, and that bush – we walk past that bush every day. This day, the CD was just standing out.'

When she played the CD she felt enveloped by tingling warmth as the Ramones' 'I Believe in Miracles' started. It was an uplifting sign, Margaret says, then adds gleefully: 'I think John's a phenomenal spirit.'

In 2013, on Margaret's birthday, she stopped by Tracey's home for a glass of wine. As she was leaving, Tracey handed Margaret a book called *Letters From the Light*, a 1914 account of the afterlife. She explained that John had given her the book before he died, and asked if Margaret would like to read it. Margaret was shocked. Not only did the subject echo a contemporary book she'd just received for her birthday, but like that title, it made much of the link between music and the spiritual realm.

'Somebody had even underlined the part about music,' marvels Margaret, who was surprised that her son had owned such a book. 'It just seemed it was confirmation of my beliefs, like I could almost hear John saying, "See, Mum, it's all true."'

Beautiful birds are his other calling card. On the afternoon John died in a car accident, Margaret wandered down to feed her chooks as she did every day at around 4 pm, and stopped short at an extraordinary sight: 'There was this bird, a magnificent coloured bird, trapped in the chook pen. It was trying to get out and I screamed to my husband to come and have a look at it, but it was gone before he got there,' recalls Margaret, describing a bird with purple plumage resembling a macaw. 'I'd never seen a bird like it before. It went up into a tree, but then it was just gone. It was just gone.'

About two hours later, the police knocked on Margaret's door and she learned her son had been killed in an accident at 4 pm.

Colourful birds also featured in a happier sign from John, who'd once gifted his mum a porcelain statue of rosellas guarding a baby bird in a nest. 'We have rosellas come to our backyard in the afternoon; they're just like the rosellas in this statue and I always call them John's Birds.' She explains that there are usually only two or three but on the day Margaret and her husband returned from visiting John's son, born after his death, a mind-blowing sight awaited them – their backyard was swarming with rosellas, their rainbow brightness lighting up an otherwise bittersweet homecoming. 'I counted eighteen!'

Margaret says. 'I've never, ever, seen eighteen rosellas here and I haven't seen that many since.'

They are universal symbols for freedom, peace, beauty and flight, so it makes sense that birds often play leading roles in 'wow' moments of synchronicity linking the departed and their grieving loved ones. The summer after her husband, Tom, died in 1988, Eileen, who in earlier chapters told of the solace she's drawn from connecting with his spirit, felt accompanied by a watchful grey heron that would alight on the paddock close by whenever she was out mowing the grass. It was meaningful because, on the eve of his death from a heart attack, Tom had insisted, to her amused exasperation, that she listen to every detail about the ride-on mower he'd purchased that day. After his death, Eileen took over the mowing, and Tom's beloved ride-on. 'I used to stay out cutting the grass, it felt like a way of being close to him,' Eileen says.

The heron – as 'tall, thin and grey' as Tom had been – would appear when she was mowing, 'very near, always at significant times', says Eileen, but also at other times when she was 'particularly sad'. She recalls on one occasion, 'I was sitting on the verandah talking with my cousin, who was visiting from Scotland, about our respective husbands, both deceased. Suddenly I heard a scratching above us. There on the roof directly above our heads was a grey heron.'

Another sighting occurred far from home, as Eileen was leaving Switzerland after visiting family in winter: 'Having said my goodbyes, I was in the plane, just about to take off, and there was a grey heron standing on the grass beside the runway.'

Eileen says, 'There have been so many, many sightings at special times that I've lost count. It is so extraordinary and

I always feel it's a sign to say Tom is with us and never far away.'

On the day her father died, a feathered messenger also found its way to Deborah Pringle, pinpointing her amid a crowd of 50,000 in a football stadium in Queensland in May 2003. Sitting in the packed stands with her two sons, niece and nephew, Deb answered a call on her mobile from her husband. 'He told me that my dad had just passed,' says Deb. Her 83-year-old father, Ron, who everyone called 'Wonga', had been bedridden for years. As she took in the news, Deb was stunned to see a bird soar straight towards her, hovering in mid-air about a foot in front of her. 'I thought, "Dad, you're free now." For years he couldn't get out of bed by himself but now he was free. He could fly.'

The moment gave her 'instant relief', says Deb. She can't remember what type of bird it was, only that its appearance 'really knocked my socks off, because, like I say, a big crowd at the footy, screaming and yelling, and this bird just comes right in. I could have grabbed him!'

When she was a child, Deb's father used to say to her, 'We're always together, nothing can tear us apart' and 'I'll always be with you', and true to his word, since his passing he's made every effort to let his daughter know he's still a part of her life. Many of the signs began to arrive (or be recognised) after Deb had a reading with psychic Charmaine Wilson, who taught her to be alert to the clues he leaves. One of them is the number 511, which Deb has come to identify with her father who died on 11 May.

Deb, now 54 years old, recalls a recent sign that her father's still with her: 'In July 2012, I had an operation and I said to Dad as I was going in, "Dad, be with me. Make me come through this okay." Well, I entered on floor five and when they wheeled me up, my bed was number eleven. Of all the beds I could have gone to . . .'

Other times, when she's driving along and thinking of her father, Deb may spot a car with a 511 numberplate. On one occasion, as she hunted for parking on a rainy day, she saw a car reversing from an ideal spot – its plate was RVW, her father's full initials. And then there was the unforgettable time when she was heading into the local hardware store with her mother, who'd been bemoaning her husband's absence from her life, and a car with the plates RON 511 was parked right outside the entrance. 'Goosebumps,' sums up Deb. 'You can't believe it but you can, because it's right in front of you.'

Deb's children, too, have been awakened to their grand-father's presence. Once, her son lost his way on the streets of Sydney and pulled over to check his map. Looking up at the street sign to see where he'd stopped, shivers coursed through him when he saw he was in Wonga Street. Another time, he shook his head in wonder when he received his race number for a marathon he was taking part in on Remembrance Day: 0511.

Each moment is like a gift, an offering of hope to usher in, or encourage, healing – a reminder that a loved one is never far. 'Souls are joined, you can't say they're not,' says Deb, who has also seen her dad's spirit jump up and click his heels together, in the classic gesture of joy, at the foot of her bed. 'These signs keep you going, and you can help others if they're going through the same thing. You can sort of guide them in the right direction and say, "Look, I can tell you – I've seen. I've done. I've heard."'

Deb's belief that 'signs keep you going' echoes beyond the experiences in this book. As 2012 yielded to 2013, other voices in the media were also telling of wisdom and transcendence grasped amid darkest grief. When all seems lost, embracing love as an antidote to despair was a theme woven through many of the saddest news stories to break as I was working on this book. Time and again I was moved to tears and humbled by the towering courage and grace displayed by people in unfathomable circumstances, and, in many cases, inspired by the open-hearted way they shared their belief that their loved one's spirit survived to comfort them – and soar anew.

This was one such story: on 25 October 2012, Marina and Kevin Krim endured the unthinkable – their children Lulu, six years old, and Leo, twenty months, were murdered at their home in New York while Marina was at swimming lessons with their other child. How to go on in the face of such monumental loss? Yet the Krims, with exquisite grace and dignity, went further, establishing the 'Lulu and Leo Fund' to benefit disadvantaged children. On their Facebook page, they share warm and personal updates, including their conviction that their sweet children live on, that they paint golden sunsets to make their parents smile and plant little keepsakes in their path as signs of their presence. Their lives were short, but now, like beams of sunshine, the legacy of Lulu and Leo reaches far and wide, warming thousands with their credo of love and hope.

Less than a month later, headlines again blared incomprehensible news of innocent lives snatched violently. This time, a gunman murdered twenty first-graders at a primary school in postcard-pretty Newtown, Connecticut. This act of unimaginable cruelty committed against tiny children with the excitement of Christmas in their eyes was too hard to absorb. But to turn away from coverage of the atrocity was to risk forgetting the children who were gone – and what they had to teach us. Like the Krims, the parents of Newtown were united in their determination to find a shard of light in the aftermath of tragedy, to spread a message of love and caring as a fitting way to honour their little ones' gentle and precious hearts.

In interviews with nine sets of parents published by *People* magazine in the US four months after the tragedy (15 April 2013), three mothers mentioned the ways their children's spirits lingered to help them heal. Jenny Hubbard, who lost her daughter, Catherine, said her little girl sends her signs. 'One day I found two tiny white feathers . . . All I could think of was, "Catherine, your wings are beautiful."'

For Deb Carr – who shared in Chapter One how her brother's suicide tore her world apart – feathers also became their code, shorthand for the indestructibility of their bond. 'Whenever I need a message, I will find a green feather,' says Deb. 'I find them everywhere. I've had hundreds of them!'

In 2006, during a particularly trying time in her business, Deb travelled to Queensland with a friend for a two-day course in professional speaking. During a break, Deb wandered into the garden to sit in quiet solitude in the gazebo and reflect on her situation. In her hands she held a painting she'd been drawn to buy of Archangel Michael, depicting him with iridescent green wings of hypnotic beauty, and a journal bound in the same colour. After taking some deep breaths, Deb voiced a plea for hope: 'Please give me a sign, please give me a sign that everything will be alright.'

As she walked back to her room, Deb found an 'exquisite green and yellow feather' – her sign – but to her dismay, when she returned to Sydney, she could not find the precious feather or her journal. Still upset as she walked her daughter to school the next morning, she was flabbergasted to find an identical feather at her feet. She picked it up and took it home, where she received a call from her friend – he had packed her journal and feather by mistake in Queensland and had them in his safekeeping.

Another occasion just makes her smile with amazement and a shake of her head: the green feather she once found at her feet as she took her seat on a plane. 'I will never be able to understand that one,' she says.

Deb, however, has no doubt what the feathers mean – 'They're signs for me.' And in 2007 she got a green feather tattooed on her lower back to celebrate her brother's abundant communications.

There is, indeed, an element of the miraculous in these events. Six months after his brother, Theo, died of an epilepsy seizure in 2007, Manny was on his way home from his office Christmas party. He'd only attended because it was a work event, but found himself feeling uncomfortable and out of place so decided to leave quickly. He could not staunch the tears on the bus-ride home and then faced a twenty-minute walk to his parents' home in Sydney's inner-east.

Manny recounts: 'I was walking – upset, crying, angry – it was like, "All these people are happy that it's Christmas and my brother is dead and it's my first Christmas without him." You get into such a state, so sad, depressed and hurt, that really, quite frankly, you entertain the idea that if you were to die, it wouldn't be a bad thing because at least all the suffering would end.

'At first, I wasn't conscious of it, then I noticed there was something kind of fluttering around me, but I kept walking; I was so consumed with my grief. I stopped at the traffic lights and saw it was a large, white butterfly and it had basically followed me from when I got off the bus.'

Telling me what happened next, on that sad summer's evening at 10.30 pm, Manny seems transformed by the wonder of it:

As it was flying, flying, flying, there was this moment where I actually stopped what I was doing and stopped what I was thinking and completely focused on this butterfly and registered what it was and what was happening. In that moment, when I did that, the butterfly came and kissed me on the lips, he says, with a burst of unselfconscious laughter. I know it sounds crazy that a butterfly would kiss me, but that's literally what happened. And then it just flew away. I thought to myself, 'There's no way that can be anything other than my brother.'

That first kiss, so to speak, heralded an uplifting new phase in Manny's life: his realisation that his relationship with his brother continues, but in a surprising and delightful new way. Like the butterfly, the only creature to completely assume an entirely new form as part of its growth cycle, Theo – and his love for his brother – endures, but he's shed his old self. He's transformed.

'Now, every time I'm really sad, really down or depressed, or every time I'm just thinking about my brother, praying he's at peace, he always comes to me in the form of a white butterfly,' says Manny.

He recalls that nine months after Theo's death, he took his mother, stepfather and brother for a trip to the south coast of New South Wales. It was his mother's birthday, and though no one felt like celebrating, the last thing Manny wanted was for her to be at home, the scene of their deepest loss, where the atmosphere was still heavy with heartache.

On the balcony of the holiday rental, Manny breathed in the ocean, drew in its tang of salt and sand and sky, let the rhythm of the rolling waves become another pulse inside him. But the sea did not wash away his sadness. As he wept and smoked, regret consumed him – that the family had never holidayed together when Theo was alive, that he was missing their mum's birthday, that his absence was as vast as the ocean – when a visitor drew him out of his thoughts.

'Out of nowhere comes this white butterfly,' remembers Manny. On a cool April evening on the blustery south coast, the creature fluttered and lingered around the grieving clan, as it went on to do again and again throughout that melancholy weekend. 'It was like Theo was still part of it, like he wanted to say, "I'm here even though I'm not here."'

Three months later, on the first-year anniversary of Theo's death, as the family gathered to remember him at the gravesite where he's buried together with his father, Manny had to smile through his tears. 'I look up and I see not one, but *two*, white butterflies,' he recalls. 'In all the years I've been going to that cemetery, I've never seen white butterflies there, and here were two! I thought, "Here's Theo now coming with our dad."'

As Manny's account demonstrates, what butterflies accomplish in the plethora of stories detailing their role in synchronistic events often defies what we understand of the creatures and their behaviour. Since the tragedy of her daughter's stillbirth in 1997, Queenslander Beau McKnight and her five daughters sense the baby's presence in the delicate sway of a butterfly's wing.

'The most amazing time was when we were driving up the highway, we were going a hundred miles an hour, you know, and in flies a butterfly and lands on my lap,' says Beau, her voice bursting with joy. 'It was crazy! I was, like, "Look at this! What's going on? This doesn't happen . . .!"'

Beau first made the link only days after Rhiannon's death, when a white butterfly danced around her as she sat crying on her verandah. 'It gave me some kind of hope that she's still around, even though I can't see her and I miss her like crazy,' she says. And the signs continue to this day, Beau adds, telling me that just a couple of weeks before our chat, during a visit to the park, a large butterfly flew around her and her two little girls and landed on her. After touching down on Beau's shoulder, it flew directly onto Beau's outstretched palm. 'The girls were laughing and saying how that was Rhiannon saying hello,' recalls Beau, whose daughters are aged between three and seventeen. 'Because they talk about her, you know, their baby sister.'

So many of the moments I've been privileged enough to hear about and share suggest loved ones appreciate knowing they're still part of the everyday lives of family and friends they've left behind – and they're very clever about letting us know it, as the next two stories show. In each, butterflies deliver reassurances from young women whose lives were stymied by illness, but whose love lives on, strong and steady as a heartbeat.

Prisms of light

'It's symbolic . . . Caterpillars kind of die and then they become some-thing else.'

Danielle Flannery runs a PR firm in Queensland. Fast-spoken and articulate, her story tumbles out with the efficiency she harnesses in her professional life, but tears come, too, for her story is as heartbreaking and touching as they get. To help primary school-aged children through grief, Danielle, a mother of three adult sons, has written a not-for-profit children's book, as yet unpublished, based on the experiences she describes below:

In 1999, my younger sister, Robyn, was diagnosed with duodenal cancer at the age of 36, when she was happily married and had a son, Tom, who was eight. It's a very rare cancer, supposedly not hereditary. The prognosis was always pretty ordinary, she had secondaries everywhere but she never really talked about it, or thought that she was going to die. Very rarely did she mention anything about it, it was just all very 'I'm going to be positive'.

She did the chemo and that was vicious and revolting and then in the following April after her diagnosis, she had finished the chemo, but she was in hospital, desperately ill – doctors were telling us, 'She's not coming out of hospital,' so we were all devastated. She was given the last rites. Meanwhile, her son, who was extremely close to his mother, would not go and see her in the hospital.

We told Robyn that Tom wouldn't come and she said, 'Don't force him.' But we, as in her husband and I, were getting a lot of pressure from pastoral-care staff telling us he would resent us later, that we had to take control and be the grown-ups and bring him to see her. Well, we were trying. Everyone was trying to get him up there, but he would literally put his hands over his ears. You could talk about his mother but you couldn't talk about her in the context of him going to see her in the hospital because for him, the last time his mother went to hospital, the world stopped spinning – disaster.

So, this day, they really spoke very firmly to us and said, 'Get that kid up here.' And we decided that I'd pick him up from school the next day with my youngest one who was seven and take him to the hospital and if he had to go in kicking and screaming, well, so be it. So the next day, I remember that was a Wednesday, I said to him, 'How about we go and get Mum something from the shop for Mother's Day?' At that time, we had absolutely no expectation that she would make Mother's Day. He was perfectly happy about that. So off we go to the shop and he went into this, what I call, a 'voodoo shop', with crystals and those kind of things.

I said, 'You can have anything you like,' and he picked this very pretty crystal butterfly that you hang from a window. It creates prisms of light. On the way home I said to him, 'Actually, what you got Mum would look really good in her room in the hospital. We could take that up tomorrow.' It was my last-ditch attempt to get him up there. 'She could hang it on the window and it will make prisms of light all through the room. It'll be so nice.' And he, once again, did his trick of putting his hands over his ears and said, 'No!' Just flat-out no.

Everybody had tried at this point to get this kid up to the hospital. I had, his father had, my mother, who was brilliant with children – everyone had tried and failed. Never in a million years would I ask a seven-year-old to intercede but my little son did. I swear to God, angels got in his mouth. He said to his cousin, 'Well, why wouldn't you go and see her?'

And Tom goes, 'Because it will make me sad.'

And my son said, 'But I think Robyn would like to see you.'

I just shut up at this point and let them go. And Tom said, 'Well, I'm sure she would like to see me but I know it will make me sad if I go up there.'

And my son replied, 'It's alright. We'll take the Pokemon cards and we'll make a cubby under the bed and we'll take lollies. Can we take lollies, Mum?'

He painted this picture for Tom of making a little party under the bed. Even to this day, I tear up thinking about how he just went forward whereas everyone else stepped back, he just went forward and painted this picture of how fine it would be.

So Tom went up to the hospital and he didn't have to be dragged kicking and screaming and he was fine and they had a lovely visit and Robyn got her butterfly crystal. Then, she surprises everybody and comes out of hospital – but only to die. With Mother's Day approaching, again I took my nephew shopping and to a different kind of shop and once again he bought something with a butterfly on it, a pretty bookmark, and gave her that for Mother's Day.

About two weeks before she died, a friend of mine, who didn't know about the first two butterflies, called in and said she'd been in a shop and seen something and bought it for Tom to give to Robyn. I opened up the bag and it was another butterfly. I thought, 'That's so weird because the last two things he's chosen for her are also butterflies.' So he gives his mum this third butterfly.

The next day, Robyn and I were at her place alone and she said, 'What's with the butterflies?'

I said, 'I don't know. It's weird, isn't it? Three out of the last three things that he's given you have been butterflies.'

Now, can I tell you that my sister and I weren't that deep, you know? We talked about kids and shoes and cooking and family . . .

She said, 'I think it's symbolic.'

And I said, 'How do you mean?'

She goes, 'Well, because caterpillars kind of die and then they become something else.'

So we then went on and had what I think was the only conversation she ever had with anyone about dying, that she would die and how she would try and send us a sign.

103

I should tell you nobody knew about this conversation that she and I had, no one knew. We were the only people in the house and I didn't talk about it to anyone. It was just a conversation between sisters.

About three weeks after she died, my nephew is sitting on the kitchen bench. It's night-time, it's winter and it's raining and all of those things are relevant. He's sitting on the kitchen bench and his dad is cooking dinner and this butterfly appeared in the kitchen, fluttered all around the kitchen and landed on my nephew's shoulder. I know enough about butterfly behaviour to know that butterflies don't appear in the rain in winter and at night, and very rarely are they inside. It was a cold day and the house was all closed up anyway. They're in their chrysalis in winter and they come out mostly in spring, I think? It certainly seemed unusual butterfly behaviour; there's this butterfly, inside the house in the middle of winter at night and when it's raining outside, sitting on Tom's shoulder. And he went, 'Dad, look at this!'

The next morning, David, my brother-in-law, dropped Tom off in the morning and I made him breakfast and made sure his homework was done because David was not coping at all well; he was in the deepest, blackest depression. He's an atheist, not spiritual at all, but he said to me, 'This weird thing happened last night. This butterfly fluttered all around the kitchen and landed on Tom's shoulder and just sat there for the longest time and then it just seemed to flutter away and disappear.'

I just got goosebumps all over my body and I went, 'Oh my God,' and told him about the conversation I'd had with Robyn.

He said, 'Don't tell anybody. They'll all think we're crazy.'

I said, 'Righto.' I didn't tell anybody.

That afternoon, Mum went over there to clean the house, which had been her routine while Robyn was sick. She'd been over there all the time when Robyn was dying. She goes around there, then she comes over to my place afterwards. She didn't know about the butterfly on Tom's shoulder. She didn't know about the conversation that Robyn and I had. She didn't know about the conversation I'd had with David either. She didn't know anything.

She comes over and says, 'Such a weird thing happened when I was around there today. I was vacuuming Robyn's room and this butterfly appeared and fluttered all around my head. Fancy seeing a butterfly in winter and inside a house! And it was still raining.'

Once again I had goosebumps all over. I said, 'Oh my God, have you been speaking to David?'

She said, 'No, he's at work.'

So I said, 'What did you do with the butterfly, Mum?' I had these visions of her sucking it up with the vacuum cleaner! [Danielle laughs.]

She goes, 'Well, I went and got Tom's bug catcher and the damn thing caught itself.' She said it just flew right in, like it wanted to be caught: 'It was the weirdest thing I've ever seen in my life.'

So I told her about the conversation I'd had with Robyn before she died. Mum went back around there the next morning and the butterfly was dead in the bottom of the bug catcher, lying flat on the bottom, its wings together. So Mum and David are both completely horrified.

Then Mum said, 'It's alright, I'll draw it.' It was very brightly coloured – black and blue and yellow and red. So she gets it out of the bug catcher, places it on the kitchen bench, and draws a picture of it with Tom's textas, which took about half an hour.

The really spooky part is, after she finished drawing it, it woke up and flew away!

But we have a drawing of the butterfly.

Not just special occasions

'It was just like Melissa – to keep the surprise for when we were least expecting it.'

In the Brisbane home of Kathy and Steve Ford, there is a corner set aside in memory of their daughter, Melissa, who died of ovarian cancer when she was only 23. Anchored by photos of their vivacious girl, it's a restful place in the house where they can go to focus their thoughts, to retreat from the world, to take an infinitesimal step towards bridging the boundless uncharted terrain that's sprung between them and their beloved 'Liss'. One morning, Steve was home alone and chatting to his daughter's photo in her 'little area' when he was overcome by a powerful feeling that he should go into her bedroom, which he'd steered clear of since her death. He walked in and immediately noticed her iPod in its dock. The device wasn't playing but it was illuminated, a miniature beacon in the still and empty room. Steve drew closer and peered down at the song that was selected. What he saw made his eyes water. It was Aerosmith's 'I Don't Want to Miss a Thing'.

Two years earlier, in August of 2009, Kathy Ford was getting ready to go to work at her job in administration/accounts. Every weekday, her routine never wavered: shower, breakfast, brush teeth, put makeup on, slip on watch and jewellery then pick up her bag and walk out the door. But this day, she'd just finished applying her makeup and was en route to the dressing table when she stopped abruptly.

'I got a message,' says Kathy. 'It was like a thought had just popped into my head and the message was this: "You are going to lose a child."' Baffled, she took a couple more steps and then the rest of the message arrived: 'Melissa.' At this, Kathy burst into tears. 'I did not know what this all meant and it frightened the hell out of me. All I could think of was maybe Liss was going to have a car accident and I felt absolutely powerless about it.'

Of Kathy's three children – Daniel, Melissa and Kellie – it was Daniel, a soldier, who seemed most at risk. Soon after Kathy's troubling 'message', he was deployed to Afghanistan, much to his mother's distress. 'I truly believed Daniel would not come home alive – I thought that the "message" gave me the wrong child's name.'

Instead, it proved heartbreakingly accurate. On 13 July 2010, Melissa was diagnosed with ovarian cancer. 'It was a complete shock,' says Kathy. Melissa had undergone routine surgery to remove a cyst on her left ovary, which turned out to be malignant. 'To cap it off, it was a rare type of ovarian cancer – less than 50 cases worldwide.'

Throughout it all, Melissa, a blonde, tall and attractive Qantas flight attendant with a stunning smile, was characteristically upbeat. On learning her diagnosis, she quipped, 'That's one way to lose weight,' and insisted the news be kept to only her family and closest friends. 'Liss was the epitome of "only the good die young". She was a very loving, very loyal young woman who loved life,' says Kathy. 'She packed so much into her short 23 years, for which I am grateful. She would do anything for anyone.'

Her battle with the disease was brief and brutal, only ten months, but Melissa fought it to the end with immense heart and courage. After enduring chemotherapy and radiation therapy, her cancer returned and on 7 February 2011, she was in surgery, while in another hospital on the same day, her little sister, Kellie, was having an emergency caesarean to deliver her baby girl at only 25 weeks gestation. It was a trying time for the Fords, but love sustained them, bonded them, kept them from buckling beneath the strain and fear of what could come. A week later, on Valentine's Day, Melissa, too, put her faith in love: she and her boyfriend, Darren, became engaged.

But hopes plummeted less than two months later, when Melissa learned her cancer was terminal. There was nothing more that could be done. Yet amid the tears and devastation, the devoted parents and groom-to-be somehow found the strength to pour their energy into planning a wedding to make their darling's heart soar, to cram a future's worth of love and happiness into one perfect day.

On 8 April 2011, Melissa and Darren sat down with their parents to set a date. 'We were never told how long Liss had to live, we never asked and we didn't want to know,' says Kathy. She explains that two dates were in contention, Friday 20 May or 27 May. 'All I can say is that something was screaming, and I mean *screaming*, in my head that it couldn't be the 27th. I had to restrain myself from yelling out that it had to be the 20th – again, I did not understand why, but I do now.'

The nuptials were set for 20 May, on the idyllic waterfront at Bribie Island, where a pair of dolphins frolicked in the waves, as if to script, as the bride and groom exchanged vows. Melissa looked ethereal in a cloud-white gown, its strapless design showing off her graceful shoulders and golden skin. She wore a diamante necklace and earrings and an ivory rose behind her ear. 'Liss was in some pain, but at the same time, she was nervous, just like a typical bride,' remembers her mum. 'It was a magical day.'

But barely 24 hours later, Melissa was back in hospital. 'We thought it was simply to top up her pain medication,' tells Kathy. 'Unfortunately, we never got to bring her home.'

Melissa lost consciousness, and on Friday 27 May, she was in palliative care. Had that been the wedding day, it would never have gone ahead. As it was, says Kathy softly, 'She got to marry the love of her life.'

And at the last, the light she'd brought to others' lives was returned tenfold, as family and friends clamoured to enfold her in their love, to let her know what she meant to them. Kathy recalls that every night in her final two weeks, Melissa had people staying with her; at least seven each night, and one night Kathy counted twelve. 'She was surrounded by love at the end.'

Love awaited her, too, at her next destination, as she had let her mother know before losing consciousness. 'She pulled me close and said, "I'm going to see Nana,"' recalls Kathy, in a trembling voice. 'They were her very last words to me.' On 4 June 2011, as Kathy lovingly puts it, 'Our angel on this earth became a real angel.'

The end of her daughter's life sparked the start of a spiritual quest for Kathy, now 48, who read voraciously and spent hours online, trying to understand the origins of the frightful premonition that had 'popped' into her mind: 'I have struggled with the fact that I did not do anything when I was first told that I was going to lose Liss . . .' Participating in a retreat with psychic Charmaine Wilson led Kathy to make peace with that: 'She helped me accept that Liss's time was up. Even if the cancer had been caught earlier, something else would have happened.'

Now Melissa herself is taking opportunities to let her parents know she is never far. The moment with the iPod was one of her first communications, says Kathy, who feels the timing was no coincidence. It happened in December 2011, the morning after Kathy and Steve attended an event featuring US psychic Allison DuBois. 'I thought, "Okay, Liss has come to realise that we're starting to think there's something going on here." That's when she really started to let us know, "I'm here! I'm here!"'

That day with the iPod, 'Steve just couldn't explain it,' says Kathy. 'There was no logic for it. It was lit up with "I Don't Want to Miss a Thing". I took that to mean Liss wants to know everything that's going on, so I just talk to her continuously, I tell her what's coming up.'

One big family event Melissa clearly refused to miss was her baby niece's naming day ceremony. Kathy recalls: 'We had it here at my home. We had Melissa's photo up and a candle lit – she was made Mia's spiritual godmother. And this big beautiful black butterfly with white spots on its wings just flew in among everybody.'

Then, on the first anniversary of Melissa's death, Kathy saw the same butterfly at her memorial site. 'We took fresh flowers down and this big black butterfly with the white spots on its wings was flying down beside us! And I've never seen it there before, though I'm up there regularly, a few times a week. That's the first and only time I've ever seen that butterfly up there. That was very comforting.'

On the second anniversary of Melissa's passing, Kathy was hoping to see the large and striking butterfly again. Together with Kellie and her two children, Steve and Kathy took flowers and balloons to release at Melissa's resting place. One balloon contained a note from Kathy to her daughter, words of love to set adrift into the winter sky, and the others were filled with flower seeds, forget-me-nots. 'The idea is that when the balloons burst, the seeds will fall to the ground and a new plant will grow – a new life,' says Kathy. 'This has become our tradition.'

After the ceremony, Kathy was bereft. The butterfly had not made an appearance and she was at a loss to understand. 'I was so disappointed and upset,' she relates. 'But I was also after validation. I had been having issues with my beliefs in the afterlife – do I believe because I really believe, or do I believe just because I want to?'

Back home later that afternoon, Kathy and Steve were sitting in the new Balinese-themed gazebo and deck area they'd built in honour of Melissa, who'd adored Bali and made frequent trips there. 'I went back inside the house to get a drink and as I came back out, I caught sight of this big, black butterfly with white spots just before it flew back over the wall,' says Kathy. 'Steve saw it all. He said the black butterfly flew into the gazebo area, did a few loops and then flew back over the wall. There was my validation. How amazing! And it was just like Melissa – to keep the surprise for when we were least expecting it.'

Now Kathy and Steve know Melissa is around for the everyday moments as well as the special occasions, that she dwells in her family's hearts and thoughts all day every day, not just at her memorial site. After all, she doesn't want to miss a thing.

*

I hope you enjoyed these stories as much as I enjoyed writing them. Researching this chapter, I was in a state of perpetual goosebumpy wonder! Rainbows blooming like a child's drawing projected onto the sky, a clock and a doll suddenly animate, celestial music as a balm for sore hearts, feathers to treasure, birds sent with love from beyond and butter-flies acting against their nature on the same mission . . . It's mind-boggling stuff.

Readers of my previous books will know I love marvel and magic – I grew up watching 1970s television shows like *That's Incredible!* and *In Search Of* – and don't necessarily believe a mystery is the better for being solved. Yet immersing myself in these stories, I became consumed with trying to understand how and why seemingly disparate events could be knitted together. I learned that science has proven everything and everyone is connected and that our thoughts are electrical impulses that affect the world around us.

'[The] spiritual is stronger than any material force,' said Ralph Waldo Emerson. 'Thoughts rule the world.'

Nobel Prize-winning physicist Max Planck, who origin-ated quantum theory, declared, 'Matter is derived from consciousness.'

This leads me to wonder, if there is a universal consciousness, and consciousness survives death, could these startling moments of synchronicity be a majestic coproduction of sorts between us and our late loved ones?

In his book *No Death, No Fear*, Buddhist master Thich Nhat Hanh says we should take solace in the scientific impossibility that the departed are no more, since energy is indestructible. 'Our beloved was not destroyed; she has just taken on another form,' he writes. 'We can see our loved one in everything.'

What an almighty idea, a healing spell encased in the ultimate mystery. 'You would know the secret of death,' wrote

Love Never Dies

Kahlil Gibran in *The Prophet*. 'If you would indeed behold the spirit of death, open your heart wide unto the body of life. For life and death are one, even as the river and the sea are one.'

5

Watching Over Us

⌒∿⌒

By our side when we need them most

'Though lovers be lost love shall not;
And death shall have no dominion.'
—Dylan Thomas

The night Sarah Williams turned 21, she celebrated with a family dinner in the back room of her parents' home in southern Sydney, where decorations from the big party she'd had with friends the evening before were still up, enhancing the festive mood. To accommodate the eleven guests, including her two grandmothers and a great-aunt, furniture was shuffled around to make room for an oversized table, which was soon laden with a baked roast dinner, vegetables and a creamy potato bake, followed by caramel mud cake, Sarah's favourite. It was the perfect menu for an exceptionally cold winter's night.

115

At the end of 'a really special night' full of chatter and laughter, Sarah was walking the last of her guests out through the hall at around 11 pm when she spotted her great-grandmother, Kathleen, nicknamed Kitty, perched in an armchair in the combined lounge and dining room. Sadly, Kitty had missed the dinner, on account of her having died a decade earlier, but she was obviously determined to make an appearance.

'She looked as if she were alive, not see-through or anything, exactly like a person,' recalls Sarah, now 27, and a social science/criminology honours graduate. 'She was just sitting in the chair, looking straight ahead. She was wearing what she would have worn in life – a cardigan, a blouse and a long skirt. She had her glasses on.'

Sarah did a double-take and Kitty vanished. 'I was like, "Wow, okay, did I just see that?"' she remembers thinking, though the level of detail in her account suggests there is little room for doubt. The momentary return of her great-grandmother wasn't frightening for Sarah. In fact, it felt right. 'I wasn't freaked out at all. I just thought she must be visiting to say happy birthday. And also because a lot of family were there, she wanted to be there, too.'

The same could be said of Lois, who sent happy returns to her only child, Kate, via a joy-filled and pointed dream months after her death in December 2012. On the wintry night of Kate's 44th birthday the following year, she dreamt of a heavily pregnant woman, which at first she took to be herself, but after waking up, she realised she'd been mistaken. Kate recalls: 'The dream started with the pregnant person in my parents' bedroom, showing Dad her pregnant belly. He was very excited and then the belly expanded and the baby's hand pushed out so far you could hold it. Dad was holding the baby's hand and then it pushed out even more and he exclaimed that he could see it was a girl. Dad was crying with excitement that it was a girl!'

The next morning, Kate, a mum of two boys aged ten and twelve, examined the dream in the stark light of day. Was her mum telling her she'd have another baby? That didn't seem likely, she says, adding with a laugh, 'I'm way past it.'

'Then I remembered that I had forgotten an important part of the dream – that the baby's fingernails were painted orange! While Mum was alive I always painted my toenails orange (since her death, blue) and she always laughed at me over the colour. This was Mum's dream to me about *me*.'

It dawned on Kate that it was a poignant birthday wish. 'Every birthday she always talked about how much she loved being pregnant and how excited she was when she found out I was a girl. The orange nails were her sign to me that she was still passing that message to me from the other side.'

The message at the heart of the stories in this chapter is simple – 'we still care' – yet deeply profound to the many people who've told me about the valuable role their deceased loved ones continue to play in their day-to-day lives: from popping in unexpectedly to celebrate a milestone, like Kitty, to showing up regularly to offer assistance where they can, like babysitting the kids, for example. I'll never forget Cherie Frazer telling me in *Spirit Sisters* how she saw her late grandmother peering into the cot to inspect her new grandchild. The lady looked radiant in the pale yellow suit she'd been buried in, said Cherie, who went on to reveal that the visit proved to be only the first of many.

Kylie Ofiu also came to count on the help of a spirit carer. The 27-year-old Canberra-based writer who works in the finance industry, and is a single mother of two girls, found spiritual support courtesy of her mother, Jennee, who'd died of bladder cancer in the year 2000, when she was only 37 and Kylie was a tender fifteen.

After giving birth to her first child in 2007, Kylie, who was in an unhappy marriage, was diagnosed with post-natal depression. Struggling with breastfeeding and troubled by her newborn's failure to thrive despite the constant feeding, there came a day when Kylie couldn't see a way out of her sorrow. 'I just couldn't cope. She was lying in her cot, and she was crying and crying and I just couldn't get up out of bed. I didn't want to deal with her. I started to cry and then I just felt my mum come into the room,' says Kylie, taking a deep breath as she recalls what happened next.

'It was like my mum walked in and just went over to the cot, leaned over and touched my daughter's face, brushed her cheek and made some cooing noises. My daughter stopped crying. She settled her right down.'

Although Kylie didn't physically *see* her mother, her presence was palpable, she says, and the effect on Halia, her daughter, was startling. With difficulty, Kylie pulled herself up into a sitting position and watched her baby's eyes 'lock onto' a sight directly above as she gurgled and made sweet baby sounds of pleasure into the empty space.

'There was an energy there. I could mentally see everything that was happening and feel everything that she was doing and so, in my mind, it was like I could see her. I was so grateful because I just couldn't get up to Halia, and it was such a relief to have my mum there, taking care of my baby,' says Kylie, her voice cracking. 'I just thought, *Thank you.*'

Over the next month, Jennee, who'd had five children, continued to pop in and help her daughter, just like any mum.

'I was able to function better, even though she wasn't there all the time, but she'd come especially when my daughter got really upset, she'd settle her for me,' says Kylie.

Kylie adds that she was her mother's 'shadow' when she was a little girl, cutting her hair, massaging her feet and always standing at her side in the kitchen, as the talented cook whipped up another off-the-cuff masterpiece in the kitchen. But when she became a teenager, things changed, to the point where Kylie feels their bond has strengthened in the wake of her mother's death, especially since she became a mother herself.

That's why the name she gave her first child, a melodious story in itself, is the perfect way to seal her own story of love beyond life: 'Halia is Hawaiian for "In loving memory",' explains Kylie, whose ex-husband was born in Hawaii. 'And her middle name is Jennee, after my mum. So her name literally means "In loving memory of my mum."'

A helping hand from the spirit world also arrived for new mum Lisa when 'earthly' support networks were unavailable, as the now 43-year-old Sydney insurance adviser reveals: 'When I was 27, my second child, Dawn, was born with Down Syndrome. There were a lot of times in those first five years when I spent my life in and out of hospitals because of her health. When Dawn was about two, my mother was in hospital having a mastectomy for breast cancer at the same time my sister's daughter was in a car accident.'

Two days after her mother's surgery, Lisa took Dawn to the hospital to have surgery. As she recovered, Lisa, who'd broken her ankle, had to enlist a home-care company to help her look after her toddler, as family members were tied up with their own problems. 'One day, early in this period that seemed to go on for about two weeks, my husband walked past our daughter's room and saw someone standing over her cot,' says Lisa. 'He thought it was me but when he walked into the kitchen at the other end of the house, I was at the sink. He freaked out and said, "I just saw you standing over Dawn's cot!" I looked at him quite calmly and said, "No, that was Neil. He is here."'

Neil was Lisa's brother who'd died of melanoma in 1977, when he was eighteen. Lisa was eight when Neil died and only remembers him in 'snippets' of childhood flashbacks. 'In the 25 years since he'd gone, I had never felt his presence, but I knew he was in my house at that time,' says Lisa. Although her father had died of pancreatic cancer when she was fifteen and Lisa had been 'the apple of his eye', she knew this presence wasn't him. She simply knew, in that enigmatic, dreamlike way particular to these experiences, that it was Neil.

Lisa recalls, 'My life had a certain calmness about it for the next four days, just a knowing that if I was sitting on the lounge, he was sitting next to me, and I was not afraid. I was happy.' But her smile faded the next day. 'My husband came home to find me sitting on the lounge very upset. He asked what was wrong. I said, "He has gone now." I felt very alone again, but when I needed someone and had no one, he was there. I haven't felt him since . . .'

That is the crux. Neil had never made his presence known to his sister before, and, so far, he has not been back, yet Lisa is certain he returned to her side during one of the most fraught and stressful periods of her life. This suggests our late loved ones remain aware of and up to date with the details of our earthly existence, from the mundane to the urgent, though only the latter is likely to involve their intercession.

Kathy Ford, whom we met in the previous chapter, had been racked with worry about her baby granddaughter, Mia, whose white-blood cell count was very low. Doctors were running tests but Kathy, whose 23-year-old daughter Melissa had recently passed of ovarian cancer, was fearful of leukaemia. In the midst of this upset, Kathy received a visit: 'I woke up at 2.30 am – I remember looking at the clock – and I said, "Oh, Melissa is here. Hello, Liss." I can't explain exactly how I knew Liss was there – I definitely did not see or hear her. The best way I can describe it is like, when my kids were little, every now and again, one of them would come into my bedroom in the middle of the night. I would wake to find them just standing beside my bed, looking at me. They usually didn't make a sound but I just sensed they were there; that is what woke me up that night – *sensing* her. Liss just said, "Mum, Mia will be alright." With that, I went straight back to sleep and slept like a baby! And yes, Mia was fine – just some weird virus.'

Leonie Hitchenor, who in July 2012 was keeping vigil at her mum's hospital bedside as her life drew to a close, received a practical solution to a pressing problem from a surprising source: her dad, who'd died in his sleep four months earlier. Leonie, a 48-year-old from the New South Wales Central Coast, explained: 'It was a long night because of my own issues with chronic illness and pain, and during the early hours, I was in a bit of trouble. I had been sitting for hours trying to keep Mum comfortable. I needed to hold her oxygen line as she felt it was choking her when it was allowed to drop. She was also annoyed by it on her face.'

Debating with herself about whether to ask the nurses for something to hold it up, Leonie, who was utterly exhausted, began to doze off. 'Then, there was a very strong tug on the machine end of the oxygen line and something fell down with a very loud clatter,' she recalls. 'I jumped up and actually said aloud, "What the heck was that?!" I looked around the darkened room and couldn't see anything wrong. Then I spotted a roll of medical tape on the floor – I knew for a fact it had not been there before as I was continually checking the floor around me to make sure my seat wasn't on any of the cords and lines to Mum.'

For a few minutes, Leonie just sat and contemplated the roll of tape. 'Then I said, "Thanks, Dad," and picked it up. I used a piece of it to tape the oxygen line to the bed frame. I know nurses often keep that tape on the back of the bedhead, but even if it had just dropped down, that doesn't explain the huge yank on the airline that woke me out of my half-sleep, or the massive noise that little roll of tape made as it fell . . .'

Literary agent Selwa Anthony has also experienced the death-defying force of a father's love. It was a Friday evening in 1965 and Selwa was running late for the wedding of her sister, Yvette. The nuptials were set for 6 pm in the eastern Sydney suburb of Randwick, so after work, Selwa's husband picked her up from her job in the city and the couple hoped for the best as they joined the peak-hour crawl. When the church came into view, Selwa realised everyone was already inside and asked her husband to drop her at the door before parking. She looked up at the church where her sister was about to take her vows. Aglow with the warmth of the setting sun, it seemed a structure out of time, a sanctuary of love – a place where a miracle could find a way in. 'Here will do,' said Selwa, already opening the car door. 'I can see Dad standing outside waiting for me.'

Reminiscent of Sir William Crookes's observation about paranormal phenomena – 'I do not say it is possible. I say that it happened' – there was Abraham, her father, who'd been buried a year before, waiting outside the church, looking as proud and dapper as any father of the bride. Selwa says: 'He was standing there. He was wearing exactly the suit he had on when I got married two years previously. He had the red rose in the lapel that he'd worn for my wedding, to match my bouquet of blood-red roses.'

Abraham, known to all as Abie, was a proud family man. He'd fathered two sons and five daughters, including Yvette, who was minutes away from walking down the aisle, and nothing could keep him away. 'As soon as he saw me he entered the church,' recalls Selwa, 'but not through the door, he walked through the church stone wall.'

Throughout the service, Selwa felt her father's presence as intensely as if he'd been sitting at her side. His joy filled every corner of the sacred space. Smiling at her newlywed sister, Selwa reflected, too, on how lucky she had been – of all his girls, Selwa was the only one Abie had given away on her wedding day. Her gown had been stark as snow against her bouquet of blood-red roses. The following year, he was gone.

As powerful as these experiences are, they tend to knit themselves into the fabric of our lives – they don't stand apart, they *are* part of us – so it was that Selwa didn't dwell on her father's return and got on with her busy life. Then the photographs were developed. 'I'd worn a black fascinator with a single red rose and there was one photo that came out all black, except for this rose!' To Selwa, this was proof that she'd seen and felt her father at the church.

'The red rose was symbolic of my wedding and my sister's wedding that my father wasn't there for,' she explains. For one daughter, as for the other, with a tenderness to tear apart the laws of nature, Abie wore a rose in his lapel, like a drop of love. 'It was absolutely amazing. To this day, it's still like it happened yesterday; I see it, I feel it and I know his presence was there the whole time. I didn't even question it. His presence is still with me to this day.'

Bea, 72, a great-grandmother from Sydney's western suburbs, knows the spirit of her identical twin helped her find the strength to stand up for herself after 50 years of marriage to an abusive man. 'I picked him up and threw him, I don't know how I got the strength to do that, but I think my twin helped me. I just lifted him up like a piece of rag,' says Bea, whose doll-like voice has a note of steel. The attacks only stopped in 2012, the petite pensioner tells me, after she consulted a solicitor and threatened to go to the police.

Now, she frequently sees her twin, Cecily, who died when she was in her 60s, watching her from outside her lounge-room window. 'She just stands at the window smiling at me. She looks just as I remember her, just the same. Her hair's dark. Mine's gone snow-white and she just looks the same. She's always got a lovely smile for me.'

The sightings always follow the same pattern: she appears as Bea is watching television and remains for up to twenty minutes, pouring her love into a brilliant smile, a gift for her sister from the other side of the glass, from the other side of life; then she turns and walks away. The only thing that changes is Cecily's outfit. 'She used to love to get dressed up, so she'll have a lovely jumper on or a lovely jacket and her earrings and all her hair fluffed out,' says Bea. She concedes, however, to feeling 'a wee bit frightened' by Cecily's visits, enough to stop her venturing outside to investigate, but she'll always smile right back at her twin and give her a wave.

'I think she just wants to let me know I'm not alone,' Bea says.

'I know she's waiting for me up there, but I think she's looking after me, too. Now I just can't stop looking at the window. I look every day, hoping she'll come back again soon . . .'

For love is always welcome. It's a theme that lights up even the darkest corners of the following three stories, featuring a grandmother returning to help heal the heartbreak of miscarriage, a caring boy whose nocturnal visits changed the life of his lonely and psychically attuned sister, and a husband whose shocking unsolved murder was not enough to tear him from his soulmate's side.

Chain of hearts

'She shows up just when I need her and I feel so lucky to have that.'

'My nan was always a big part of my life,' says Kristen McNeil, 36, who knows she can state that in the present tense and it will still be accurate. She has been warmed by her grandmother's love time and again since her death in 1998, but never more so than in 2013, when she stood by her side through a crushing loss. In her nan's calm and reassuring presence, hope flowers; as Kristen, who lives in Canberra and is studying to be a social worker, tells us:

> Nanna and I were always very close when she was alive. She lived with our family after Grandpop died, moving into our house when I was about seven. Every day, my brother and I would come home from school and there my nan would be, waiting for us with a smile and a drink. She used to help my mum with all the housework as both of my parents worked full-time, and she would often put dinner on for the family.

She lived in a caravan in our huge backyard and my dad built a big bathroom and sewing room for her. I used to go down to her place most Sundays when I was kid and have 'stripe' (tripe!) for dinner with her. There she would be with her glass of sherry and her radio on. I would just sit with her sometimes while she knitted and listened to her music. I loved those times and always felt so happy to just sit and be with her.

When my parents divorced and I left with my mum at around the age of fourteen, I didn't see my nan very often for a few years but I still used to call her and catch up with her. It was in my early twenties that I started to visit more often and moved back to live with Dad and Nan for a while and we were able to reconnect. She used to still insist on doing my laundry even when I was an adult, but she always teased me about my tiny underwear and G-strings when she hung them on the line. She used to say, 'I don't know how you can wear those tiny things! They are like string! They must be so uncomfortable!'

When I was about 22, my nan started to become very frail. She didn't get out and play her bowls or bingo very often anymore, and she rarely drove. She had a stroke and lost all the feeling down one side of her body. I would visit her in the hospital and do her nails and put cream on her hands for her. The doctors told my parents that she had cancer and had a few months left to live, but Nan wasn't told. She always said she didn't want to know if she had it.

Once she came back home after the stroke, she needed daily care as she spent all her time in bed. For a woman who was so independent and such a hardcore housewife, this was crushing. She had lost everything in herself, all within a matter of weeks. But she was one determined lady. When my dad told her she would have to go into full-time care after she fell and broke her wrist trying to use the bathroom, she adamantly refused and swore she wanted to die at home. She refused over and over and my dad heartbreakingly booked her into the care facility. On the day she was due to go, he came to pick her up. As he was putting her in the car and doing up her seatbelt, she said his name and then died in his arms. I told you, my nan was a determined woman!

When my dad took her back inside to lay her on her bed, he found that she had completed all her paperwork for her bank accounts and will and laid them all out to be found. She had decided then and there, that day, that she was dying on her own terms!

On this day, around half an hour before she died, I was temping at a reception job and the boss walked in and said, 'You can go home.' I thought I was in trouble and asked what I had done wrong. He said, 'Nothing, we just decided you can go home today, take the afternoon off. See you tomorrow.' I was dumbfounded. I got into my car to drive home and as I pulled out of the street I thought to myself, 'Oh great, I have the afternoon off, I might go and visit Nan,' and I started to make my way there. About fifteen minutes later I got a call from my mum saying that Nan had died. She had died almost exactly at the moment when I had decided to go and visit her.

When I arrived at the house, my dad was in the dining room, heartbroken, and he told me that Nan was in her room in bed. I asked for some private time with her.

When I went in there it was the strangest thing I have ever experienced. A lot of the women in my family have psychic visions, dreams and feelings but I had never experienced anything like this. Nan was laid out on the bed but to me she looked like a shell, an empty body . . . but the room itself was full of her! The air was thick like electricity and buzzing on my skin. I could hear a buzzing like an electric razor and I felt all the hair on my body stand on end. It was like white-hot fire when I thought of touching anything in the room. Yet when I looked at her she looked so empty and pale. I said goodbye to her and told her she was going to be okay and not to be afraid. I was just so worried that she would be alone and afraid.

Over the next year or so, I moved in with my dad into a new house for a fresh start for us and tried to be a support and comfort to him. Even though she was gone, she was still on our minds often. It was about a year later that she started to show up in the house when I was alone. It started with a few times when my dad was staying away for the night and I was in the house by myself. I used to leave a light on in the hallway while I slept so that I didn't freak out in the dark if I had to get up in the middle of the night for the bathroom. Well . . . when we were kids my brother and I used to tease my nan and call her the 'electricity police' as she used to walk around behind us, turning lights off after us. Imagine my surprise when I woke up one morning to find the hallway light had been turned off when I had left it on. I started to keep track each time when Dad was away and I was alone at night and left the light on, and sure enough it was turned off in the mornings. Oh Nan! This was really lovely and it let me know she was around (though it was a little bit freaky, too!). Another night, she decided to take it one step further . . .

One Saturday night I was alone again and I was doing laundry. I was washing, drying and folding the clothes on the sofa and bringing loads into the lounge room. When I got back into the lounge room after putting another load on, I walked out to my piles of dry unfolded laundry and found one of my G-strings laid out flat and smooth, dead centre of the coffee table, nowhere near where I had been carrying the laundry! Obviously my nan was teasing me again, just like she did when she hung the washing on the line. I couldn't believe it! I was so shocked I retraced my steps and tried to see if there was any way I could have dropped the underwear myself . . . nope. It was my nan alright!

It was during this time that Nan also 'visited' me in my sleep. I know it was her. I was dreaming and I could literally feel the warmth of baby-soft wrinkly skin in my hands, just like her hands had felt in life. I looked up and it was her smiling at me, holding my hands. I said to her, 'It's you! It *is* really you! You really are here!' and she smiled and said, 'Yes darling, it really is me – here I am! I am here!' and then she faded away and I woke up with a jolt into my body. I think she was letting me know that she is around.

I haven't felt that much of her lately, but I do know she is around and takes care of me often. She shows up just when I need her and I feel so lucky to have that. It was only recently that I suffered a terrible heartbreak when I was almost three months pregnant and bleeding. When I was at the hospital waiting for my ultrasound, my husband went out of the room and I was alone on the bed. I was lying there wondering if my baby was okay, and my nan appeared at my left side. She was standing there with me and she put her hand on my belly and said to me, 'It's going to be okay, it's okay, it's okay,' and she patted my belly. I didn't see her with my eyes, I saw her with my mind, feeling her there; it is like staring at a point in the room and seeing her in the corner of your eye. My husband then entered the room and my nan was gone.

129

I thought my baby would be okay based on what Nan had said, but sadly they told me it had passed away. It was then I realised that she wasn't telling me the pregnancy was okay, she was telling me my baby would be okay because Nan was going to take care of it. I fell to pieces, not only for the anguish of losing my baby but also for the burst of love I felt for my nan after that private moment we shared. I know she is looking after my amazing little baby and I know that she is watching over me, smiling, and will be holding my hand through the days, weeks and months ahead when we try to bring another little life into this world.

It gives me great comfort and peace to know that my nan was there for my little one and that she will take care of it just as she took care of me.

Stand by me

'He sat there quietly, just smiling at me.'

A four-year-old girl wakes from a nightmare, her lawn-green eyes stretched wide in fear. Trembling, with sweat trickling down her back, she sits straight up and sobs with relief to see she's not alone. Someone has come to sit with her, a little boy whose smiling face is a lighthouse to guide her safely back from terrors that wait for darkness to fall, for her eyelids to block out the day. She says, 'Matthew?' He replies with a smile and a thought, not spoken words, which blooms effortlessly in her mind: 'You are not alone.'

There is a secret Erika Müller has kept beneath her skin for two decades. Like a photograph stored in the breast pocket, made supple and warm by tears, years and its guardian's beating heart, it is a powerful and private emblem of solace. Today, she is sharing it for the first time. Love may never die, but sometimes, as we've already explored, love doesn't even take its first breath . . .

'As far back as I can remember, I've known about Matthew,' says Erika, speaking of the eldest of her parents' four children, a son who was stillborn in 1984. The first time he appeared, presenting as a blond boy of eight, was after she'd had one of her most frightening nightmares. Four years of age is very young to be enduring recurring dreams of death, but for Erika it was her desolate reality. The nightmares varied – little Erika trapped in a coffin, a teenaged Erika falling into the jaws of a shark, Erika as an old woman at the close of a pitiful life where 'there was nothing after, there was no point to being alive' – but all left her breathless and mute with terror. She was only in kindergarten.

Calling them back from the basement of her memory, Erika, who grew up in Perth and is now 24 and working in a café, fights back tears again. In the same way her secret is a salve for her pain, these bleak nightscapes retain the power to wound: 'I still get shaky when I think about them,' she says. Erika adds that the visions of how she'd look in the future – petite, with a head of thick, dark curls setting off her pale complexion and green eyes – have so far been eerily accurate. She cannot explain why the nightmares began. Her Lutheran grandmother telling her the dead 'wait in the coffin until God comes back to Earth' may have been the culprit, but she is not sure if she heard this before or after the first nightmare. She only knows they eventually stopped once Matthew came to her side.

'He looked solid to me,' she remembers, explaining that she somehow understood there was nobody there in the physical, but that the image in her mind was as sharp as a high-resolution photo. As others have echoed in their stories, it was more the implicit sense of his presence than anything witnessed – these experiences are multi- and extra-sensory. Erika recalls: 'He sat there quietly, just smiling at me. I could understand what he was trying to say to me, though he wasn't using his voice. I could only hear it with my thoughts. But it's mainly his presence that helps me understand. That first time made me realise that I won't be alone when I'm gone.'

Three months after Matthew first appeared, the nightmares stopped, but not his visits. It would be nine years before she saw him again, however. When Erika was thirteen, her great-grand-mother, whom she adored, died and the teenager plunged into grief and guilt, berating herself for not having intuited her death. 'I remember being so angry at everyone and so angry at myself for not knowing,' says Erika, who was an ultra-sensitive young-ster. One Christmas, she had snuck out of a family gathering and walked to the nursing home where her great-grandmother lived. 'I remember Great-grandma loving the fact that I visited her, but being so furious that I was there by myself.'

When the old lady died, it was Matthew's gentle presence at her bedside once again that put Erika on the path to healing. 'He helped me realise that what was important was that she wasn't in any more pain.' This time, Matthew looked about seventeen or eighteen, his hair now a blend of blond and light brown. 'He was becoming handsome,' says Erika. She last saw him in 2008, when her beloved grandfather died of cancer, and Matthew looked to be in his twenties. (Many of the people I spoke to have described spirit children who appear to be growing and thriving in spirit. Most mediums believe this is the case, too.)

'I haven't seen Matthew in years, but I've felt him every now and then,' says Erika, who shares a story of how he helped her walk away from a near-miss with a bus in Chapter Eight, 'The Power of Love'. Though Matthew's visits are few and far between, they have always been perfectly timed to support the sensitive, psychically gifted sister he never had the chance to know in life, during moments when she needed him most. He has found a way to be a brother to her from the other side.

'He's my angel who is always with me and my family,' says Erika. 'His presence calmed my nightmares, helped me realise there was no reason to fear death. There would be no endless darkness.'

Scent of a soulmate

'I've been living with a spirit husband.'

It happened on the edge of dawn, when an enchantment had fallen upon the morning, emptying it of its usual sounds of traffic and the street. In that otherworldly quiet of her apartment in Sydney's eastern suburbs, Emilia Bresciani drifted in the realm where dreams melt into waking, and waking into dreams. Soon she became aware of sounds pulling her out of sleep. What were they? She tried to decipher them. Murmurs of love? The sigh of the wind? 'Then there was something streaming under the door,' recalls Emilia. 'There was a scent that streamed, that rippled, under the door, and then the door opened and there he came, gliding in, wearing his wedding shirt.'

It was her husband, Richard Diack, who'd been murdered during a bushwalk in the Blue Mountains three weeks earlier. Where in life he'd lost most of his ginger hair, now it was returned to him in abundance. 'He came and sat next to me on my side of our bed, and I looked at him and said, "Richard, you've come back," and he said, "Yes, I'm here."' Though Emilia asked, he did not want to discuss the details of his death. Instead, he took his wife's hand and they set off on a voyage. 'I stood up, and we flew,' says Emilia. 'We flew across the city, across the bridge and over the water, like two birds.' Richard was on a mission that morning in 1992. His purpose would eventually become clear to Emilia, but first he took her back to where their story began.

The lifts opened at the headquarters of SBS Television in Sydney's Milsons Point one weekday in February 1991, and Emilia, then a reporter on the program *Vox Populi*, could not peel her eyes from the tall, pale, red-haired newcomer who'd pressed the button for the sixth floor.

'Who are you?' she asked, with a bravado born of knowing that in that moment everything in life was going her way. ('I lived very happy,' she recalls. 'Like Carrie from *Sex and the City*.') In the soft voice that would come to imprint itself on her heart, he said he was the new guy in marketing. She responded with her name and added cheekily, 'I'm a star reporter here. Give me a call, we'll have a coffee and I'll show you around.'

Today, the memory makes Emilia, now a counsellor and writer, chuckle into her coffee, as she weaves her story of mystery, murder and death-defying love at a café in the Queen Victoria Building. 'I was full of confidence then. You know how TV journalists can be,' she says, still looking ready for her close-up in a jaunty Fedora-style hat, her signature accessory.

A week after their meeting, Richard left a message at Emilia's desk and when she called back she discovered he was actually an executive. 'I accepted his coffee and said, "You never told me you were the big boss." He was very unassuming and said, "You never asked."'

From there, things progressed quickly. Perhaps it was a prescient urgency that propelled the couple forward. To Emilia, their bond seemed forged in another lifetime – a recognition of souls across dimensions – for how else to explain the energy that pulsed between them? How else to explain the effect one had on the other throughout their intense, all-too brief, time together? 'It was as if I looked at him with my third eye and I said, "This is it." Some marriages last twenty years, ours lasted seven months and the totality of time we were together was eighteen months. Yet, I find myself doing many things that he did, and I don't know if that's my way of remembering him, of being near him.'

In the fourth month of their romance, Scottish-born Richard proposed and the wedding was set for the early months of 1992, an auspicious year for Emilia, who hails from Peru. 'It was the celebration of 500 years of Latin America, so I thought, "Let's celebrate the union of two worlds."' After visiting Emilia's family in Peru in the sunset of 1991, the couple flew to Antigua, the Caribbean island where Richard's brothers lived, and exchanged vows in that idyllic setting. The bride, who was 33, wore a red and black dress and a dazzling smile, while the groom looked dapper in his shirt that mirrored the colour of his eyes and the sea surrounding them.

But a tempest brewed around the newlyweds, whose union was marred by 'confrontations and fights' alongside 'moments of great intensity and love', says Emilia, who shared their story in her bestselling memoir, *The Raw Scent of Vanilla*, published in 2000. Stress was a third party in their relationship, with Richard's high-pressure job at the network consuming most of his time and energy, which in turn compromised his wellbeing and his capacity for intimacy with his wife – a situation that troubled Emilia, but not overwhelmingly so. 'I didn't care,' she says, with a shrug. 'It was beyond that.'

To address the problem, Emilia introduced her husband to alternative therapies and healing techniques, though he preferred seeking peace and relaxation out in the open, bush-walking and photographing nature. On the eve of his death, something happened which augured a breakthrough, a return to a more balanced way of life for the pair, who hadn't given up on their dream of finding harmony, buying a new home and starting a family.

That day, Emilia kept an appointment with a past-life regressionist, more in the spirit of curiosity and adventure than staunch belief. 'My question to her was, "Where had I met him?" I told her, "This relationship goes beyond the physical. The more we fight, the more I realise how much I love him. The moment he takes off, I really miss him, it is as if he has become my oxygen."'

The hypnosis session revealed the couple had spent a previous lifetime together, which ended in 'a violent separation, and that was why I was still angry,' says Emilia, who couldn't wait to get home to tell Richard that they'd met before. 'He laughed, he was not really into this sort of thing, but he said, "Okay, let's go have Thai food to celebrate."'

The evening proved to be a joyous return to everything that was wonderful about their relationship. Over dinner, they discussed their future, and afterwards, snuggled on the couch to watch a movie. All was well.

The following morning, Richard got up early and left for his bushwalk, as planned. 'I understood. He had so much stress, he needed to be in the bush,' says Emilia, who's been haunted ever since by the sound of the door clicking in place behind him. The ominous 'click' even features in a scene in the novel she's writing. 'That sound is so present. It was the last physical connection I had with him.'

When Richard did not come home that night, Emilia, who'd been waiting by the window for hours, raised the alarm. The news, when it came the following afternoon, was unfathomable. A bushwalker had discovered Richard's battered body. He'd been robbed and bludgeoned to death. He was 40 years old. Something inside Emilia cracked, never to be repaired. 'I was in shock for days, you know, shock meaning there is a kind of veil of denial.'

While outwardly she remained stoic, calling on the lion hearts of the Amazonian women of her bloodline to keep her upright and functioning, when night fell, Emilia would weep for hours, riven by the loss of the man she'd mapped out her life with. 'Death is the worst abandonment. It's so final!' she says. 'For days, I would look at the door of my bedroom expecting him to come in again. Two weeks later, he did, when he came to say goodbye.'

Seeing her husband's spirit, clothed in the outfit he'd worn for his marriage and funeral, was a transformative experience for Emilia. Though she's always been drawn to the mystical and the magical, inheriting from her late *mamá* an appreciation of the invisible world, she had never experienced anything like this. After he glided in, looking healthy and robust in his shirt of ocean blue, Richard told his wife, 'I'm here to pick up my computer,' and up they soared, hand in hand, to the place where they'd met and worked, the SBS offices. But dreams have a language of their own, as Emilia points out: 'In this experience, the office was a white building, with a garden on the left-hand side.'

In this garden, three trees bloomed, made not of wood, but marble. The 'trees' were actually a trio of huge sculptures of hands, each covered in hieroglyphics traced in red, like fine veins on alabaster skin. Entranced, Emilia stepped closer to inspect them while Richard entered the temple-like edifice, in search of his computer. Then he called out, 'Come on, come on, we have to go up,' and Emilia, sensing his haste, rushed to join him.

'We went into the lift and he pressed five and we went up,' she remembers, adding that when they'd met in the lift on that first fateful day, she'd alighted at the fourth floor while Richard continued to the sixth. 'In the dream, on floor five, he gave me a hug and we united,' she says, her downcast eyes as black as her hair and the coffee in front of her. 'He dissolved into me and in that moment, I opened my eyes and I looked for him, and I was on my bed. It was so real that I could still smell him.'

A week later, Emilia returned to work, where she was given a box of Richard's belongings. 'In the box, there was a little square disc with the word "Personal" on it,' says Emilia, who'd discovered her husband's electronic journal entries. Afire with grief and the pain of learning that Richard had kept secrets from her, she deleted the files. This, coupled with the contents of some of the journal entries, where Richard vented about the ups and downs of their marriage, was enough for the police to declare at the 1996 inquest into his death that she was the only person with a motive to kill Richard, to Emilia's utter astonishment and horror. Suddenly, the pieces of the puzzling dream fell into place. Richard's urgent mission to return to the office and retrieve his computer 'was a warning', she reflects. 'It was a kind of communication.'

The state coroner later cleared Emilia, but the accusation and the public ordeal scarred the young widow, who sank into a deep depression. Two years in therapy helped her recover, and sparked a new career in psychology, which now subsidises her heart's calling – her dream of becoming a novelist. Once she's finished her book, she may attempt to have the investigation into the still-unsolved murder of her husband reopened.

Though Emilia would like the mystery solved, she's secure in the knowledge that Richard's spirit is not uneasy – rather, it's imbued with joy, inspiration and infinite love. In the first year after his death, especially, 'he was very present at home', says Emilia, who would often catch a whiff of his Paco Rabanne aftershave as she was driving. One evening, she came home at 11 pm and was preparing for bed, when at exactly midnight her CD player came to life and an enchanting melody flooded her apartment. It was the flute solo she had selected to accompany Richard's coffin as it was carried out from his funeral service. These moments, and the extraordinary dream of flight – or 'experience of altered consciousness' as Emilia calls it – proved to her that Richard had not abandoned her after all. 'He was sad about the pain I was going through, so he tried, however he could, to contact me and say, "I'm still around and I'm sorry for what you're going through." That helped me heal.'

Though Emilia was in the prime of life and beauty when her husband died, for her, there has never been another. 'I never fell in love again, and I've always been a woman who loved male company, because I grew up with four brothers so I've enjoyed being spoilt, I've enjoyed being protected, I've enjoyed being helped at home with a hammer and a drill, you know.' Pondering that, she muses that each of us has one soulmate, and that even if that person is no longer here in the physical, the bond continues in another way. 'I've been living with a spirit husband,' she declares, with a smile that transforms her back into that apple-cheeked bride exchanging vows in paradise.

The man she married is by her side as she writes her novel, cheering her on from the place where his spirit dwells. He will be with her wherever she goes, which may soon be closer to the nature he idolised. To simplify her life, and complete her work in tranquillity, she's considering a move to the very mountains that claimed him, or down the coast, where she'll pour out her story to the beat of the pounding waves, under the all-knowing gaze of her cat, Moche. 'I discovered that we fall in love with people whose qualities are in us, so that they are catalysts for these qualities to emerge,' says Emilia, explaining that Richard, who was a skilled writer, is inspiring her to new heights with her craft. 'So now, when I write, I'm very connected to him.'

Two years before Richard died, Emilia's mother passed at the age of 66. Fearing for her father, left to fend for himself in the house that once hummed with the chatter of his wife and their five kids, now bare of warmth and love, Emilia would phone him and half-jokingly suggest he find a 'girlfriend' to share his days with. 'And he said, "No, because your mum is here and I would never offend her, so I am not alone." And now I understand exactly what he meant! Because I am never alone,' says Emilia, who glimpsed eternity that portentous day she met Richard in the lift, when whispers from a hidden past urged her to change her future. 'There was something special about him, and that connection is still with me.'

'To me, it's more a sense of him being inside myself, and it's no longer a "he". It's the substance of his spirit that joined mine,' she says, echoing the climax of her visionary dream. 'Once upon a time we had been one, and then we split to live different experiences, and then we came back together. Life is wonderful – it's also very mysterious. Why we had to split again, I don't know . . . but now, we are one.'

*

If there's any chapter that most simply sums up the message of this book, it's this one, with its tales of deceased loved ones returning, sometimes many years after they've passed, to prove they're as much a part of the family as anyone in the physical, in times of celebration, as Sarah and Selwa found, as well as sadness. Throughout the most trying times in our lives, they're there, providing support and a spiritual 'shoulder' to lean on.

As new mothers struggling to cope, Kylie and Lisa were buoyed by the steadfast presence of their mother and brother, respectively. When earthly support networks were non-existent, these spirits stepped in; Kylie's mum helping to settle her grandchildren, while Lisa's brother bolstered her with his kind and caring presence, making all the difference to her wellbeing.

Knowing her adored nan is looking after the baby she mis-carried means everything to Kristen, who can plan for the future knowing that no matter what, her grandmother will be there for her. What a powerful and freeing thought. It's the case for all of the people who shared their stories in this chapter. Their loved ones died, but they came back when it counted. What better way to show they've never stopped caring? And they continue to care because they continue to *be*.

'Our spirit is a being of indestructible nature,' said the writer Johann Goethe. 'It works on from eternity to eternity; it is like the sun, which though it seems to set to our mortal eyes, does not really set, but shines on perpetually.'

6

A Parting Gift

Love lights the way at the edge of life

'We're all just walking each other home.'
—Ram Dass

Ionce met a nurse who was a stunningly gifted medium. To her, the dead appeared as real as flesh-and-blood people, but she was very shy and private about her abilities. It took some coaxing to secure an interview. Perhaps if she'd taken bookings, she could have made a fortune and become an Australian Allison DuBois; instead, she led a humble and anonymous life in rural New South Wales with her husband and three children. Hers, she told me, was a gift she wished she could return.

With one exception . . . she took the greatest delight in seeing deceased relatives waiting to accompany patients to the other side of life. It was her favourite part of nursing, and made

143

up for all of the hardships and anxiety that were part and parcel of her 'gift', she told me, eyes brimming with tears. Her story, 'The Reluctant Medium', appears in *Spirit Sisters*. One moment she described has hung like a framed photo in the halls of my memory ever since. An elderly woman was ill and a young man, dressed in the scratchy, slinky fashions of the 1970s – gaberdine flares, a skintight shirt and platform shoes – waited patiently in the chair at her bedside for hours. Was he a son, brother or former lover? The nurse couldn't tell, but what mattered was what he was there to do. 'It's just really nice,' she said, 'to know that a family member comes to pick you up when it's time.'

The nurse had the rare privilege of seeing the spirit who'd returned to collect his loved one. More frequently, it's the patient themselves, usually someone who's terminally ill, who reports, or is witnessed, seeing or speaking to someone invisible, like a deceased friend or relative, usually to the surprise and – depending on point of view – delight or disbelief of the living friend or relatives who witness or are made aware of this. Sometimes, patients who've been immobile and moribund suddenly appear momentarily lucid, and reach their arms up or out towards a wonder only they can see. Reported as far back as ancient Egypt, these events, known as 'deathbed visions', cross the divides of culture, religion, age, gender and socioeconomics.

The late co-founder of Apple, Steve Jobs, marvelled at something only he could see in his final moments on 5 October 2011, as revealed in the eulogy delivered by his sister, Mona Simpson, at his memorial service. Her words – she permitted the *New York Times* to publish the eulogy – evoke the mystery and wonder characteristic of these anecdotes. Explaining how she rushed to his side after Jobs asked her to come as soon as possible, she arrived to find, 'His tone was affectionate, dear, loving, but like someone whose luggage was already strapped onto the vehicle, who was already on the beginning of his journey.' After making it through one more night, he began to let go. 'Before embarking, he'd looked at his sister Patty, then for a long time at his children, then at his life's partner, Laurene, and then over his shoulders past them. Steve's final words were: "Oh wow. Oh wow. Oh wow."'

Six little words, yet how dense with possibilities they are! They raise gooseflesh whenever I read them. What *did* Steve Jobs see? The answer, it seems, will be revealed to each of us in due time. 'The secret of heaven,' said the nineteenth-century writer Oliver Wendell Holmes, 'is kept from age to age.'

A mystery unfurled at the bedside of Karen Davis's mother-in-law, too. Visiting two days before she died, Karen watched her chat happily to unseen relatives. 'Her mind was sound, it was just her liver that was dying,' prefaces Karen. 'She introduced me to Jack. I said, "Who is Jack? There's no one there," and she said, "Jack's my uncle twice removed. Don't you remember Jack?" And I'm going, "No, no." But then I just played along with her, sitting there, thinking, "Wow, this is weird." And she just kept staring at the wall. I said, "Do you want me to put the TV on?" She answered, "No, it's alright. I'm happy." She was talking to people. People were coming to see her.' Yet Karen was the only person in the room.

Stan Simpson's wife, Helen, was diagnosed with terminal cancer in October 2008, 'so I took her home and nurtured her', says the 80-year-old retiree from Mudgee, New South Wales. 'I still loved her dearly after 47 years married.' One afternoon two months later, he was sitting in his regular spot on the bed beside her when she opened her eyes and asked, 'Who's your friend, love?'

'You are, darlin',' he replied. 'Always will be!'

'No, I mean that man!' she said. Stan looked around, thinking they had a visitor.

'There's nobody here, love,' he said.

'Oh, right,' she said, and went back to sleep, with a smile.

Stan says, 'The next morning, Helen passed away in her sleep, and I've always wondered . . .'

In his 1926 book, *Deathbed Visions*, physics professor Sir William Barrett includes a firsthand account by his wife, obstetrical surgeon Lady Florence Barrett, about a patient, Doris, who'd just given birth and was haemorrhaging. Nothing could be done to save her. Lady Barrett described: 'Suddenly she looked eagerly towards one part of the room, a radiant smile illuminating her whole countenance. "Oh, lovely, lovely," she said . . . "Lovely brightness, wonderful beings." It is difficult to describe the sense of reality conveyed by her intense absorption in the vision. Then, seeming to focus her attention more intently on one place for a moment she exclaimed, almost with a kind of joyous cry, "Why, it's father! Oh, he's so glad I'm coming; he is so glad . . ." Her baby was brought for her to see. She looked at it with interest . . . then turning towards the vision again, she said, "I can't, I can't stay; if you could see what I do, you would know I can't stay."'

Lady Barrett left the room, but describes how Doris lived another hour, during which she 'retained to the last the double consciousness of the bright forms she saw and also of those tending her at the bedside'. Had Lady Barrett been able to stay a little longer, she would have witnessed what is the perhaps the most intriguing part of this now quite famous tale, as the matron of the hospital, Miriam Castle, related in a letter to William Barrett, which he published in *Deathbed Visions*:

'Her husband was leaning over her and speaking to her, when pushing him aside, she said, "Oh don't hide it; it's so beautiful." Then turning away from him . . . [Doris] said, "Oh why, there's Vida," referring to a sister of whose death three weeks previously she had not been told.'

Barrett also includes a testimonial from the late sisters' mother, who confirms every detail, explaining that as her daughter Doris's pregnancy was delicate, it was decided to keep the news of her elder sister's death from her. She added that when Doris saw the vision of Vida – the name means 'life' in Spanish – she wore a 'puzzled expression'.

But Barrett was not the first to probe the enigma of deathbed visions. In 1882, Francis Cobbe compiled many such experiences in her book, *The Peak in Darien*, including that of a man who was dying from 'consumption' (tuberculosis), which has much in common with Barrett's story as well as modern-day accounts: 'Suddenly, while we were thus talking quietly together, he became silent, and fixed his eyes on one particular spot in the room, which was entirely vacant, even of furniture. At the same time, a look of the greatest delight changed the whole expression of his face, and, after a moment of what seemed to be intense scrutiny of some object invisible to me, he said to me in a joyous tone, "There is Jim." Jim was a little son whom he had lost the year before.'

Whether a 'radiant smile illuminating her whole countenance' or 'a look of the greatest delight', as recorded in the early literature above, many accounts of deathbed visions highlight the almost beatific expression of exaltation which transforms the face of the sick person who's glimpsing, perhaps, what awaits us all behind the veil. Occasionally, there is a sense of presence or 'energy' in the room of someone who's dying or has just died, palpable to medical staff and visitors alike.

Sydney aged-care nurse Gabriella, 53, specialised in the one-on-one care of people who were approaching the end of their lives at home. One patient was a 63-year-old dying of liver cancer and the stretch of time preceding and following her death has carved a niche in Gabriella's memory. 'I've never seen this before but she was looking up between her eyes and breathing in a certain pattern. She was sitting up in bed, looking up,' remembers Gabriella, adding that the patient had three adult children present, two of whom were 'accepting of her death – they knew it was her time', and one who resisted it.

Gabriella, who says she has learned how to 'intuit' a situation, or 'tune in', took a seat by the distressed daughter and explained how a loved one's stress and resistance may complicate the dying person's transition (and here I was reminded of Ban Guo's story of his comatose father in Chapter Three). Gently, she told her, 'It's your mother's time to go. Release her, tell her you love her and that it's alright to go.' Then together, they sat on either side of the lady, who was still gazing heavenward, and held her hands. 'The daughter said, "Mum, it's time to go, I love you . . ." and then the mother passed away.'

What she'd accomplished with her utterance of love amazed the daughter, as did what followed: 'There was absolute joy and bliss in the house, we felt her spirit, it was tingling joy! The doctor walked in to do the death certificate and he felt it, too. He said, "It happens, sometimes,"' says Gabriella, who once also experienced a hallway of lights flickering in farewell following the passing of a patient.

Lydia is a palliative care nurse from Adelaide who's witnessed events which, she says, are 'so magical and beautiful, it blows me away'. She will never forget the look on the face of one elderly patient she was caring for in what turned out to be his final hours. 'I was speaking to him about his wife and he was telling me how he'd lost her three years prior, and that she was the absolute love of his life,' remembers Lydia. 'Then the hairs stood up on the back of my neck because when I was getting him back to bed, his face became euphoric and he looked through and past me and focused on something behind me. I couldn't *see* anybody in the room, but the look on his face! I just knew she'd arrived.'

An hour later, Lydia checked on him and noticed the 'mottling' of the skin around the extremities, which indicates the body is beginning to shut down. Although sometimes a patient survives a couple of days after this, Lydia began to notify his family that the time was near. Her instincts were spot on; he died that afternoon, just as Lydia was finishing her shift at 3.15 pm. 'I just had a feeling – she had arrived for him and I knew it,' she says. 'The look on that man's face! The euphoria . . .'

Lydia, who has an eleven-year-old son and moonlights as a makeup artist for weddings, is one of those people whose innate serenity sets others at ease, explaining, perhaps, her success in her dual careers. 'I'm really bright and cheerful,' says the 42-year-old, with an open smile. 'I see it as my place to inject sunshine into the room, where I can. I used to know nurses who would sing while they work and they're the kind of people I love to be around.' Her voice shines with warmth and empathy as she shares details of profound moments she's encountered caring for people with life-limiting illnesses such as cancer and motor neurone disease. These are tear-stained days for family and friends who must farewell a beloved person, but they can also have a celebratory touch, when it appears there's a welcoming party 'over there' just waiting to kick off . . .

This seemed the case with a patient who was sitting up in bed as he carried on an animated conversation in another language with a corner of the room, as Lydia and his many family members who were gathered around looked on in awe. 'His daughter was saying, "He's been talking only to all of those who have died: his brothers and sisters."'

The sight would make your skin tingle and heart burst, insists Lydia. 'It was almost like a party atmosphere in the room, it was really extraordinary! He would also respond to the people that were sitting there, but then he'd go back to looking to this particular area and his eyes would dart back and forth and he'd be chatting,' she adds. This reminds me of Lady Barrett's description of her dying patient, Doris, who retained 'the double consciousness of the bright forms she saw and also of those tending her at the bedside'.

As before, Lydia observed 'that sense of euphoria about him, almost like being reunited. It was happy talk, he was smiling away.' He died within two days, but not all deathbed visions happen in the immediate vicinity of death.

Another patient of Lydia's was admitted to the same room in which his son had been treated for liver and pancreatic cancer. She recalls: 'This man was in his 80s and he was very, very fearful of death. He said, "My son was here and I miss him terribly." I told him, "I looked after your son, he was a beautiful person." When he talked about his son, the man would wipe tears from his eyes.'

One day, as Lydia was doing her rounds, she was relieved to see the frail man's eyes alight with happiness. 'He told me, "He was just in here! He was sitting on my rollater frame and he was doing burn-outs," and he laughed and I just had these beautiful visuals.' This vision, Lydia noted, was in keeping with his late son's signature humour and larger-than-life personality. Over the next few weeks the man told staff several times, 'My son was just in here,' and Lydia says she 'would just get shivers'.

'This older gentleman was so frightened of death, so frightened of what he was going to experience. I think his son wanted to come and help him along,' she says, and the man appreciated the gesture. 'He was very moved by it. And I talked about that with him. I would say things like, "How beautiful that you're going to see him soon" and "Typical of him to be thinking of you, of making your transition better". Three weeks later, he died.'

At a palliative care conference Lydia attended in 2012, one of the topics was deathbed visions, she tells me, in a heartening sign that the scientific and medical communities are beginning to embrace the significance of this widely reported phenomenon. 'What the research – albeit little – suggested, was that these events are different to visual hallucinations, which caused the patients distress and agitation,' says Lydia. 'Deathbed visions, on the other hand, occurred during times when people were quite lucid and experienced little distress, and usually they were not in a drug-affected state.'

Enmeshing heartbreak and humour, jubilance and pain, awe and humility – like life itself – these moving scenes, so quietly played out in hospitals and homes every day throughout the world, have left their mark on Lydia. 'It's a gift to witness these special moments, so they have left a legacy for me, too,' she sums up. 'I don't think we die alone. There are plenty of people on the other side to help us over.'

World-renowned grief specialist David Kessler agrees these moments have much to teach us. 'For all we know, the veil that separates life and death is lifted in the last moments of life, and those who are dying may be more in touch with that world than ours,' he writes in *Visions, Trips and Crowded Rooms: Who and What You See Before You Die*. 'If you find the concept of a dead loved one greeting you on your deathbed impossible or ridiculous, consider what I finally realised as a parent . . . What if there really is an afterlife and you receive a message that your son or daughter will be dying soon? If you were allowed to go to your child, wouldn't you?'

Sandra Milton has firsthand experience of the power of that sentiment. The 60-year-old psychiatric nurse, who lives in Albury-Wodonga, New South Wales, and is a mother of three and grandmother of four, shares a breathtaking story that speaks volumes about the indelible nature of parental love. In 1997, her husband, John, died at the age of 58 following a failed heart transplant, and his experiences – and Sandra's – in the months leading up to that support Kessler's argument.

Sandra tells me: 'Six months before my husband died, I was in bed with him one night, he was quite ill at the time, and I saw this man standing at the end of my bed, with this little person above him with the brightest bluest eyes. It was just amazing. This man had a suit on, I couldn't actually see his face, and he didn't say anything and I didn't feel frightened or threatened. When my husband woke the next morning, I told him about it and he said, "You've just described my father, and my brother Leslie, because of the blue eyes."'

In the darkness of the room, Sandra says, the child's eyes shone like searchlights as he wavered, enveloped in an aura of purest white, above the man. 'His blue eyes were what stood out. I've never seen a photo of him because he was sick and died so young, I don't even know what he passed away from him.'

Neither does she know what woke her that night, what ethereal invitation she accepted to open her eyes and behold the simple beauty of a father's eternal love for his sons; one who kissed the earth for a mere two years, the other whose journey took him much further. 'I just had this sense of somebody there, but he wasn't actually on my side, he was standing at the foot of my husband's side of the bed,' she recalls. 'It was a figure of a man dressed in a suit and, sort of, not much hair. His face was in shadow.'

Leslie was 'a menopause baby', the youngest of John's siblings, Sandra later learned, along with the fact that her late father-in-law, Edward, who was 57 when he died of renal cancer, had a bald patch and was never seen out of his suit.

As John's condition deteriorated, he confided that he, too, now saw his dad, who would reach out and tell him everything would be okay, as parents will do. 'Towards the end, for about two months prior to his death, he was on oxygen and was unable to sleep in the bed, so he'd sit in the lounge in his recliner. In the daytime, sometimes, but mostly at night, he said his father was putting out his hand [to him], but he never really described anything to me, only that he was saying, "Come, it's a good place, don't be afraid." About two days before he died, he said to John, "You need to come with me, I'll look after you." I think it helped him with his journey.'

Sandra, too, drew solace from the experiences in the bleak days following John's death, when it was left to her to console their three children, aged only eleven, twelve and thirteen. 'I knew he wasn't going to be alone,' she says. 'I felt he was at peace. I was upset for the children, but I didn't feel, "Why him? Why did it have to happen?" None of that, really. I just felt that he was still here with me. And I still feel that now.'

As for the extraordinary sight that greeted her that long ago night: 'It's like it happened yesterday, it was so vivid,' says Sandra, who only has to close her eyes to see it again – her elegant father-in-law and the shining figure of Leslie, a boy hugged by light who carried the sky in his gaze.

In one sense, Sandra's experience has echoes of what's known as a 'shared death experience' or 'collective experience', in that she witnessed the spirits of loved ones who'd arrived for her ailing husband as his time drew near. Yet where it differs from those accounts – but also adds to its enigma – is that her husband did not share in the experience with her, and that it took place six months before his passing. The 'shared death' experience is more likely to occur closer to the time of death, with both the dying person and his or her surviving loved one/s sharing part of the transition into death together.

This was the case for Brisbane psychic-medium Charmaine Wilson, 48, who tells the extraordinary story of her life in the final chapter of this book. In 2006, ten minutes after her mother died, 'Mum took me through "the gates", which was lovely,' says Charmaine, who explains what happened.

'I'm half-Italian. I cry like a fishwife when people die. I do the wailing,' she says cheerfully. 'Mum hated the wailing. She was always quite a reserved woman. The next thing, I felt this thump in my heart – I could hear her say, "Shut up. Listen. Feel." And she took me through the gates with her and it was the most exhilarating feeling of relief and love. It was just amazing. She met my brother, Martin [who'd died in a motorbike accident at the age of twenty], and I could hear her say, "It's Martin, it's

Martin!" I've got these tears of joy running down my face, and then she said, "It's Crystal!"'

Crystal was Charmaine's only daughter, who'd died when she was four. 'I cried tears of joy, it was the most amazing feeling. It lasted possibly three minutes and then it was gone,' says Charmaine, who'd been sitting in her brother's kitchen during her adventure to another realm. 'Basically, it was a gift, you know? She showed me something and since that time, I don't fear death anymore. I know that when I pass, then they're all going to be there with me.'

This remarkable phenomenon has been documented relatively recently in books including Dr Raymond Moody's *Glimpses of Eternity*. In general terms, the shared death experience takes place when a person spending time with their loved one in their final moments has an out-of-body experience, where suddenly they find themselves aloft with the spirit of the person who's departing their body, and together they travel partway to the afterlife. At some point, the living person understands they must turn back while the outgoing spirit continues towards the light or to a heavenly realm, which the visiting party can only glimpse.

In one case study in *Glimpses of Eternity*, a woman called Dana describes what happened at the deathbed of her husband, Johnny, who died of lung cancer at the age of 55: 'I was holding onto him when he died. When he did, he went right through my body. It felt like an electric sensation, like when you get your finger in the electrical socket, only much more gentle.

'When that happened our whole life sprang up around us and just kind of swallowed up the hospital room and everything in it in an instant. There was light all around . . . everything we ever did was there in that light,' recalled Dana, who went on to describe a 'wraparound life review', like a diorama, depicting in a flash everything she and her husband had ever experienced, together or apart. 'In the middle of this life review, I saw myself there holding onto his dead body, which didn't make me feel bad because he was also completely alive, right beside me, viewing our life together.'

The 'life review' is a hallmark of the shared death experience, writes Moody, alongside a change in the physical surrounds, an all-pervading 'mystical' light, the sound of music and an out-of-body experience. Some of these are also traits of the near-death experience (NDE), where a person who is seriously sick or injured, or has been resuscitated, reports travelling (commonly through a tunnel) towards a welcoming, blissful light, where they meet deceased family members and/or an angel, spiritual guide or deity, and see their body lying below, before being instructed or deciding to return to life.

Both phenomena enclose lessons about life, death and what lies beyond. People who report these experiences are usually transformed – for the better – having learned that, not only does love transcend death, but that love is 'the only meaning', as the American playwright and novelist Thornton Wilder so beautifully put it.

Almost everyone who's experienced an NDE 'stresses the importance in this life of trying to cultivate love for others,' write Doctors Craig R. Lundahl and Harold A. Widdison in their book, *The Eternal Journey: How Near-Death Experiences Illuminate our Earthly Lives*. Their subjects shared post-NDE insights highlighting the supreme significance of love. Being kind and caring for others in ways large and small in your day-to-day life were also found to be of much more value than status and wealth in the context of the 'life review', where every thought and deed will be called to account, they said. Teaching others and gaining knowledge were also high on the list of purposes of post-earth life, with human incarnation seen as a means to learn lessons and progress.

This is something that Denise Mack, who shared the story of her mother's 'healing presence' in Chapter Three, has experienced. More than 40 years ago, Denise regained consciousness after her NDE with the deep conviction and desire to fulfil her life's mission, as she tells below:

After giving birth to my second son, I suffered a post-partum haemorrhage. Before collapsing I called for help. The attending nurse responded to my complaints of intense, sudden pain and bleeding with, 'Don't be stupid. Just get out of bed and sit on the pan.'

While my body lay on the bed in an unconscious state, 'I' found myself in the corner of the ceiling looking down at the scene. My GP and the attending nurse and two other nurses surrounded the bed. I saw that my doctor had a bald spot, something I'd never noticed as he was very tall.

The attending nurse was wringing her hands and crying hysterically: 'I can't find a pulse. There's no heartbeat. It's my fault.'

'Nurse. Keep calm. There must be a heartbeat. Try again,' my GP responded with calm.

I felt great compassion and detachment for the medicos and the grey and lifeless body lying on the bed.

Then I felt I was falling into a velvety, warm blackness. This blackness became darker and darker until it was suddenly light. And the light intensified and expanded until I was the light, and the light felt like pure and unconditional love, unlike anything I had experienced.

This love had no boundaries, no limitations. It was beyond intellect, beyond word description. And this sense of light and love contained all the knowledge of the universe.

And I knew in that instant that this love is eternal, the essence of all life, the power from which all else emanates, and is available to all of us. It was incredibly beautiful.

Suddenly the atmosphere changed. With soul-instinct I knew it was time to go back. 'No . . . I can't go back to that body. I want to stay here. Don't make me go back.'

Then I felt/heard a voice, that was more like a supreme, godlike vibration, and I felt compelled to do as it said: 'You must go back. There is more to do. Don't be afraid.'

I regained consciousness briefly as I was being wheeled into the women's hospital, where I'd been transferred. Then I fell into unconsciousness and remained in intensive care for five days, at the end of which I, at last, met and held my son.

This NDE experience impacted my life profoundly. I feel that all humans have a purpose. And this purpose is to evolve through service and love. Whatever else we achieve in life, evolution through service and love is paramount.

For me, the journey is a breath-by-breath, day-by-day process. I frequently stumble and lose my way. But the NDE experience remains as vivid and compelling as it was 40 years ago, and it draws me onwards with joy and hope and an eternal curiosity.

Raymond Moody classifies the NDE – he coined the term in his pioneering book, *Life After Life* – and the shared death experience under the umbrella of 'near-death and related experiences'. Further to what we've covered, these pivotal moments, laden with meaning and healing potential, may also incorporate other phenomena: from synchronistic events and visions of 'mist' rising from a patient's body, to out-of-body travels and premonitions. The two latter points – combined, they equate to a 'crisis apparition' – feature in two of the final three stories closing this chapter.

The 'crisis apparition' occurs when a person who is close to death appears to a loved one for a final farewell; their soul or spirit, now free to roam, bridging in a millisecond the divides of space and time. A hallmark of the phenomenon, which has been reported for centuries – Napoleon is said to have appeared to his mother at the moment he was killed – is how solid and lifelike the vision appears, so much so that often it's only in retrospect that the percipient acknowledges something inexplicable and uncanny has taken place.

As Maria Kolettis tells below, not only did her husband's spirit 'come to say goodbye' in the hours *preceding* his death, but after the fact, in a dream visitation to her sister, the young man revealed that at the moment of death he was in the middle of a conversation with his late father – he'd had a deathbed vision, that quintessentially human experience, an affirmation of love.

Reflecting on the countless stories of deathbed visions he's heard about or witnessed in his career, David Kessler writes in *Visions, Trips and Crowded Rooms*: 'In each case, the vision brought hope to the dying person and to his or her family. It gave them a different way to view death. Life ends, but love is eternal.'

That message forms the beating heart of the next stories: a young husband and father's forewarning of a tragedy about to upend his family's world; as her life slips away, a mother sends her spirit to fulfil a promise across distant shores; and a deathbed vision sparks the healing of a lifetime of bitterness and misunderstanding between a daughter and her dying father.

Harbinger of heartbreak

'He was standing in my room that day.'

In the golden hours that embraced the first dawn of autumn 2009, Maria Kolettis opened her eyes to Sunday morning. Her skin had woken first to a sense of being watched, then the rest of her followed. She winced and put her hand to her forehead – inexplicably, her head was pounding. She glanced up. Her husband, Stan, stood at the threshold of their bedroom, staring at her and their seven-month-old son, George, who lay in the middle of the bed, his lashes a silken curtain concealing the closed windows of his eyes. His tiny chest rose and fell with the tidal rhythm of breath.

'What are you doing? What are you looking at?' she asked, not meaning to be brusque but she was feeling out of sorts.

'Ah, nothing, nothing, I'm just getting ready to go soon,' said Stan, whose tall, slightly paunchy figure filled the doorway. Maria could see the blueprint for their son in his rounded cheeks, olive skin and thick, dark hair, now receding at the temples. He was wearing jeans and a T-shirt she'd bought him, she noted with pleasure, one with brown-and-white stripes and a tiger on the front.

Maria nodded. She knew he was waiting for her dad to pick him up to run an errand, about an hour's drive away. A second later she heard a car horn. Her dad had arrived.

'I'm going now. Bye,' said Stan, and he turned and walked away.

Maria put her head back down on the pillow, but she couldn't get back to sleep because of her headache. She lay there for a few more minutes then gave up and climbed out of bed. At about 8.30, half an hour after she'd seen Stan, she called and asked him to buy headache tablets on his way home. 'Yeah, we're on our way now, we're going to be home soon,' he said. He hung up and Maria stared at the phone, confused. How could he be on his way home, she thought, when he'd just left? Their destination was an hour away.

Again she picked up the phone, this time she called her mother. 'Mum, something's wrong,' she told her. 'I don't feel right today, something is really wrong. Please just come and help me with the little one.' Her mum said she'd be right there.

Soon afterwards, *too* soon, Stan was home and complaining of a sore back. 'No, it's *really* hurting,' he said. 'Can you just go to the chemist, please, and pick up something to rub my back? I think I've caught a cold.' He was wearing overalls, not the outfit he'd had on that morning, but he was in so much pain, and having such trouble breathing, that Maria barely gave it a thought.

Leaving her baby behind with her father and husband, she rushed to the chemist. When she got there, her phone rang. It was her dad: 'You need to come home now. Stelios [Stan] is not well. You need to get home now.'

Maria replied, 'Yeah, okay,' then spent five minutes looking for the cream, before finding one and paying for it.

When Maria walked into her home, she knew in an instant that her husband was gone. His lifeless form lay on the couch, the very couch where they'd watched the news, fed George, eaten dinner, laughed and snuggled up to watch a movie. What had happened? How could it be that the breath had fled him?

'I went into a state of shock, I think. I panicked,' says Maria, remembering how she dialled triple-zero and tried in vain to follow their instructions to attempt CPR. Stan's lips were clenched tight and she couldn't prise them apart. 'Then the ambulance arrived and that's when my knees buckled,' she recalls. 'I just collapsed.'

The paramedics, who'd arrived at the same time as Maria's mum, worked on Stan for 45 minutes, then transferred him to the hospital and tried for another half-hour, says Maria. 'Then they said, "Look, we're sorry. We just can't bring him back."' Her husband had died of a heart attack at the age of 34.

Returning to her house, the broken shell of Maria walked like a robot to their bedroom. 'I just wanted to grab something of his, something to hug, to smell his clothes, so I opened his cupboard and I see the T-shirt he was wearing when he was staring at me from the doorway that morning. It was hanging in the cupboard, fully cleaned and ironed. He hadn't worn that T-shirt that day.'

Clutching the T-shirt, she sat on the bed and replayed the events of the morning, though it felt like a century ago. It was so unnaturally quiet – like she'd walked into an inexpertly rendered facsimile of her house, a museum display of the domestic aftermath of cruel and sudden loss – but the silence helped her think. Running her fingers over the soft fabric of the shirt, she went over and over the day, accounting for every second. That's when she realised that when she'd seen Stan in the doorway of their room that morning, he had actually driven away hours earlier. In the exact moments the couple had exchanged those few words in their bedroom, in 'reality' the ailing Stan and her father were already on their way home.

Her heart clenched and the walls seemed to contract and expand around her. She understood. 'His spirit knew what was going to happen and was coming to say goodbye to me,' says Maria. 'It was the only thing I could think of because he was standing in my room that day. I saw him solid, he was there.'

Stan and Maria's story began in 2004, in the south of Greece, where Maria had moved to Melbourne with her mother and sister to open a shop. Stan, a local welder and an old friend of her mum's, was enlisted to help with the fit-out. 'He goes, "I'll come over tonight and we'll discuss it,"' remembers Maria, with a giggle. 'So he came over and we all drank two bottles of Bacardi. We were laughing like little kids and we just had the best time. Then he said, "I'll show you girls around," and he did.'

After three months, friendship turned into romance. 'I loved his personality,' says Maria. 'Oh, he was the life of the party. He knew everybody! Even after we moved back to Melbourne, so many miles from Greece, we're walking in Richmond one day, shopping, and he ran into two people he knew! He knew everybody and everybody loved him. He was a joker, he was generous, he was amazing. His energy just drew people in.'

When the couple learned they were going to be parents, they decided to return to Maria's home city, where she felt more comfortable with the hospital system and had a better support network. They'd only been settled in their new home for a year before Stan's shock death – though the coroner would reveal he had a blocked artery, he'd displayed no symptoms.

Suddenly the new mother was a widow, and had to cope with the stress of organising two funerals, including one in Greece, where Stan would be buried. Throughout, she was frustrated by her inability to detect her husband's presence, though he'd turned up in the dreams of other family members, including Maria's mother and mother-in-law, and had appeared, plain as life, to her sister.

'One week after my husband's death, it was morning and I hadn't slept at all and was just sitting there, crying, and my sister rang me,' recalls Maria. 'She saw my husband in front of her that night and he told her [his death] was so quick, he didn't realise what was happening because he was having a conversation with his dad, who'd passed eight years before. She waited until morning to tell me. It brought me some comfort.

'My biggest fear, when I left his body at the hospital and then went home, was that he'd feel all alone, do you know what I mean? I thought to myself, "I have to go back, he's all alone . . ." I didn't want him to feel abandoned. So it was comforting to know that he is with his dad and he is okay.'

Though it eased her pain to know Stan's father had come to collect his boy, still, she struggled to come to terms with why Stan didn't deliver the message directly to her. 'Everyone except me had seen him, and I was punishing myself,' says Maria, who, like her sister and mum, has experienced psychic phenomena since childhood. 'I thought, "He must be so angry with me, he must be upset with me. Why isn't he coming to me?" But it wasn't that. I think it was because my grief was just so raw.'

Eventually, the dreams of Stan began, the first of which was set in their backyard, which had been drought-ridden and patchy when he died, but appeared verdant and lush in the dream. 'Stan was sitting on a bench and he was just looking at me, smiling. I said, "Oh my God, oh God, you're here! I need to know you're okay, I *need* to know." And he's just sitting there, smiling this big smile at me, and I felt peace, I knew he was happy.'

Whenever he visits his wife's dreams, Stan appears in the brown-and-white T-shirt he wore on the Sunday morning he projected his spirit to her to say goodbye in peace and privacy, in the quiet of their bedroom, as the leaves turned amber and crisp outside their window. Somehow, he knew he wouldn't get a chance to do it later, that all would descend into chaos and agony, that by the time Maria returned from the shop it would be too late. 'I always see him in that T-shirt and I don't know why,' she ponders. 'That was not a favourite of his.'

Perhaps not but, I suggest to her, it was one she had bought for him, so it could be his sign of abiding love and appreciation for her.

On this side of the divide, 36-year-old Maria, a legal secretary, reciprocates by making a point of telling George, now four, all about his father, how much he loved him and how high his spirit soars. 'When he's sleeping, I'll check on him and sometimes he'll be laughing in his sleep or smiling. The next day, he doesn't tell me about his dream but he'll just say, "I talked with Daddy."'

Those are the moments Maria tastes the salt of her tears as they spill into her smile. 'I'm proud that he knows who his father is. He says to me, "I know my daddy lives in the sky. He's playing in the clouds."'

The promise

'I was absolutely shocked at her unexpected arrival.'

On a typically muggy day in the Philippines in July 2007, Pastor Eugene Balbon was putting the finishing touches on an orphanage in Pagadian City he was hoping would soon be ready to open its doors. Looking up from his work, he was stunned to see his collaborator on the project, Pat Pryor, breeze in wearing the ear-to-ear smile that was her calling card. The Australian missionary and philanthropist had been due to visit the following month, so this was a delightful surprise for the pastor, who sprang up to greet her. Sparkling like the open skies of her homeland, her blue eyes shone with vitality and enthusiasm. Pat had always been a human 'pick-me-up' with the knack of bolstering hopes and spreading cheer to anyone she turned her caring gaze on. That grin of hers was contagious.

Touring the site, the pair discussed how it could best serve the needy kids it would shelter. Pat had devoted years to helping the Philippines' poorest, including the children who lived in the festering rubbish dump known as 'Smoky Mountain'. She'd often taken teams of Australians and New Zealanders there, teaching them that though the task of helping those people seemed as insurmountable as the mountain of muck that sustained them, simply showing love and compassion was a good way to start.

They were in the middle of chatting when, without warning, Pat got up and walked out the front door. Pastor Eugene chased her, calling out, 'Pat, Pat! Where are you going?'

Without breaking her stride, she glanced over her shoulder and said, somewhat cryptically, 'I must go ahead. It will all be finished in a week.' Then she said it again.

The pastor lost sight of her impeccably blow-waved silvery hair as she vanished into the crowded street. Baffled, he stepped back inside and picked up the phone.

Meanwhile, in a home built on the shores of a lake in Coolangatta, Queensland, a family encircled their mother, who was succumbing to cervical cancer. She'd chosen to spend her final weeks at home, where the walls hummed her lullabies of a life well lived. This was the nest she'd created for her husband and four children, who were raised to appreciate the beauty of spirituality and of nurturing an inner life, of the value of growing your heart to accommodate others. Now it was her time to rest in the cradle of her family's love, this beloved matriarch. Her name was Pat Pryor.

The sound of the phone ringing sliced through the cathedral quiet of the house. Naomi Pryor rushed to answer it so that her mum wouldn't be disturbed. The caller identified himself as Pastor Eugene Balbon, and said he was working on opening an orphanage with Pat. 'I couldn't quite understand him,' recalls Naomi. 'He was frantically yelling, saying that he'd seen my mum and asking where my parents are staying. I knew they had planned to go there next month, though that was clearly cancelled. I told him I would get back to him. I knew my father would try to keep his commitments, if possible.'

After telling Naomi that he'd send an email, Pastor Balbon hung up and Naomi resumed her place at her mum's bedside.

On the last day of her life, Pat swam in and out of consciousness. 'She lay asleep in her bed but every now and then she'd wake up, smiling, and have a conversation with people I couldn't see. I wondered if she was seeing a place beyond this dimension,' remembers Naomi. 'At one point, as I sat holding her hand while she slept, she suddenly opened her eyes and said, "Wow, a purple piano in yellow cornfields," like she was looking straight at it. She almost became childlike in her manner again, giggly and full of wonder. It felt like she wanted to give me updates on wherever she was and whatever she was seeing.'

Pat was safe in her family's arms when she closed her blue eyes for the last time, on 9 July 2007. To Naomi, it was heartening that her mother seemed to have had 'such a wonderful experience' in her closing moments on earth, which marked a turning point in her daughter's life, too. 'There was definitely something about her crossing that comforted me and made me no longer fear death,' says Naomi, adding that at the moment Pat died one of her friends received a missed call from her number. Stranger yet was what Naomi uncovered when she eventually did find time to check her emails . . .

Among them, though she'd almost forgotten about it, was Pastor Balbon's message, expanding on what he'd had trouble making clear to Naomi on the phone that day when her heart was in pieces. Within the familiar black type on white lay the seed of a miracle.

'Can you please tell me where your mother is staying in town?' he asked. 'I was working on the orphanage when your mother walked in. I was absolutely shocked at her unexpected arrival. She said she was keeping her promise to come and see the new orphanage . . .'

Staggered, Naomi read and re-read the email. 'It will all be finished in a week,' her mum had told the pastor. She double-checked the dates. He'd seen her exactly one week before she died.

'Did she somehow know when she would die?' wonders Naomi. 'How did she physically appear to her friend in the Philippines while she was lying in her deathbed in Australia?'

There is no firm answer to Naomi's questions, but theories abound. What Pat accomplished is a well-documented phenomenon known as a 'crisis apparition', though it's no less astounding for having a precedent. As a missionary and pastor of her own non-denominational church, Pat was a supremely spiritual person, says Naomi. 'She invested most of her time teaching others about God's love and the spiritual aspect to their lives, the importance of spiritual gifts and how to use them – it was quite controversial in the church scene – yet people loved her because she had such a heart for others. She constantly gave of herself to inspire and build others.'

Did her spirituality and enlightenment – her compassion which seemed to encompass an innate understanding of the oneness of humanity – assist Pat to more readily access an aspect of herself we all possess but most of us are asleep to?

Yes, says Naomi, recalling her mum's monklike serenity as her transition came closer: 'She spent so many hours in prayer and meditation towards the end of her life, I feel that her spirit became so much stronger as her body became so weak. I believe this is part of the reason she projected to other places, because her body had become of no use anymore; her spirit found its freedom to journey and discover its possibilities.'

Pat's busy-as-ever spirit wasted no time in getting back to work. It was only a few months after she passed, Naomi says, when her mother made her presence known: 'My father, William, had been booked to speak at a conference in Sydney. The host came running in to tell him, "William, I don't believe in this stuff, but your wife appeared to me and I just had this funny feeling she was going to be around you at this conference to help and work with you." He didn't know that only moments before, my father had felt someone touching his hair, just like Mum used to, and a few people had seen a woman walking behind him.'

Pat has also appeared to her family and friends in dreams, says Naomi, chuckling at the time her husband awoke, the week after their wedding, 'to see her floating above us, smiling'. He also spotted her standing beside the chest of drawers she'd gifted Naomi.

A singer-songwriter, Naomi, now 32, would also embark on a journey of uncovering her psychic potential, facilitated by her mum's spirit. 'Eventually, she led me down the path of working as a clairvoyant and medium, something I never thought I'd do,' says Naomi, whose musical dream is still very much alive – she muses that her next album cover may show her playing a purple piano in yellow cornfields . . . 'I have learnt so much from my mum in spirit, it's a beautiful relationship that continues on. It seems that no distance or dimension can keep her from her family.'

Or stop her from fulfilling a promise.

After she read Pastor Balbon's email, Naomi recalled her mum sitting up and inexplicably shouting, 'Two pesos!' (Philippine currency) as her body was shutting down. Naomi remembers, 'I wondered if she had stopped off at her favourite markets on the way back for one last shopping trip.' The pastor might have thought the same thing, as he watched Pat meld into the crowd, not a hair out of place, on that typically humid day in 2007. Only later did he learn of the gift inside the everyday vignette of a friend dropping in unannounced. Says Naomi: 'He felt so special that she had chosen to see him on her way out.'

Peace offering

'My grandmother was at the end of my father's bed, waiting.'

Listening to the accounts of the people who I spoke to for this book, it became clear that, sometimes, relationships blossom and thrive after one party has died. Sometimes, the two were distant relatives who may have never met in life (I'll look further into this in the next chapter) and in other cases, there were close genetic links marred by an emotional chasm, and only after death is an understanding reached. Like Ban Guo, who told in Chapter Three of making peace with his father's spirit when he respected his wishes on his deathbed, so it was for Wendy Dunn. She arrived at an understanding with the father she'd been at odds with her entire life, starting from the moment his life ended. Wendy, 54, a historical novelist who lives in Victoria, tells her story below:

My father died on a grey, rainy Anzac Day, in 2002. We knew his death was coming. The doctors had made that very clear to us – my mother and his four children. Three days before his death, he had been brought back to hospital stricken by a massive heart attack, only ten days after his first. Then, we were given little hope for his survival, only to see him make a miraculous recovery. The second heart attack returned my brother, two sisters and myself to the hospital, taking turns to stay by his bedside, this time knowing death was the only outcome we could expect.

On the day he died it was the turn of my brother and I to keep watch. Not long after we arrived, his nurses examined him and told us he would last an hour, if that. Now I believe that Dad stayed with me for days after he died, and there are other things I find more difficult to explain.

I had a complicated and fraught relationship with my father. He was a tormented man, damaged by childhood experiences; experiences that influenced a style of parenting that went on to damage his own children. It was through writing I learnt to finally forgive him; at last, coming to understand why my father believed with all his heart that life was cruel. More than anything, he wanted his children

171

to survive. He told me many times – when I wept and railed against him – that it was better to learn about the harshness of life when you're young. So often, I simply hated him, and cried at night because I wanted a father who loved me, a father I could love without fearing.

He died when I was in my early 40s. I knew by then of the eleven-year-old boy evacuated in World War Two, to suffer starvation and abuse. I knew he truly loved his mother, but put us first when she was dying, refusing to place his financially struggling family in greater debt by paying for a trip to London to be by her side. At seventeen, I viewed his choice with great bitterness. Through always-remembered birthdays, regular letters and annual, thoughtful gifts, none of us doubted our grandmother's love. When my uncle wrote she had died refusing to give up hope that my father would walk through the door, it was just another confirmation that he deserved my hate.

Twenty-six years later, I no longer hated him. Adulthood had opened my eyes to a simple, undeniable fact: despite a very unhappy marriage, he never deserted his children. Now I was just a grieving daughter, watching the shallow rise and fall of my father's chest, thinking of what could have been if life had dealt with him more kindly; life had embittered him by robbing him of so much. Class and times gave him few opportunities to reach his full potential.

Just before he died, I felt a moment of confusion. My brother was out of the room at this time, but I seemed no longer alone with my dying father, and strangely comforted. Even more strangely – something told me that my grandmother, my father's mother, was at the end of my father's bed, waiting. Distracted, I looked that way, blinked, thinking I saw a woman in dark clothes. Time stilled and hushed; I turned back to my father to realise I gazed at his dead body.

But the story doesn't end there. Until his funeral, I couldn't shake the sense that my father was angry. Angry about dying, when he had fought so hard to live after his first heart attack, angry with me. I told myself it was only my imagination, likely stemming from my guilt when, as a miserable teenager, I prayed for his death. But I found myself talking aloud to him, trying to reason with him – begging him to lift this oppression that followed me, darkening days already too dark. Only when I wrote his eulogy – sensing that he stood behind me, proud of me, loving me – did I feel the oppression dissipate.

I rationalised it all. Sensing my deceased grandmother at the hospital, followed by days of disturbance by what seemed my father's unquiet spirit, was simply because of sorrow. But that same afternoon, after I finished his eulogy, my then five-year-old son pointed to a darkened corner in my bedroom and told me, 'Poppa's there.'

After that time, I have felt my father watching over me. With love.

*

As I finish this chapter my thoughts go back to the little boy with the blue eyes. He stole my heart. Alongside his father, he journeyed from the light, as his brother's time neared, in a gesture of raw and purest love. For days I pictured little Leslie, trying to imagine what Sandra saw that night in her bedroom, as her critically ill husband slept. I tried to conjure those eyes that shone, bright as lamps, in the darkness. The toddler's eyes like lighthouse beams aptly encompass the theme of all these stories: in their promise that in our final moments we'll be collected by loved ones who've made the crossing before us, these experiences of celebration and reunion light the path towards peace and joy, and away from fear.

Many nurses, like the lovely Lydia, whose stories I had the privilege of sharing, have seen that very light reflected in their patients' eyes, stretched wide in bliss at a private wonder. Maria wasn't with her husband, Stan, at the end, but learning that his deceased father had come for him gave her a measure of relief amid the tears, shock and gut-wrenching grief of her quick and cruel loss.

Naomi also breathed easier, knowing that her mum, Pat, set her spirit free a week before she lost her battle with cancer. Her body lay weak and bedbound, but her spirit flew, untroubled, to check on a friend overseas. In the Philippines, far from home, Pat was doing what she did best: caring for others, flashing her brilliant smile – and handing out big helpings of hope.

7

Family is Forever

∽

Love in the lineage

'The connection with our ancestors transcends time and space.'
—Lee Lawson

The story that concluded the previous chapter told how the death of Wendy Dunn's father ushered in a rewarding new phase in their relationship. This was not the only experience I've heard or read about that taught me relationships improve, thrive and even start afresh after death. In chapter five, we met Kristen and her late grandmother, whose love for each other is undiminished. As Kristen told me: 'She always turns up when I need her most.' In the previous chapter, I introduced Naomi and her mother, Pat, whose bond not only continued after Pat was gone, but blossomed into something entirely unexpected, delightful and life changing.

Equally breathtaking is the discovery of such a rapport even if you hardly knew the family member when they were alive, or in fact, you never had the chance to know them at all! Yet if we can accept that, after death, we all return to a spiritual home where we're met by family members who've gone before us – as per thousands of accounts of near-death experiences, and the consensus of most psychic-mediums and spiritualists – then perhaps it's not so outlandish to consider that these same loved ones who've predeceased us may have cared about us all through our lives, regardless of whether we were close to them.

'Family in the spirit world is more than the immediate siblings, parents, grandparents, cousins, aunts and uncles,' write Craig Lundahl and Harold Widdison in *The Eternal Journey*. 'A family includes all individuals who are related to each other in any way, and this includes distant ancestors.'

Acknowledging their presence can be a powerful healing tool.

Racked by grief after her daughter, Rhiannon, was stillborn in 1997, Beau McKnight had a 'comforting' dream: 'My late grandfather came to me, and because I wanted to see where she was, he took me into this room. It was a big room and it was separated into two halves by see-through metal shelving. I looked through the shelving and there's Rhiannon with two parents,' she says, with a happy laugh. 'Yes! She had a mum and a dad!'

Then Beau noticed: 'They were wearing 1950s clothes. I couldn't see her face because the "dad" was holding her, just holding her up and looking at her really lovingly, and the "mum" was too. And they were just looking at her and smiling and they were just in love, you know? And my grandfather said to me,

"See there? She's just over there and you can't be over there at the moment, but she's fine." That was just amazing.'

Before our conversation, Beau, who's unacquainted with a large part of her family, hadn't considered the possibility that these adoring surrogate parents of her baby's might have been related to her. 'You never know,' she muses, adding that her grandfather, who'd pointed out the couple in the dream, was also technically a stranger. However, she maintains, 'I've really seen him as somebody in my life that is around a lot, even though I never met him in this life.'

A grandparent also guided bereaved mother Naomi Kalogiros towards healing, appearing with the message that love – and family ties – transcend death. A few weeks after the passing of her beloved grandmother in 2009, Naomi was cooking dinner when she 'felt the urge' to look towards her staircase. There stood her grandmother and grandfather, holding hands with William, the son she'd lost in the 21st week of her pregnancy in 2003, though he now presented as a little boy. Ethereal and achingly tender, this was a family portrait like no other. 'Shivers flew through my body as I stood and looked with love, sadness and – strangely enough – joy, knowing that my son was with family and being looked after,' says Naomi. 'A sense of love emanated from the three of them.'

Love is the glue that binds a family and death is no match for it. On the first day of the last month of winter 2013, beneath a cloudless sky of brightest blue, I rode the train to work and lost myself in a book that explores that very idea. In the *The Ancestral Continuum*, Natalia O'Sullivan and Nicola Graydon investigate all we have to gain from tuning into and honouring our links to family members who've gone before us, no matter how long ago they lived. The authors write of 'guardian ancestors [shining] a light of wisdom and compassion' who come to us 'full of their best intentions and advice'.

Reading their insightful words, my thoughts are full of my own late ancestors, especially those I hardly knew – a lifetime of connections sacrificed to immigration. Where are they and why have they been so silent? Where is my maternal grandfather, Manuel, his green eyes lush of lash and brimming with warmth? Where is my mother's cousin – my godfather – Roberto? In an instant, I remember a psychic reading I had many years ago, and the chills that ran across the back of my neck when the woman said she could see a pot-bellied man smiling as he stood with his hand on my shoulder, protectively. I knew him straightaway: Roberto. Yet why can I not sense his guidance, or see in my dreams his chipmunk eyes as dark as chocolate drops, his tummy big with Uruguayan pastries and melancholy?

Where is my paternal grandmother, who howled her farewell into my hair that tear-mucked day at the port, or my uncle Jorge, with his jolly cheeks and springtime eyes a mirror of Manuel's? What about my gentle paternal grandfather, Coraldino, who would carry me to the park taking tiny shuffling steps, a legacy of the Parkinson's disease that would eventually claim him . . . And though I only met her a handful of times, my one-of-a-kind great-grandmother Aurora, her name like a fairytale and her face a riot of wrinkles and gums?

The Ancestral Continuum maintains our ancestors are with us always, but keeping a respectful distance until we ask them to step forward. This idea has been prominent in all of my reading: the spirit world is utterly respectful of our free will and our journeys that must unfold – yet if we invite their communication and guidance, they will respond. So I call down the love and wisdom of the family I lost that day we crossed the skies. There is nothing to fear and everything to gain.

More than anything, I'm hopeful, because it's clear that some of us are more likely than others to connect with relatives on 'the other side'. Why that may be is the proverbial million-dollar question, alongside 'Is there an afterlife?' Mystery seems to be part of the plan – the answers we seek are deliberately obscured, perhaps so that each of us will continue seeking, striving and learning – but part of the answer may lie within each of us, and where we fall on the spectrum of psychic awareness. Though we all have the potential, some are simply more naturally attuned to sensing that hidden realm. Others discover their ability (with a nudge from a late loved one) as part of an awakening to their spirituality and true purpose in life. This was the case with Marcus Lang and his spirit brother, Les, whose story is coming up in this chapter.

For me, I've always known that my mother and sister are more in touch with the unseen than me. Mum has had countless spiritual experiences throughout her life, some of which I documented in *Spirit Sisters*, and my sister has inherited her gift. The night before we'd learnt my uncle Jorge died of cancer, she dreamed he came, looking restored to health, to utter a signature refrain, *'Bueno, me voy a laburar,'* in a voice as warm as woodfire. His parting words – 'Okay, it's time to leave for work' – grew dense with meaning when the news reached us the next day.

It is said that the younger we are, the flimsier the veil between the two worlds, and children indeed play a starring role in many poignant and startling accounts of afterlife connection between far-flung relatives. Sandra Milton's granddaughter was a year old when Sandra's father died aged 84 in 2009. When

179

she was three she began to frequently mention 'Grandpa', though Sandra's dad had been known as 'Pop' to his great-grandchildren.

Sandra was struck dumb when the toddler could 'clearly identify' her father in photos. He'd also figure heavily in her games, with the little girl setting a place for him at her tea parties and travelling beside him on car trips. 'I'd ask her, "What's Pop saying to you?" and she'd say, "Go to sleep, little girl, and wake up and be good for your mummy tomorrow," and I can just hear my dad saying that! My mum confirmed that would be something my dad would say.'

Danielle Flannery's son Otto was two when her aunt Christine, her mother's youngest sister, died at the age of 44. 'Of all her great-nieces and great-nephews, she shared a particular bond with Otto,' remembers Danielle. One afternoon when Otto was four, Danielle was reading him a story ahead of his nap when he asked, completely out of the blue, 'Anyway, Mum, where is heaven?'

Taken aback, Danielle answered, 'Well, I don't know. Some people think it's all around us. Some people think it's up in the sky. Nobody really knows – why do you ask?'

Her son answered, 'Oh no, it can't be that. It can't be as far away as up in the clouds because I wouldn't be able to hear Christine when she talks to me!'

The preschooler's 'matter-of-fact' delivery stumped his mum: 'I would never put a thought like that into a kid's head,' says Danielle, who learned that Christine's comments to Otto were along the lines of, 'Don't climb so high, be careful, that could be dangerous . . .'

Interestingly, seven years later, Otto casually mentioned his great-aunt Christine had 'caught my pants' in the nick of time when he was falling off a high beam in the park, preventing him from hitting his head. Is Christine Otto's 'guardian ancestor'? The little boy seemed in no doubt of the fact. We'll explore more instances of deceased family members taking on a guardian angel role, stepping in to save a loved one from harm or certain death, in the next chapter.

Almost half a century after it happened, Colyn, a 76-year-old retiree from New South Wales, still shakes his head over the meticulously detailed message his late Uncle Hal nonchalantly laid in his lap one leisurely Sunday evening. Just as mind-blowing as the substance of the message was the way it was delivered . . . Though it's wise to not meddle with a ouija board, and I would never suggest otherwise, I'm sharing Colyn's story because it is one of the few examples I've come across where a positive and proven communication has come through this medium.

It was a Sunday afternoon and Colyn, a car salesman, and his wife decided to take their two young children, a toddler and a preschooler, for a drive. Whether something led him there, Colyn can't say, but somehow he ended up in the suburb where an old mate of his, Sam, lived with his wife, Margaret, and their two kids. Colyn recalls: 'We weren't looking for him, we didn't even know exactly where his house was. When I saw him out in the yard, I thought, "Well, I'll stop." If he hadn't been out the front, I would have kept going.'

Afternoon tea at Sam's gave way to dinner, and soon, the kids were tired and put to sleep on makeshift beds. When Margaret suggested they try to communicate with the spirit world with a ouija board, Colyn and his wife exchanged unsettled glances, but agreed in the spirit of fun. Says Colyn: 'I just thought it was a joke, you know?'

Immediately the upturned wineglass began to repeatedly spell the full name and surname of Colyn's cousin, Ron, whom Colyn hadn't seen or heard from in years, though they'd been the closest of childhood friends. Over the next hour or so, the spirit of Ron's father, Hal, revealed in specific detail his concerns over a stressful situation his son was in: the gist, as he told it, was that Ron, a builder, had laid down a floor at a basketball court (he named the suburb), there was a dispute and he was in danger of going bankrupt. As the wineglass flew from letter to letter, a wonderstruck Colyn madly scribbled every word down on a scrap of paper.

But Hal wasn't just offering an overview of the scenario, he delivered a solution, too: the answer to Ron's woes lay in a legal manual that made clear how a subcontractor in Ron's situation could not be culpable. Then, to everyone's astonishment, Hal gave the name of a friend of Ron's who owned this very book. Colyn could not believe what he was seeing. Nobody in the room could have guessed this information – Colyn himself hadn't spoken to his cousin in years, and it had been just as long since he'd even been in touch with his old friend Sam. It was pure coincidence he'd shown up on his doorstep today. Or was it?

Colyn was sufficiently rattled by the bizarre turn of events to take action. 'The next day, I said to the wife, "Look, get the kids ready. I'm not going to work this morning. We're going to see Ronny. I'm going to give him this information because if he's in trouble, he probably needs our help."'

When they pulled up outside Ron's place, the first thing they saw was piles of timber stacked in the front of his yard. Ron's wife answered the doorbell. 'I hadn't seen her in ages, but she knew me straightaway,' recalls Colyn.

They waited hours for Ron to return – his wife admitted she had no idea what was keeping him. When he did show up, 'He was so happy to see us, he was all over me, sort of thing,' says Colyn, chuckling. They chatted and caught up, then Ron chilled Colyn with a comment that, had the previous 24 hours not played out as they had, would never have survived to play a part in a decades-long reminiscence. 'I've just had the best bit of luck ever,' Ron remarked. 'This mate of mine has just given me this book and it's got a clause in it —'

'The clause means that the subcontractor can't be fined for what happens,' said Colyn, finishing his cousin's sentence.

'How did you know that?' asked Ron, jaw agape.

Handing him the piece of paper where he'd jotted down the previous night's message from Hal, Colyn simply said: 'Read this.'

Awestruck, Ron revealed that the timbers stacked out the front of his home were the ones he'd laid at a basketball court, only to learn later that he'd laid them the wrong way – sparking a dispute, exactly as his father's spirit revealed to Colyn.

All these years later, Colyn is content to file the experience away as something magical that may never be explained: 'I've accepted it as a fact that it happened to me. There could be things out there that we don't understand, you know?'

So far, I've shared stories of unexpected interaction between family members occurring when the spirit person propels themselves into *our* present, be it through dreams, or auditory/visual phenomena, but in some of the most intriguing case studies I've come across, the reverse is true: sometimes, the living travel back in time to take the stage in their distant ancestor's lives.

Sydneysider Mark, 48, a father of four who has a high-pressure job in computer software sales, was born in the UK.

He tells an enthralling story about a series of vibrant, lifelike and evolving dreams he's been having for more than twenty years. In the dreams, he is a boy of around eight in 1880s London, who is waiting for his mother, who works nearby, to finish her shift. He passes the time in a narrow lane surrounded on either side by red brick walls at the end of which lies the river Thames, busy with boats steaming back and forth. The panorama of the Houses of Parliament are directly over the river. Dressed in wool breeches, suspenders and newsboy cap, he plays on his own as he waits for his mum. Reaching into his pocket, he always finds something different – some string, a small ball, a couple of wooden pegs, a handkerchief. Some days, it's marbles he finds, clinking sonorously together, so smooth and cool in the palm of his hand.

The briny smell of the river permeates the scene, mixed with the soot of burning coal, which is, Mark tells me, as real as life. 'As soon as my mum finishes work, I run to hug her, and I can smell her clean fresh aroma, see the spotless white of her starched apron and feel the slightly scratchy fabric. In the dreams, I can never see my mother's face, but the joy of being reunited with her is palpable.'

In 2009 when Mark and his family travelled to London, he never imagined he'd uncover the setting for his enigmatic dreams. Out of sheer curiosity, as they were near the spot where Mark felt his dreams were set, the family went hunting. To his great surprise, right there next to St Thomas Hospital on the banks of the Thames were the remains of a red brick laneway – sprouting inexplicably amid the modern buildings. The location was exactly as in the dreams: opposite the Thames and the Houses of Parliament. 'Parts of this lane are still visible today, even on a satellite map,' Mark says.

Is Mark dreaming of a past lifetime in Victorian London? Or is he tapping into another dimension, or an ancestor's memory bank, with the well-tuned psychic antenna he's long been aware of, yet rarely acknowledges? He's adamant it's not the former.

'I don't believe I have lived before,' says Mark, who's a Christian. 'I believe we are all absolutely unique, one-off creations . . . I do believe, though, that human beings are powerfully complex, that we possess a soul, a conscience, and that this truly spiritual side of our nature – of which we have yet to learn much – is what sets us apart. So then, just as the blood, the DNA, the essence of my father, my father's father, my ancestors and indeed all people before me runs through my veins and makes up in small parts my own being – so, too, I believe that, like reflections in a mirror, the very experiences, visions, thoughts and feelings of those that went before me echo down through time in my spirit and my experiences.'

There is burgeoning research to support Mark's argument that memories, like physical traits, may be inherited. While science races to unravel the mystery, Mark continues to experience moments when the past and present collide – and he doesn't have to be dreaming for it to happen. Mark recounts an occasion when he was working out at the gym one evening, near closing time when the place was unnaturally quiet: 'I was sitting on a bench doing bicep curls in front of a mirror, when suddenly a completely different scene unfolded in the reflection – it was my grandfather, who'd been in the navy, sitting on a ship's deck in the bright sunshine wearing a white singlet and exercising the same way, a big smile on his face. It was a bright, warm day, with crystal blue sky, and everything including the ship was busy and sparkling clean.

185

'While the scene was very brief, it was absolutely clear who and what I was seeing. I could make out the tattoos on his arm, his belt and trousers, people behind and around him, the guns on the deck, flags flapping in the sunshine and even the steam from the ship itself.'

To Mark, the moment 'felt empowering, unifying, like a continuity of manhood – an eternal brotherhood of fathers that spans aeons'. Is it possible that the solitary, almost meditative, act of exercising led Mark into an altered state of consciousness? That a moment of affinity – the bicep curls – facilitated the temporary dissolution of the divides of space and time, so that the two men could reconnect? Whatever the answer is, it's clear that not all of us can see and hear these 'echoes' across the aeons.

The disparity doesn't bother Mark. 'Why some of us see more than others is no more mysterious to me than why one person can dance, while another can sing and yet another can do neither but is great with a hammer and nails,' he sums up. 'Why this happens in some situations and not others is no more confounding than why one person likes sun and another likes rain. To me, all of this speaks to the miraculously complex beings that God made us to be.'

In Chapter Five, Sarah Williams told of her surprise and joy at seeing her great-grandmother, Kitty, sitting in her living room on the night of her 21st birthday dinner. In 2012, she returned the favour, crossing the divide to witness a scene in Kitty's life – this time, via a dream. 'I can always feel the difference between a random dream and a spirit dream,' says Sarah. 'I went back in time in this dream.'

It began with Sarah driving in busy inner-Sydney, but then the car transformed into a vintage model and 'the years were literally ticking back, descending to 19-something – the numbers were going back in front of my face', remembers Sarah. 'And then I was at a house in Paddington, at the moment my great-grandmother received the news that her son had been killed in World War Two. I was there as the family received the telegram and it was very upsetting.'

In her dream, Sarah was sobbing with the rest of the family in the front yard, and the indescribable grief lingered long after she woke up: 'I was *so sad*. I felt really, really sad, like I had lost him as well. I was experiencing what they experienced.' In hindsight, Sarah feels that sharing this tragic snippet of her life was her great-grandmother's way of enhancing their bond. 'In the dream, I felt like I belonged,' she muses. 'It just felt like I was part of the family.'

Experiences like these made me examine classic ghost stories in a new light, including one of my favourites: in *Spirit Sisters*, Amy told of waking during a childhood sleepover to see a family – a father, mother and their young son – in colonial clothing watching her curiously. Today I wonder, could Amy have been distantly related to her otherworldly visitors? Perhaps they were just checking in on her?

There are many reasons why distant relatives would suddenly play a part in our earthly lives – chief among them to offer wisdom, healing and guidance. In the following two stories, family members step out of the shadows to connect – in vastly different ways: Kate's great-grandmother led her on a mission to untangle the branches of their family tree, and Marcus's brother helped him come to terms with his gift, lighting the way with love to a profound and meaningful new life.

The family tree

'She came to see me . . . before she left.'

Jack is five years old, with honey-hued hair all akimbo and wide-set dark eyes that aim for the floor when a camera's near. He likes fish and chips with salad and he drinks his milk out of a Paddington Bear mug. He lives with his parents and younger brother, Tyler, and baby sister Susie in a little town steeped in history in rural New South Wales. The family's home is tiny – two bedrooms converted to three – but that hasn't stopped the influx of relatives who come and go at their leisure. In Jack's house of history, the people in the sepia portraits of the family tree his mum is compiling have climbed down from the branches and into the rooms of his house, where they chart his life with enthusiasm and pride. Who could blame them? Jack is a very special little boy.

Around Christmas 2012, his mum, Kate, was worried about a dear grand-aunt, Eleanor, who hadn't been in touch for some time. As she and her mum were talking about her, Kate recalls, Jack butted in and said, 'She's dead.'

Kate couldn't help herself – she squealed. 'What?! What did you say?' she asked. Her son was still four months off his fifth birthday. How could he possibly know that?

In the same blasé tone, Jack repeated, 'She's dead in the hospital.'

Eleanor, a sister of Kate's grandmother, had never met the children, though just a few months earlier, she'd asked to see them. But being so busy with a new baby daughter, Kate didn't get around to taking them. No one in the family even knew Eleanor was in hospital, or that death was imminent. But now, though he'd heard scant mention of Eleanor in his short life, Jack filled in the blanks about her whereabouts and death with, as Kate later found out, astonishing accuracy: she had died at 6 am that morning in hospital (this was confirmed by a nurse). She had been in bed when 'some people' came in. When Kate asked Jack if these people were nurses, he replied, no, they were people she knew. 'She looked up at them and she just went with them,' he explained.

Kate asked how he knew all this and he said, 'Because she came to see me and Tyler before she left.' Then he added, 'She's gone. Gone.'

Though Kate and her mum were gobsmacked – especially when, after urgent phone calls, they discovered that Eleanor had indeed passed away in hospital after a sudden illness – Kate admits she realised from the moment her first child was born that he was a beacon to a loving tribe only he could see.

'I'd get up to him in the middle of the night, or any time, he'd be crying and I'd go in to settle him and, all of a sudden, his eyes would fix on something next to me and close to him. He was looking at someone else. And he'd start giggling and laughing and cooing and gaga-ing at them.' On certain nights, she could feel them approaching, says Kate, and sure enough her baby would begin to gurgle in delight. 'Sometimes I was very uneasy about this, scared, because I didn't know who or what was there.'

Eventually, it would become clear that guardian ancestral spirits were drawn to Jack, and that there was nothing to fear, though he also communicates with spirit people who are not related. One of the first he mentioned, even before he could properly talk, was the quaintly named 'Bessie' – as his vocabulary improved, he was able to tell his mum she was a little girl who 'lived next door'. For years, she was his invisible playmate.

He no longer mentions her and Kate doesn't ask. 'I sort of just let him talk, if you know what I mean?' she says. 'I try not to put words in his mouth. I want to see what he says.'

Not long after Jack started talking, aged around three, a new name began to pass his lips – 'Jenneman', a cushion of a word he took to repeating so often, it quickly faded into the background of his parents' busy lives (29-year-old Kate and her husband run an air-conditioning business). One day, Kate was sitting at the kitchen table, sorting through a wad of vintage family photographs, searching for one in particular she wanted framed. Casually, Jack wandered over and pointed to a photo and said, 'Oh, there's Jenneman.'

Kate had never considered the possibility that 'Jenneman' could have been anything (or anyone) other than babyish babble. She looked again at the photo, which showed, in that muddied palette of yesteryear, eight people sitting around a fireplace in a handsome living room full of art-deco features. Four were women – and in between a young, smiling brunette with glowing cheeks, and a stern matron whose eyes slid away from the lens, sat Kate's great-grandmother, Lillian, her head and collar just peeking through. Unsmiling, with grey hair pulled back from her face, she tilted her chin subtly upward as she stared straight at the camera.

'All those photos, all those people and Jack was pointing straight at her,' remembers Kate. She wondered, was 'Jenneman' actually what Jack called her great-grandmother; she decided to test the theory.

'There's another one of her in there, see if you can find it,' she said to Jack.

He happily sifted through the thick pile of tactile old pictures. 'And he finds it,' Kate says, her voice still disbelieving. 'He said, "There she is."'

This time he held a photo of a happier and younger-looking Lillian, leaning on a verandah rail beside her husband and her son, Kate's future grandfather. Anyone taking a guess would have been hard-pressed to pick the two women as one and the same, but Jack did not hesitate. 'No doubt about it, pointing straight at her,' recounts Kate, with a laugh. 'My heart stopped. I couldn't believe it. I was just lost for words.'

Just as she was trying to compose herself, and a response, Jack dropped another bombshell. Walking to the hallway, he pointed to two picture frames that had once belonged to Lillian. 'They're hers,' he announced, indicating the two frames.

'I said, "What's hers?" and I picked him up to make sure I knew what he was talking about. He put his fingers on the glass and said, "These are hers. She doesn't like what you've done to them."'

Since the frames had been empty when Kate inherited them, she picked out Renoir and Monet prints to display inside them. Perhaps her choices hadn't gone down too well?

The young mum, who's in quiet awe of her son's gift, jotted down everything that had just happened in a notebook she keeps for documenting these moments, which is just as well. More than a year later, in August 2012, a cousin emailed another batch of vintage photos, along with contemporary snapshots of her family's everyday life, which Kate printed out. Then she left the inch-high pile on the kitchen bench.

Two weeks went by, and she was watching TV when she heard Jack yell out, 'Jenneman! There's Jenneman!'

Skin afire with goosebumps, Kate 'jumped up' from her seat. 'I thought, "Oh my God, this can't be happening again, this is too weird."' But she stayed outwardly calm.

'Where?' she called out to Jack. 'Bring it over here and show me where.'

He toddled in and handed it to her: 'There. Right there.'

Kate emails me the photo. It's a group portrait taken at her grandparents' wedding. There are six guests in their church finery flanking the newlyweds – a tall and beaming groom (Pa) holds the gloved hand of his bride (Nanna), who radiates the creamy, wasp-waisted beauty of an old Hollywood siren. In the back left corner, in gloves, hat and corsage, is mother-of-the-groom Lillian, her lips holding the ghost of a smile.

'Are you sure that's her?' asked Kate, in a voice as tiny as her son.

'Yes,' answered Jack. 'That's her.'

Her stomach flipped. She had a thought: Was 'Jenneman' Jack's way of saying 'Lillian'? Kate compared them. The rotund words rolled from her lips, landing with a thud on the matching last syllable. Kate hadn't made the connection before because her mother had always called her grandmother 'Nanna Sweet' and so the family did not refer to her as Lillian. Now, though, Kate had to consider the possibility that her son was in contact with his great-great-grandmother – because he told her it was so.

This proved the beginning of a trip back in time for Kate, who displays an impressive familiarity with the lives of those who've peopled her past. Partly, this was due to conversations with family members and online ancestry research she'd begun, at her grandma's request, before anything Jack had said. The project lapsed because Kate is time-poor, but Jack's chatter (and what it signified) helped revive it. Like the colourist of antique prints who, with a dainty dab, could rouge ladies' cheeks and turn their babies' hair to coal or golden wheat, the little boy illumed the details in the portraits fanned out across the kitchen bench.

'One day, we were at the supermarket and I was buying packet-cake mix,' recalls Kate. 'Jack said, "Jenneman's cranky at you for buying that." I said, *What*?"'

She was right there, explained Jack, right there and telling him so. His mum put the packet into the trolley anyway, or threw it in with a hint of defiance, might be more accurate. Kate drove home and phoned her mum. She could almost hear her shaking her head in disbelief down the line. 'She said that Lillian had loved to make cakes! It was her hobby.'

This fact, unknown to Kate, had never been revealed to Jack either. So how could he have known? It's a telling episode, because it's hard to imagine why a preschooler would say something so specific – and push the point.

It wasn't the only time Jack resurrected a slice of the formidable lady's personality. 'He says that she's very bossy, sometimes he gets very cranky,' says Kate. 'I think she tells him what to do and I don't think he likes it.'

('Well, she was a very bossy lady,' confirms Kate's mum, Lillian's granddaughter.)

But Lillian means well, too, and through her great-grandmother's connection with Jack, Kate has learned a great deal about her family, and herself. In late 2012, a young woman, who'd been studying Jack as part of her course in primary school teaching, confided in Kate (with reluctance and reservations, as is often the way) that she believed he was demonstrating signs of mediumship. Kate had never mentioned her own suspicions. The student advised Kate to seek out a psychic, the only one she knew of in their small town, and the appointment was made.

'I'd never met this woman before, never seen her around town, had no idea who she was,' recounts Kate, whose youthful voice still pitches excitedly when she recalls the uncanny details the psychic poured out.

The woman spoke of Kate's 'firstborn' having the gift, that 'lots of past grandmothers visit him', female ancestors who 'come and go and help you look after the kids'. Among many other validations, she described 'a man in a hat with a boy' who is Jack's guardian angel.

'That was weird because Jack had been speaking about this man with a hat and a baby for as long as Jenneman's been around,' says Kate. She explains that a year before her grand-aunt Eleanor's shock passing, the elderly lady told her of a family secret, a tragedy buried deep in a shroud spun of tears and years. She'd had a brother, Eleanor said, a baby who was gone before his first cry. His death sent out ripples of pain that stilled the voices of his family. 'No one spoke about it,' says Kate softly. 'But when the psychic mentioned it, I instantly thought, "I wonder if that is the baby that Jack can see?" Because he always tells me, "The man's angry about the baby."'

Or perhaps he's just cracked by sadness, this man in the hat, who could be Kate's great-grandfather, Richard, as he carries his baby that never drew breath. Perhaps, to a little boy with gold-tipped, zig-zaggy hair, expressions of anger and grief might seem interchangeable? Or could it have been supplication – a father's appeal to his pint-sized descendent that his son not be forgotten?

Postscript: On the eve of submitting this book, Kate sent me an interesting update about her two younger children. She writes in an email: 'Last week, out of the blue, Tyler [now aged three] sitting at the kitchen bench, spoke of Jenneman. I said to him, a bit surprised, "Oh, Jenneman! Do you know Jenneman?" He said, "Yes, she talks to me." I asked if he meant the Jenneman Jack knows and he said, "Yes, she talks to us before we go to bed and she's just around." As he said this, he looked around and flung his arms about. I asked what she looked like and he said, "She is a big woman."

'And I now have an old family portrait hanging in our hall. Recently I was holding my fourteen-month-old daughter and I got stopped by one of the boys in the hallway. While I was talking to them (something like, pick up your shoes), Susie started giggling. I looked at her and saw she was looking at the portrait. I moved her a little closer and she pointed straight at Eugenia (my great-great-grandmother). I watched her for a bit and she kept looking straight at Eugenia and pointing at her. I tried to get her interested in other people in the photo but she wasn't.

Each time we walk past it now, if she's looking that way, she stares and points straight at Eugenia.'

Housemate from heaven

'There is such thing as magic.'

You'd be lucky to find a flatmate as attentive as Les. He stocks the pantry with decaf coffee, Milo and herbal tea, and doesn't need an occasion to shower his fellow tenants with mementos to remind them how much they mean to him. The fact that Les died in 1981 has faded into insignificance for his brother, Marcus Lang, the man at the coalface of these everyday miracles. Marcus has no explanation for how Les upturns the laws of physics every day in the humble granny flat in Sydney's western suburbs, where he and his partner, Vickie, live anonymously, hearts ablaze with gratitude and awe. To them, the message Les trumpets is far more important than any quest to decipher how it's conveyed: 'Love,' he would have us know, 'is all you need.'

Marcus's eyes of sparkling blue are the first thing I notice when he stands up to greet me at a café in Sydney's CBD. Transparent as water and loaded with discoveries, they're the eyes I've come to associate with people who have a story to tell me, people with psychic and mediumistic talents – 'clairvoyance', after all, means clear vision – as I tell Marcus.

'I'm about as psychic as a toaster,' he responds with a chuckle, but physical mediumship? Well, that's what we're here to chat about.

Tall and rugged, with close-cropped light hair flecked with silver, Marcus has a smile that spells uninhibited joy and expectation – like a child on Christmas Eve. It's how he feels all the time now that 'I have me bro back', says the 44-year-old friendly and chatty ex-biker, a former 'card-carrying sceptic'. As he adds with a grin, 'There is such thing as magic.'

His soulmate, and fellow 'explorer' of the uncharted realm he's navigating, sits to his right. Vickie, 42, has skin, hair and eyes of caramel, as if the warmth and sweetness within has spread outwards, right to the tips of her long lashes. I have Vickie to thank for alerting me to their story via a Facebook message in September 2012. 'Now we know that we don't die – our bodies do, but we don't,' she wrote, telling me about the 'loving' presence of Les, and how he's been by Marcus's side, 'helping him cope and giving him hope' since he narrowly survived a motorcycle crash in 2010. 'I know you might think it's too good to be true. Well, I'm here to tell you it's real.'

Both Marcus and Vickie push away the remains of breakfast,

as we draw closer into our bubble of anticipation and revelation, heedless of other diners nearby. There's an air of peaceful knowing, a state of grace, about this couple and I'm keen to hear how they found it. Or how it found them. I press the red button on my digital recorder and . . . nothing. It refuses to work.

'I'm not surprised,' says Marcus cheerfully, sipping on a cappuccino (he's usually decaf all the way, but today is a special occasion).

At the same time, Vickie groans; her iPhone won't load photos. She wants to show me the latest pictures of Les's communications, but it seems we'll need to be patient.

It's only the first of Les's lessons for us today.

Marcus took the first step towards his new life in 2009, when 'an overwhelming urge' led him to his brother's grave for the first time in close to three decades. He was ten when Les took his own life, aged 34, in 1981. 'I said to my parents, "Get in the car, I've got to go and visit all my dead relatives,"' recalls Marcus. 'Maybe it was the fact that I went to visit, but it was at that moment that he came back into my life.' However, it would be some time before Les began to speak up.

Soon after this graveside reunion, Marcus and Vickie moved to Surfer's Paradise for a sea-change, but the move proved disastrous, with frightful paranormal activity plaguing the couple and their children in their new apartment. Looking back, Marcus is certain he had to live through those events as part of his spiritual awakening, but in the eye of the storm, explanations weren't forthcoming, to the frustration of the lifelong science and physics enthusiast. One night, like a Hollywood cliché, the family fled in the dark, without even packing their belongings. But the return trip to Sydney took a near-fatal twist for Marcus, who was riding his Harley-Davidson while Vickie drove their car behind him.

'I was hit by a car and nearly killed, but something stopped me,' he says. 'Vickie saw the accident happen, and she said it looked like I was curled up in a ball, like in the palm of a hand, as I flew through the air. Even the hospital staff could not work out how I wasn't killed. They kept coming up to me and asking, "Why are you okay?"'

Though outwardly there wasn't a scratch on Marcus, inside he was a broken puzzle, with injuries including smashed shoulders, four crushed nerves in his neck, and bulging spinal discs. His recovery has been slow and difficult and he's still in agony much of the time, but he's weaned himself off the strongest painkillers. 'I prefer the pain, that's who I am now,' he says with a shrug. 'I can't deny that. But I can walk, at least. I've got to look at the positives.'

The accident stripped him of more than a pain-free life, it took his livelihood as well – he had to give up his job as a communications technician – but Marcus believes that everything is as it should be, part of the fulfilment of a greater plan.

'I wouldn't change a thing. I've learned to appreciate so much that I didn't before. Being humbled was the greatest thing that happened to me,' he says. 'Now I have the time to sit, to listen and learn a lot.'

His education began after the near-miss on the highway, when he threw away his membership to the sceptics association he'd been involved in for a decade, because he could no longer deny that something mysterious and transformative was taking place in his life.

At first, when 'strange things' began to happen after he'd moved back to Sydney, Marcus admits he was afraid that the force in the Queensland apartment had followed him. But this time 'it didn't feel nasty', he reasoned. On the contrary: it was positively courteous. Marcus shakes his head and still seems amazed, incredulous even, when he recounts how Les first began to demand his attention.

'We were out of decaf coffee and Vickie had gone to borrow some next door because we were stone-cold broke. She went back to put it in the cupboard and a big, full jar of unopened decaf was there – it wasn't there and then it was,' he marvels. 'I had to accept this was happening, but how?'

It was Marcus's mum, Melvene, who came up with the solution. Les recalls: 'She said, "Look, if this is smart enough to be trying to communicate with you, maybe it's smart enough to spell something," so she gave me her Scrabble kit and said, "Leave this out and see what happens." I was dubious, but I left it out on the floor. Later that day, my son and his friend were here, and all of a sudden there was a word formed. My son and his friend freaked out because they'd seen the letters all scrambled, they were just all over the place. And then a minute later, it said LES.'

Diving deep into his well of memories, Marcus salvaged scraps of his brother – long strands of 'beautiful' black hair, a moustache, the wiry hedge of a beard – 'a real bushy look', he recalls with a sad smile, for their time together was fleeting. On the eve of Marcus's tenth birthday, in the dawn of the neon 1980s, Les's body was found on a park bench, a cigarette still dangling from his lips, sending grey snowflakes into the winter sunshine.

'Les was a loner,' says Marcus, taking a deep breath. He prefers not to specify how Les passed. 'He had his problems. One day, we got the phone call. It was heartbreaking.'

Yet an aura of peace cradled Les and when he was alive he was never too consumed by his own pain to extend a hand to his kid brother. 'When things were stressful at home, he'd just say, "Come on," and walk all the way with me to the shopping centre, or take me to Luna Park, just to cheer me up.'

He's still leading him to a better place, alphabet tile by alphabet tile. Where in life, their brotherhood was crushed by the weight of Les's sorrows, in death, Marcus feels their bond renewed and strengthened, thanks to his astounding communications via a Scrabble board. It is as simple, he explains, as leaving it under the bed and pulling it out in the morning to read what is on Les's mind. His messages range from the practical – 'It will happen, don't rush it', regarding an insurance matter – to the profound – 'Love is all there is'. Mostly, the notes are 'personal, directed towards me', says Marcus, whose brother calls him 'Bud'. Here's a selection of Les's telegrams from another place:

> God is within
> Don't doubt Urself
> He will be safe with me
> Love u Bud
> Love all equally
> Its ok Bud Tonite we hugs connect u n me

'I believe he's here just to guide me now through my own spirituality and learning,' says Marcus.

He shows me some of the hundreds of photos he's taken of Les's messages. In some, the tiles are on the board; in others, letters spell words on the carpet. Sometimes, the words sit amid a jumble of tiles, so that you have to pick them out like in a find-a-word puzzle, but other messages – like 'NO PAIN' – are stark and alone. 'The Scrabble letters just became an easy way for him to speak,' Marcus believes.

But it's not Les's only way.

Marcus has heard his laughter, albeit rarely, and seen him in dreams. On cold nights, Les has switched on their electric blankets. But it's the apporting objects – including, but not restricted to, fresh roses, feathers, coins, cigarettes (even though Marcus no longer smokes), pantry items and even medication – that are the calling card of this one-of-a-kind 'flatmate who comes and goes as he pleases'.

'There have been times when we've been sitting on the lounge at home and I've had big white long feathers stuck in my hair like an Indian and I've not even felt it,' says Marcus. This reminded me of our first phone conversation, when Marcus startled me mid-sentence by yelling 'Ohhhhaaaahhh!' when a fluffy white feather dropped from the ceiling. I remember how his voice swelled with excitement and wonder, and how my heart quickened, too. Then he'd told me, laughing, that earlier that day, 'eight herbal teas were thrown onto the floor in front of me'.

Coins also feature in Les's unique alphabet of love. In fact, they were one of the first signs of his presence. 'Coins were turning up everywhere, and a lot of them had the year of his passing – another way of him saying, "It's me." They'd turn up in our shoes, Vickie's had them turn up in her hand . . . coins were turning up in the oddest places.' Funnily enough, says Marcus, on the train to the city today, a five-cent piece dropped from above; and, as we're drinking our coffees, Vickie lifts her napkin and a ten-cent piece winks back at us. There had been nothing there a few seconds ago. We all laugh like old friends, without a trace of nerves or shyness, at these signs of Les's arrival. There's a festive buzz about Marcus and Vickie, like summer in the air, the morning of a wedding, or the birth of a child. Goosebumps sprout on my arms and the atmosphere fizzes with ineffable buoyancy.

'Love is the theme,' Marcus tells me, and with that, something pings loudly on the ground beneath the table and ricochets against my knee. I look down and am stunned to see a ten-cent coin spinning, as if expertly flicked, at my feet. Marcus whoops in delight. Each of us had our hands above the table and I'd been the first to hear the noise and spot its source. Once it stills, I pick up the coin, noting how it glistens like something newly minted, and store it in the case with my recalcitrant recorder, where it lives still.

But what part does Marcus play in these prolific displays?

It turns out he's the enabler: the man who spent ten years debunking paranormal phenomena and exposing charlatans is a physical medium of the rarest sort, a discovery that came as something of a shock at first, but now the knowledge sits comfortably within him. A physical medium is a person who facilitates the manifestation of *physical* communication from the spirit world, such as apports, usually when they are in a deep trance – in the heyday of psychical research, they worked inside a 'cabinet' and ectoplasm was involved. But Marcus works without any such trappings – no séance, trance or stout ladies lolling in cabinets required.

He's proud to say that he's written to Robin Foy, a respected British researcher of physical mediumship, who replied that he knows of only one other person in the world who receives regular and spontaneous apports in full light, a man in Italy.

He suggested that Marcus is developing a new, 'energy-based' form of physical mediumship. 'I feel like a pioneer,' says Marcus. 'It feels like I'm not walking my path, I'm bloody well sprinting!'

Behind the scenes of Marcus's awakening, like a director in the wings, is Les, and his magic words. 'He talks about the most spiritual and deep things – he looks after me. I know it's hard to believe, I feel funny talking about it cos I don't really discuss it with too many people.' Not that Marcus is concerned with convincing sceptics or presenting proof, despite paranormal investigators clamouring to visit and document the phenomena. 'I've decided against it. My life is not paranormal – it's *normal*. This is not something to be investigated, it's something to be loved and appreciated. This is all because of Les.'

He's sharing his story with me because, 'people need to know the truth,' he says, his calm-sea eyes balancing the passion in his voice. 'It's important that people realise our loved ones don't actually leave us alone when they die. They don't forget us. Ancestors influence our lives to this day.'

Even if – like Les – they were only a fragment of your past. Or a missing piece of it, like Vickie's brother, Christopher, who died three years before she was born. Since Les spelled out 'Christopher loves you a lot', her brother has been very present, says Vickie: 'My father has also been coming to visit and leaves messages. Les is bringing them to us.'

His bag of gifts isn't empty yet. Just before our meeting, Les spelled out, 'Next level stage two' and 'I told you exciting times ahead', Marcus reveals, and his kind and open face seems close to bursting with bliss. Knowing his story is still unfolding – letter by letter – makes Marcus the happiest man on earth:

'I wake up with wonder every day. I've never experienced this sort of joy before in my life. Every now and then, I'll be sitting on the lounge and a tear will fall down my cheek and Vickie will say, "What's wrong?" And I'll say, "I just can't believe how lucky I am. I have Les back."'

*

Over the course of writing this book, I was twice woken in the middle of the night by the unmistakable sound of a coin falling onto the floorboards. My heart pounded wildly for a few minutes, but then I'd fall back to sleep, secure in the knowledge that there was nothing to fear. The next morning, after crawling under the bed on my hands and knees, I'd find the coin, turn it around in my palm and wonder if the culprit was Les. If it was, I like to think he was letting me know he's happy with the story of his brother's awakening to the understanding that family is still family, even if some members are no longer around to share their love in person.

And don't they go to extreme lengths to show it? The story of Colyn and his meticulous late uncle, consumed by concern for his son, is unlike anything I've ever heard, but the power of parental love can't be underestimated, as we've explored. Yet the stories I find most mind-blowing – and touching – have to do with the ways more distant family members, and even those we've never met, manifest their love.

From Jack's assertive ancestor, 'Jenneman', who's assumed a guardian role in his life – and, it seems, his siblings' lives, to Beau's grandfather, a stranger in life who in death tenderly steered her towards healing after the heartbreak of stillborn baby Rhiannon. In a dream Beau felt blessed to have had, he pointed out a retro-looking couple cuddling her baby. Beau didn't need to recognise the man or woman to take comfort from the sweet scene.

Mark's astonishing dreams of the long-gone past hint that not only does love never die, it's never forgotten, as evidenced by the way he just 'knew' the woman he rushed to hug after she finished work was his mother – the surge of love he felt for her, and from her, told him so. Emotions and feelings are just as potent and significant as the tangible in these one-of-a-kind experiences that sing of the indestructibility of blood bonds, of the power of love that's older than sepia pictures, of love that was snatched from our arms in a tear-stained second, and of love that is yet to be.

8

The Power of Love

∾

Guardian angels reach out to help

'Everything that comes from love is a miracle.'
—Marianne Williamson

A shaft of sunlight picked out the berry tones in my mother's midnight hair as she sat in my grandmother's, my *abuela*'s, kitchen, her chair pushed back a little to accommodate her blooming belly. It was the winter of 1971 and I swam inside her, feasting on sugar-dusted pastries, dreams and stories. Always stories.

The little Formica table was laden with traditional fare for morning tea – quince paste, or *dulce de membrillo*, glistened a deep claret from its bed of brown-paper wrapping; *dulce de leche* (caramel) begged to be swirled over chunks of French bread stick or 'Maria' tea biscuits, and freshly sliced salami and cheese were savoury touches. Meanwhile, the *máte* – tea sipped communally from a steel straw – was passed around the table, its rhythm as round as the seasons.

From my mum it went to my dad, who finished and handed it to my mum's cousin, Roberto. In the garden through the back door behind them, my grandfather, Manuel, tended aviaries where his raucous charges chirped, flapped and jostled, filling the air with their silken song and the sharp whiff of seed, waste and feathers. My grandmother, Alba, hovered at the sink, sighing with contentment because her little kitchen thrummed with chatter and eating.

Without preamble, Roberto put down his *máte*, reached into his overcoat and pulled out a gun.

'What are you doing with that?' said Mum in an even voice. 'Put it away. You know that weapons are the devil's playthings, like Abuela Aurora always says.'

The vintage revolver had belonged to his father, Americo, a man whose matinee-idol looks made neighbours' wives smooth their skirts and fuss with their hair. Roberto turned it this way and that, then holding it with palms outstretched, like an offering, lifted and lowered it, enjoying the weight of it in his hands.

It had only been a month since Americo died of cardiac arrest, aged only 42. On the morning of his death, a bunch of Roberto's friends had come to pick him up for a fishing trip and the group made their way to the bus stop, laughing and smoking. Ten minutes later, Roberto was back – he'd forgotten to kiss his father goodbye. His lips brushed his cheek, then he ran to catch up with his friends. When he returned that evening, Roberto walked into the living room to find his father's body laid out for viewing, neat and cold in his coffin, as a wheel of weeping women kept watch.

He would never be the same again.

Winter sunshine fled and the marrow-chilling grey of Montevideo in July snuck back into my grandmother's little kitchen. Silence hung, dense as rainclouds. Roberto's family understood his trauma, the depths of his grief, but this was a new and alarming development.

With a grin punctuated by babyish dimples, he looked up, as if remembering the others in the room, the morning tea he'd interrupted. He cocked the weapon, pointing it at my mother.

'No,' she said. In the second it took to say it, she'd seen it all – being wrapped in a yellow shawl and handed to her mother on the day she was born, the Bible she'd won for topping the class at school, the high heels she'd bought with her first pay packet, the plans for the imminent move to a faraway place and the small life tumbling inside her.

He laughed and for a second he sounded like the old Roberto, the cousin she'd adored and grown up with.

'It's not loaded, silly,' he said. 'See?'

He pulled the trigger and, in an almost languid movement, my father reached out and nudged the gun a few centimetres to the side, where the bullet tore past Mum's shoulder and through the back door, raising hell in the aviaries and maddening the family dog, who strained at his chain and barked until he collapsed.

My grandfather ran in from outside. 'What happened?' he shouted. You could see the pulse in his neck jumping.

'Nothing,' the trio around the table declared in unison. '*Nada*.'

My grandfather was not a man you wanted to worry, especially since he, too, was grieving the recent loss of his brother. Smoke and the acrid sting of gunpowder made liars of them. Without a word, my grandmother turned back to her cupboards and pans, but her eyes recorded the moment. Sometimes, in the quiet before sleep, she would call it up and replay it, eyes stinging at what could have been.

Roberto's sobs rang out. Pulling her close he pleaded for my mother's forgiveness – he couldn't fathom how he'd almost destroyed the person he loved most, he said. He swore to dispose of the gun and, true to his word, no one saw it again until decades later, when he used it to turn the lights out on his own life.

Today, a concave scar in the back screen-door of my grandparents' house is all that's left of a day that started in the sweetness of tea and hope and sunshine, but almost ended in bitter heartbreak.

In her book *Messages From Spirit*, Australian psychic Georgina Walker explores the idea that each of us is born with a quota of 'exit points', opportunities to 'opt out from this life,' she writes. Whether we stay or go depends on where our free will steers us, and the earthly lessons that may yet still be in store for us.

Perhaps my mum used up – as did I – one of her exit points on that cold day when her cousin almost made the biggest mistake of his life?

Walker cites the case of a man who twice emerged unharmed following road accidents that should have killed him. Instead, he felt guarded by 'a power source greater than he would ever understand'.

Megan McAuliffe knows what that feels like. The 40-year-old ex-Sydneysider is still haunted by what could have been, almost two decades ago in London's West End: 'I had to get the late bus home as the tubes had finished. I was 21, and very new to London and overseas travelling. The journey home was long, and

I must've fallen asleep as the bus driver woke me at the last stop. He just ushered me off the bus, like I was a nuisance.' Megan asked him where she was and he grumbled a response, but she'd never heard of the place. It was three o'clock in the morning.

Feeling hopelessly disoriented, Megan says, 'I got off the bus, noticing how deserted and dark the streets were. I felt incredibly vulnerable. There was the odd person walking along the street and at one point two policemen walked past. I stopped them to ask them where I was and told them I was lost. They were really rude, and told me that my home was half-an-hour walk "that way" and pointed in the direction I had to go. And then they walked off. I remember thinking I couldn't walk half-an-hour in the dark, feeling the way I did, so I decided to try to find a taxi rank.'

It was utterly silent on the street, the policemen nowhere to be seen.

'There was no one about – except this one man walking towards me. The closer he got, the more menacing he became, and he was gazing straight into my eyes. I realised at that point that this man's intentions were sinister and my whole body seemed to curl up on itself in protection. As he got within about five metres of me, I felt this presence appear behind me. It was about ten-feet tall and it felt like a big mass of energy. It was enormous and powerful. I immediately felt my body straighten and lift out of its protective stance and I felt incredibly strong, almost invincible. And as the man walked closer to me I stared at him straight in the eyes. Instantly, he averted his gaze, and as he walked past me he seemed to cower, and tried to move away from me.

'There was no doubt in my mind that man felt threatened at that moment by an energy that was right behind me. I felt it, and he felt it. I don't know what it was. But, whenever I think of it, I have always got the feeling that it was an archangel. That's what always comes to me.'

For Danielle Flannery, the source of her spiritual help was also unknown, but most welcome. Three weeks after she awoke, feeling 'hysterical', from a nightmare in which her toddler fell from the 29th floor of a building while she tended to her new baby, the awful dream almost became reality. Bathing her newborn son in the kitchen of her Brisbane home, she looked across the room to check on her eighteen-month-old, smiling to herself to see him quiet and entertained. Danielle recalls, 'He was standing on the couch looking out the window, watching the kids playing next door. He was doing exactly what he should be doing.'

She finished bathing the baby, wrapped him in a towel and turned to carry him into the nursery but was stopped. 'I literally felt someone touch me on the shoulder three times and a voice in my head say, "Remember the dream." I couldn't actually tell you if it was male or female, but it wasn't a request, it was an order,' says Danielle.

Obeying, she turned around. This time there was no smiling when she saw what her little boy was up to. 'He had unhitched the glass windows and pushed out the screen – I don't know how he did it – and was leaning with his belly on the windowsill looking down.' But instead of panicking, as might be expected, Danielle acted assuredly: 'With the baby dripping on my shoulder, I calmly walked across, grabbed him by the ankle and pulled him back in. It was only a one-level house but if he'd fallen, he would have dropped headfirst onto the concrete path below.

'It was only later I realised that we lived at number 29, and in my dream he'd fallen from the 29th floor,' she adds, with the laughter borne of a happy ending.

There is another remarkable postscript to Danielle's story: her grandmother had once lived in the house where these events unfolded, and her great-grandmother had actually designed the gracious Queenslander! Danielle had no knowledge of these facts when she and her family moved in. To this day, she doesn't know if it was an ancestral voice that spoke out to ward off disaster: 'I don't know who that voice belonged to, or what, but it was definitely not a mother's intuition. It was a command.'

For Mark, who told of journeying to the past in his dreams in the last chapter, the command arrived as a physical sensation. Driving one night, he stopped at traffic lights. Waiting for the green signal, he noted the hush that hung over the moment, the thin wedge of moon pasted on a starless sky, the pervasive silence. When the traffic light changed, he couldn't press the accelerator. 'It was as if my foot was frozen, heavy as lead, it just wouldn't do what I wanted,' he says. 'It felt like something was holding it back.'

As he tried in vain to push down on the pedal, the sound of thunder snapped his neck up. It was a rubbish truck, barrelling past the red light at a speed that would have mowed Mark down if he'd been able to accelerate as normal. He says: 'I do believe there are times when God leaves us to the consequences of our broken humanity and yet other times when he directly intervenes to stop something happening, maybe through what some might call a guardian angel. A silent, invisible, yet unstoppable power.'

Stories of near-misses, where survivors describe feeling protected by a higher power, are plentiful. Yet in many cases these survivors are left in no doubt of who's responsible for their good fortune – deceased family members. In the previous chapter, we met Marcus, who was catapulted from his motorbike in a collision that should have been fatal. His partner driving behind him, who watched the horrible scene unfold, says it looked as if he was cradled 'in the palm of a hand' as he flew through the air. Marcus is certain the spirit of his late brother, Les, played a part in saving his life that day, though he didn't see him.

For others, like Ban Guo, the guardian presence of their late loved ones in dangerous situations is made specific in a vision. Ban remembers the day he 'absentmindedly' crossed a road in busy Marrickville, in Sydney's inner-west. 'The lights said "Don't Walk" and I walked across and a car turned around the corner and he didn't see me, and, oh, it was very close,' Ban says. 'I felt something push me back and as I fell onto the asphalt, I saw my dad. He made a pushing motion, and I *felt* it. He pushed me out of the way. I landed on my back and the car just stopped maybe a foot away. I remember the expression on my dad's face, like, "You should be more careful."'

One summer's day in January 2012, Erika Müller, whose ongoing bond with her late brother, Matthew, is featured in Chapter Five, caught her usual bus after finishing her shift at the café where she works. 'I got off at my bus stop and I was crossing the road and I saw that the bus still had its indicator to the left so he wasn't turning out yet,' she says. 'When I was walking in front of the bus I saw that it was starting to move,' but, oblivious to the danger unfolding, she 'just kept walking forward, with my earphones in, listening to music'.

Surprisingly, for it was a warm day, Erika felt 'cool breezes' around her. 'I thought that was a bit strange. At the moment

214

I felt that weather change, I was almost stepping onto the kerb on the other side of the road.' She did so, without incident.

The next day, an elderly lady who regularly catches the same bus as Erika leaned in to whisper, 'I cannot believe you are still alive.'

'What on earth are you talking about?' said Erika, not meaning to be rude but she was startled by the woman's comment.

It emerged that each woman had a different experience of the same event. 'She said that the bus had stopped indicating and was pulling out onto the road. She freaked out, said she was about to scream at the bus driver because she saw me walking right in front of it; she blinked and I was on the other side of the road. She couldn't explain it,' recalls Erika, who then remembered something else about the moment she stepped onto the road. 'It wasn't until I spoke to that lady that I realised I had *felt* my brother Matthew smile when I crossed the road. I thought, "Could it have been Matthew looking after me?" I still can't explain it, but every time I think about it, I see Matthew's smiling face.'

Sunshine Coast radio presenter Mary-Lou Stephens knows that her late dad, Dick, had her back when she was losing her way in her twenties, as she described in Chapter One. After he helped her kick a heroin habit, 'I felt him looking after me,' says the vivacious 52-year-old. 'There were a couple of incidents where I would have ended up dead and I really felt it was his presence that kept me alive.'

One unforgettable occasion occurred when she was driving in Sydney. 'I got my driver's licence late in life. I was a very bad driver,' Mary-Lou says, with a cheeky laugh. 'I was approaching an intersection but instead of going up to the white line, I stopped a few metres behind it, and I had no idea why. I just stopped where I was told to stop: "Just stop here, darling," I heard. And then this car came through, careening out of control. It would have totally wiped me out if I'd pulled up at the white line.'

In a heart-stopping encounter that echoes both Mary-Lou's and Megan's experiences, Perth's Shayne Wallace survived what she's certain was an attempted carjacking, thanks to the quick-thinking actions of her late teenager, Jamie, who died in a motorbike accident in 2007. Four years later, Shayne was driving to her Perth home one night in a bright yellow SS Commodore with thick black stripes that sixteen-year-old Jamie had fantasised about owning. Five months after his death, Shayne's partner purchased (without knowing of the desire Jamie expressed to his mum) the boy's dream car. They called it 'Bumble-Bee' after a character in Jamie's beloved *Transformers*.

At a large intersection surrounded by thick bushland, Shayne pulled up at the traffic lights. There was no one else around. She recalls: 'I had a "feeling" so I hit the auto door lock while waiting for the light to change. Then a little green Hyundai Excel pulled up beside me, with a woman driving and a man in the passenger seat. The man started staring at me. I just tried to ignore him, but it felt quite intense. My fear started to swell when I saw him unclip his seatbelt, all the while looking at me, and open the car door. I started asking silently, "Jamie, come to Mum, mate, I need you! Jesus, angels, God, please help me . . ." I was starting to panic, and the man was getting out of the car. As he went to stand, his arm caught in his seatbelt and he dropped his phone, but he kept looking straight at me.

'I shouted – in my mind – for Jamie again. As the man untangled his arm, and bent to pick up his phone, his foot shuffled and he kicked the phone along the length of the car. Still looking up at me, he bent to pick it up and accidentally tapped it with his shoe again. Then finally he picked it up.'

Almost weeping with fear, Shayne watched as the man made his way towards her. Still no other vehicles had arrived, but then suddenly a police car appeared and pulled up at the intersection, indicating to turn right. Shayne went limp with relief. 'The man turned, walked around the back of my car, tapped the boot very loudly as he walked past and headed off into the bush. By now, my heart had almost completely stopped – I was an emotional mess! The light turned green, and I drove off slowly to allow the Hyundai to get ahead of me before the lanes singled out. The police car turned on its siren and followed me around the corner, so I started to pull over but it raced off after the Hyundai.'

The Hyundai, tells Shayne, swerved into a side street with the police in pursuit. 'The whole incident lasted less than three minutes, but seemed to take hours. I have never been so frightened in all my life! I still don't know how I held it together during the drive home, but I do know that Jamie was in the passenger seat beside me. I have no doubt whatsoever that my son's hijinks with the man's seatbelt and phone prevented him from making it to my door before the police showed up.'

Guidance. Warning. Protection. All three are powerful manifestations of love. Most of us, especially parents and grandparents, can relate to the instinct to shield the people we care about from pain and suffering. As all of these stories demonstrate, the drive to guard our family from danger doesn't fade after death. Next you'll meet Cassie, whose father's dogged determination to send her to the doctor may well have saved her life, and Kat, whose late grandfather acted like an airbag in a car accident that should have carried her to him.

Father knows best

'He'd say, "You need to speak to the doctor," and he just kept stroking his throat.'

Of course Cassie MacDonald used to be a nurse, I think, when I meet her for breakfast at a little organic café in my old neighbourhood of Rockdale, south of Sydney. Warmth spills from every pore and her gap-toothed smile is a kind of hug. Her green-grey eyes glimmer and heave like a wintry sea teeming with secrets and life beneath the surface. When Cassie's breakfast wrap arrives, it grows cold as she unspools a story she probably would not be here to tell me about, were it not for the persistence of her late father, Ray.

Family figures heavily in Cassie's life. The 52-year-old Glaswegian mother of four is one of twelve children, her ties to her siblings still as strong as her accent, though she moved to Australia with 'the boy next door', her husband, Robert, when she was 21. Her beloved dead populate her thoughts when she's awake, and return under cover of night, too, says Cassie, whose story begins and ends with a dream.

In 2009, she learned from her youngest sibling that her dad was seriously ill. Fretting about how she'd keep things running smoothly for her husband and four daughters while she returned to Scotland in time to visit her father before he passed away, Cassie was electric with stress. Then she had a dream. In it stood three loved ones she hadn't seen in years: her mum, Lorna, who was 64 when she'd died of a stroke in 1997; her brother, Cameron, who'd died of a brain tumour aged 36; and her nephew, Gordon, who passed of kidney failure when he was 30. 'My brother was at the front, my mother was behind them and my nephew was to the side,' says Cassie, who remembers noting that her nephew 'still wore his Harry Potter glasses'.

At first, she panicked at the sight of them, because she thought they forewarned of her father's imminent death. 'Then Cameron said, "Calm down! It's not his time, we're only here to tell you it's not his time."'

She woke up, awash with relief. 'When Cameron said it wasn't his time, I thought, "Okay, okay, I can do this. I have time to get back and be with him."' She called her younger sister, Darla, to let her know she'd booked her flight and would be there in a week.

'I'm really pleased,' said Darla, 'because he's getting worse.'

To Cassie's astonishment, she explained that the family feared for his mental health because he'd claimed that the previous night he'd been with Lorna, Cameron and Gordon. 'They'd visited him and me at the same time,' marvels Cassie, a film of tears trembling on the surface of the sea inside her eyes.

Cassie spent time with her father in Glasgow in April 2009; that July, after she'd returned home to Sydney, he died of prostate and secondary bone cancer, aged 84. Cameron had been right to set her mind at ease in that dream, she reflected, because her dad indeed had months left to live. He'd been right in reassuring her that there was no need to rush. Now the grieving daughter took shelter beneath her memories of her father, who she describes as, 'A real family man – a man of few words. He didn't need to speak sometimes because the look told you exactly what he wanted to say.'

It was an expression she'd see again, when seven months after his death, Ray began appearing to Cassie in increasingly vivid dreams. At first, recalls Cassie, 'It was just a nod and a smile, just an acknowledgment, he'd just be there. One time he goes, "Everything is good, everything is well." Contrary to the frail old man he'd become at the end, in Cassie's dreams, Ray was a smiling man of 48 'in his prime'. This was reminiscent of the earlier dream of her mum, brother and nephew: those family members, too, had appeared youthful and healthy.

The other thing the two dreams shared in common was the setting: 'a light-filled void, no interference, it's almost like a meeting place,' muses Cassie, sipping her coffee. 'It's not this world, it's not their world, it's just some void.'

When she began having them, the dreams were nothing more than a pleasant reunion. 'When I woke up in the morning I was, like, "Wow!" and of course I'd share it with my husband and he goes, "Um, okay,"' recounts Cassie, laughing.

But then the dreams began to take on a more sombre, urgent tone. Her father began to speak and her mother appeared with him, but always keeping to the background. 'He'd say, "You need to speak to the doctor," and he just kept stroking his throat, and that's all he'd repeat: "You need to speak to the doctor, you need to speak to the doctor." I'd wake up in the morning thinking, "What is he going on about?"'

Now Cassie was dreaming of Ray two or three times a week. 'It was like he was saying, "You're not listening, *listen!*"' says Cassie, who at first thought Ray was urging her to call *his* doctor in Glasgow, as he'd had difficulty swallowing for two years prior to his death. Perhaps there was something the family hadn't found out about his condition? Ray had kept them all in the dark about his diagnosis for months so now Cassie wondered if there was more to learn. 'Two or three times I was about to ring his doctor, I still had her phone number. So I was taking notice of the dream but I wasn't doing anything about it.'

Meanwhile Ray continued to appear in the in-between world,

looking vital and alive, stroking his throat and pleading for his daughter to speak to the doctor.

By now, Cassie had begun to wake up with a sore throat and a husky voice. 'Of course, I'd have a couple of lozenges and it would be fine by about 11 am.' But her thoughts were never far from the dream. 'I said to Robert, "He keeps stroking his throat. Have I got a lump? Feel it." And then I'd think, "No, Dad's talking about himself." The next time he came through he said, "You. Need. To. Speak. To. The. Doctor!"'

But she didn't obey.

Three nights later, Cassie's youngest daughter, Rosie, asked her mum to watch the TV drama *Brothers and Sisters* with her. It was an unprecedented and never-to-be-repeated request. Rosie knew her mum didn't like watching TV. When Cassie argued as much, Rosie begged, 'Come, please, watch it, watch it.' (Today, though, Rosie has no recollection of having ever watched this show, which she remembers thinking was 'for oldies'.) Finally, after some discussion, Cassie acquiesced. She thought it would do her good to turn her mind off for an hour, let herself drift far from her increasing preoccupation with her recurring dream. Instead, she was in for a shock.

'One of the lead characters finds a lump in her throat, and I thought, "God, that's strange." The lump was thyroid cancer,' says Cassie, whose skin bristled as she automatically reached for her own throat, stroking it as her father stroked his in the dreams. 'It was a light-bulb moment.'

The next morning, at breakfast, Cassie sat opposite Robert and stretched her neck out for him to inspect. 'Can you see if there's anything,' she asked, her eyes pinned to the ceiling. He couldn't see anything but suggested Cassie make an appointment with their doctor anyway. As it happened, Cassie already had one lined up for Friday, in two days time. She'd had X-rays on her elbow after a fall and was due to pick up the results.

Though he'd only 'been to the doctor three times in his life', 53-year-old Robert, a plant operator, accompanied his wife without comment. Her X-ray was clear. After a routine blood-pressure test and standard questions, came this exchange:

'Anything else?' asked the doctor.

'No,' said Cassie.

'Sure?'

'Yes.'

'So there's nothing else?'

'No, there's nothing else.'

The doctor nodded and stood up to open the door. 'Are you sure there's nothing else?' he asked again.

Cassie exhaled: 'Oh, while I'm here, I know it's probably a bit silly, but can you just check my throat? I've had a wee bit of a sore throat, on and off. Can you just check it?'

The doctor asked her to put her head back and swallow. As she did that, she heard Robert say, 'Oh shit.'

'How long have you had this?' asked the doctor.

'I don't know, I don't know that I've got anything, I just thought it was my throat.'

'Uh-huh.'

Though she felt 'out of it', another part of Cassie acknowledged 'everything was coming together'. The doctor booked her in for an ultrasound and biopsy that afternoon – tests uncovered a nodule on the left side of her thyroid. 'I get it now! I get it!' Cassie remembers thinking. 'It was like getting hit on the head by a plank of wood.' The Wednesday after her routine visit to the GP, Cassie was in surgery: 'They took out half my thyroid and the nodule. The cells had started changing, it wasn't cancer, but that's where it was leading.'

Life has changed in many ways for Cassie since she resolved to trust her father's message. She's joined a mediumship development circle and has been using Reiki, also known as 'hands on healing'. With her girls grown up (their ages range from 17 to 23), she's begun to slowly shed some of the volunteering work she's done for years, for play group, primary school, high school and youth club – which alone took up 36 hours a week – and claim back time for herself to think about the direction she wants to take her life in. Before falling pregnant with her first child, Cassie relished her job as a community nurse and there's a chance she'll pursue something like that again, perhaps looking after mothers and babies. I tell her that seems like the perfect place for her comforting and reassuring presence.

After breakfast, we're saying our goodbyes outside the café when Cassie starts telling me about the last time she saw her mum, Lorna. Returning to Glasgow in 1997 for a brother's wedding, she looked into her mother's eyes: 'I just knew she didn't have long to live,' she says. 'I told my brother and he asked how I knew. I said, "Her eyes aren't dancing anymore."'

Lorna died ten days after she returned to Australia, says Cassie, whose eyes dance, too, just like her mum's once did.

Shielded by love

'Before this experience, I never believed in anything like after-death communication.'

One grey morning in 2010, with the smell of last evening's rainfall still seasoning the air, Katherine Dumont was five

223

minutes into her one-hour drive to university from Perth to Fremantle when her bite-sized Hyundai Getz skidded on the slick freeway into the path of a miracle. Travelling on the right, she bounced off the car in front of her and veered into the left lane, where she rear-ended another car. Meanwhile, a motor-bike flying up behind her swerved to miss her and the rider came off, landing in the right-hand lane. Glancing into her rear-view mirror, Katherine saw a semitrailer hurtling towards her. 'I don't think I had any feelings of fear,' recalls the 24-year-old. 'It was just a split-second that I knew I was going to be hit.' She braced.

What happened next should not have been her story to tell – by all accounts, the young woman should never have survived the impact of being pushed by the truck into the metal railings of the highway barrier. Yet, here she is.

'My car was a complete write-off. Every single window was smashed and every single panel crushed in. The truck had caused so much damage to the back and side of my car that the metal had been torn apart,' says Kat, who kicked open the driver's door and walked to the side of the road, where she stood and cried. Soon she was joined by the truckie, a 'big, tough' 50-something bloke who was bawling in relief, so certain that the driver of the little car would be a mangled corpse. He explained he'd had to make a horrendous choice between hitting the motorbike rider, lying helpless and exposed on the road, or the car in front. Choice made, he shook his head and said to Kat, 'I can't believe that you're standing here.'

Kat's mum, Di, was getting ready to leave for her job as a teacher's aide when her phone rang. It was Kat. 'She said, "Mum, can you come? The traffic's pretty bad and I need you to come,"' remembers Di. 'She didn't say she'd been in a car accident.' About 100 metres from the crash site, Di recalls, 'I see her car all smashed up and I got off the road and just ran.'

Di found her daughter on her feet, shaken and covered in glass but otherwise well. There was not a nick on her skin. No bruising, whiplash, broken bones or internal injuries to report. The paramedics, police and truck driver all agreed it was a 'miracle' she had survived, let alone walked away. 'Well, we know now why Pop was hanging around,' said Di, referring to her late father. 'He was warning us that something was going to happen. He was looking after you.'

In the days preceding the accident, Kat and Di, who lived together, had both sensed a presence in the house. Kat was the first to mention it. 'I said, "Mum, I can feel something in the house. I don't know if it's one of the dogs that's passed away, but I feel something."'

Her mother's face lit up in response. So there *was* something!

Kat recalls her mother then said: 'Oh my God, Kat, I'm so glad you said it because I've felt the same thing. I think it's Pop. Don't be scared. Don't be frightened. He's just here for a reason. I think he's just trying to get a message across.'

Kat's grandfather, Charlie, had died eleven years before and neither woman had ever sensed his presence until now. Though Kat inherited many of his traits – from his bright blue eyes and prominent cheeks to his smart way with money and low tolerance for fools – in life, he hadn't gone out of his way to bond with his granddaughter.

'To me, Pop was always a very mysterious character, but I just idolised him,' says Kat, who together with her parents and sister would spend most holidays at his home in Dongara more than three hours away. 'He wouldn't greet you with open arms, or hug or kiss you – I think he found it hard to express love – but if you ever needed anything, he was there. Once, when I was little and my parents were struggling financially, he came down from the farm and rolled up $200 in notes and put them in the bathtub plug. He didn't say anything. It wasn't until Mum went to bathe us that night that she found the money. That was his way of saying, "I'm thinking of you."'

So to Kat it made perfect sense that her quiet grandfather, who always found a way to help people in need, but 'in his own way', would have found a way to be there for her. Just as he'd been in life, says Kat, 'He stayed in the background until he was needed.' She is certain he 'shielded' her from injury and death that day on the highway.

'If she'd gone off the road just five feet earlier, it was a major embankment, probably a good twenty-foot drop,' adds Di. 'It wasn't her time.'

Only hours after the impact, Charlie himself owned up to his part in the rescue of his granddaughter. Asleep at her boyfriend's home that night, Kat woke up disoriented and with a pounding heart when the TV snapped to life in the middle of the night. 'This has never happened to me, at all,' she says. 'I totally freaked out. I said to my boyfriend, "What the hell? Are you playing a game with me?" He said, no, that it was probably just an electrical current.'

Though Kat was still troubled, the couple went back to sleep, only for the TV to burst into picture and sound again minutes later. 'I just thought, "This is ridiculous!" and then I heard the remote control fall onto the floor off the side table. I asked my boyfriend, "Did you just push that off?" but he was sound asleep.'

Answering 'a sudden urge', Kat began to speak out loud. 'I said, "It's okay, Pop. I know it was you. You don't need to do anything more, because it's scaring me, but I know it was you."' The night went back to sleep and Kat hasn't experienced anything uncanny since.

'He wanted to make sure that I knew he was looking after me,' she says. 'Before this experience, I never believed in anything like after-death communication, but since this happened to me, no one can ever take away the fact that I know Pop was there and that he protected me that day.'

*

Writing and editing this chapter, one song played on a loop in my head, the 1984 hit 'The Power of Love' by British band Frankie Goes to Hollywood. As a scrunchie-wearing teen navigating the bumpy, lumpy (and pimply) road of early adolescence, I barely gave a thought to the ballad's depth and meaning. But art has a way of revealing new layers of meaning to us with the passage of years. Three decades later, the song is telling me a different story.

For what force other than 'the power of love' could have pushed Ban, with a shove that was nothing less than physical, out of harm's way on the day he absentmindedly crossed a busy road? The same force that manifested the scolding, but loving, face of his dad at the instant of rescue, no doubt. Erika had an almost identical experience, when time itself seemed to bend out of shape to ensure her safety. Logic says the bus should have knocked her over; but there was no impact because the moment that would have housed the collision was seemingly erased, as the witness later recounted. Erika, though, doesn't remember the giant vehicle bearing down, she only remembers her brother's smiling face.

Love is all-powerful. Cassie will never again be slow to heed the advice of a relative who returns to counsel her in a dream visitation. Her father's spirit saved her life and the knowledge rests inside her like a gift of reassurance, like an awakening. Kat, too, is certain that she wouldn't have survived to share her story with us if her grandfather hadn't intervened that day on the highway. The rescue services shook their heads and called it a 'miracle' that she walked away, but ultimately that word applies to all the stories in this chapter – they are miracles, powered by love, unfolding in plain sight around us, every day. It's up to us to acknowledge them.

The phrase 'the power of love' is sleek and slight, deceptively compact and neat, but what it purports to define is the opposite: how to harness an idea that's boundless as space? Perhaps only in moments like these, moments that shine, fleeting and beautiful and unfathomable as shooting stars, in the trajectory of our lives – mothers and fathers, grandparents, children, siblings, friends and others whose identities remain elusive (for now), hurtling through the barriers of time and space to push us out of harm's way. It's almost comical, but in this sense they remind me of superheroes – and their superpower? It's love.

Years after he co-wrote 'The Power of Love', Frankie Goes to Hollywood's Holly Jones reminisced about the song. Reading his remarks, it struck me that he might agree that love can make anything possible, how it might swoop in to save us in the nick of time, how time itself may snap and stretch like an elastic at its bidding. 'I always felt like "The Power Of Love" was the record that would save me in this life,' he reportedly said. 'There is a biblical aspect to its spirituality and passion; the fact that love is the only thing that matters in the end.'

9

Love Will Find a Way

∽

Psychic-mediums bridging the divide

'Life on my side seems so extraordinarily easy compared to earth,
because we simply live according to the rules of love.'
—Sir William Barrett, in a 1929 sitting with a medium,
four years after his death

Not long after I'd finished writing *Spirit Sisters*, in 2008, I was at work when my mobile rang. The caller was a lady aged in her 80s. Sounding frail but speaking articulately and purposefully, she explained that she'd just spotted an ad I'd placed months before, asking for people to contact me if they had a story they wanted to share. I'd delivered my book, but when she started talking, I grabbed a scrap of paper and began scribbling, responding to that familiar rush of a good story unfolding. And to the valley of goosebumps sprouting on my arms.

229

She told me that a few days after a child was abducted, in a case that made national headlines, the victim appeared at her bedside. 'Tell my mum it's all over,' the child instructed.

'Why me?' answered the lady.

'Because you're the only one I could get through to.'

To me, this perfectly encompassed the experience of so many of the women I'd been interviewing for my research, women who inhabited a strange borderland between our world and the next. Unless you asked, unless they deigned you safe to be entrusted with their extraordinary truth, you'd never know that they were mediums – people who shone like a beacon to spirits who were lost, troubled or at peace, but desperate to get a message through to a loved one left behind.

Though I spoke to many who lived anonymously with their gifts, I also interviewed some who made a living from it. I was keen to peer into the lives of both kinds, without judgement, for what really intrigued me was the part they played in helping deliver a message from spirit to the bereaved – and how that often proved to be the first step on the long road to healing, particularly when the suffering of a person in mourning creates a barrier too dense for a spirit to penetrate (as my caller's story showed).

'There are times when a person's grief or expectations can have a "blanket effect" over them which causes them to overlook the subtle signs and gentle reminders that their loved ones are right by their side,' explains acclaimed Australian medium Mitchell Coombes. 'It's a bit like when you lose your car keys – no matter how much you desperately search for them, you can't seem to locate them. It's only when you stop straining to find them that they show up. The world of spirit is similar in the sense that grief and expectations can block spirit – but when you least expect it, they will come through with a special "Hello from Heaven".'

This was true for novelist Jess Tarn, who in Chapter One told of her lingering grief following the accidental drowning of her baby brother, David, when she was four. During a writing retreat in October 2012, an impromptu reading from a fellow author, Cathleen Ross, who also happens to be a psychic-medium, helped assuage Jess's long-held guilt. Jess hadn't mentioned a word about David or his death to Cathleen prior to this.

The reading began with Cathleen holding two of Jess's rings in her hand – this is known as 'psychometry', gaining knowledge psychically via an inanimate object. Then she placed her wrist over Jess's and shut her eyes. 'At first she said I was going to sell lots and lots of books, that she can see all these contracts. So I said, "Oh wow, thanks. Do you know when that will start?"' Jess recalls with a laugh. 'Then she says, "And now I see a little boy, maybe three or four." And I thought, "Oh my God." I'd never told her about David before, ever. I just burst into tears and it was like, "Oh my God, she is real and she can see him . . ."'

Next came a message from David, via Cathleen: 'He's happy where he is and he loves you and he wants you to know that.'

At that point, Jess says, her mind began to play a 'movie' of his final moments: 'It was him coming up to me while I'm holding my mother's hand to ask if he can go for a swim, and I just felt this massive guilt.'

Then Cathleen opened her eyes, telling Jess, 'David doesn't blame you, that [jumping in the pool] is what he was going to do anyway. He just walked over because he wanted to talk to you.'

As she recounts this, Jess begins weeping. 'It felt like a huge weight had lifted off of me.'

The reading is etched onto Cathleen's memory, too: 'I could see a little boy holding the hand of his grandmother and wanting to say hello to Jess,' she tells me. 'Jess was carrying a lot of guilt around . . . it's important to do worthwhile work.'

Sometimes, it is lifesaving work. Mitchell Coombes will never forget the moment he collided into a lady at a shopping centre, 'practically knocking her to the ground'. As he apologised and helped her to her feet, he saw the spirit of a little girl by the woman's side. Now he knew that their meeting was no accident, and told her so, explaining his gift. When he asked if she'd lost a daughter, the lady began sobbing and Mitchell reached for her hand, telling her: 'Your daughter wants you to know that you are not responsible for her passing and that you are needed here – she wants you to be happy and at peace with yourself.'

As the mall thrummed around them and people loaded with bags and trolleys darted this way and that, Mitchell and the woman stood together, savouring the magic of a meeting orchestrated by love. 'She explained to me that one afternoon she turned her back for just a few moments to answer the phone. In those few moments, her daughter ran out onto the road and was struck by a car – she passed instantly,' says Mitchell, who describes this event in his book *Sensing Psychic*. The woman could not see a way out of the guilt and grief that consumed her, he tells me. 'She said "I was going to end my life tonight, but this has changed everything." She thanked me from the bottom of her heart. I thanked the world of spirit for putting me in the right place at the right time.'

Such 'reunions' are being facilitated in all corners of the country by mediums such as Mitchell Coombes and Charmaine Wilson, two of the best-known and respected Australian names, in private and in public. In one year alone, his tally of readings may reach 'well into the thousands', says Mitchell. 'Many times after a public platform or private one-to-one, people often remark that they "feel much lighter in heart and mind than when they first arrived". Others have also said they now feel at peace and can move forward with their life and finally experience the happiness they have been longing for.'

To be the instrument of such life-changing breakthroughs for people in pain is a privilege. 'For me, this is not just my job – this is my life,' says Mitchell, who was three years old when he saw his first spirit. 'To reach out and offer love, comfort and healing to another person, whether they are from this side of life or in the spirit world, is not only humbling, it's extremely gratifying. I am simply the messenger or vessel for their heartfelt words to flow through.'

Many of the people I've interviewed have told how spirits go to great lengths in their interaction with mediums to ensure a message reaches its target. Margaret Marlow, who's shared stories of contact from her 36-year-old son, John, says: 'A local psychic who knew John got in touch to tell me she had received a message from him. He was concerned about somebody in the family's health and he wanted the message to get to me.'

The way he snagged her attention, Margaret learned, was at a seminar the woman was holding: 'He cornered her and then the message came.'

Later, when the woman stopped at a service station on her way home, a feather fell from the sky in pouring rain and she heard the words, 'Don't forget to tell Mum'.

Margaret admits the turn of events 'freaked me out a bit and I became worried'. The psychic sensed the message about ill health was for Margaret's husband, but wasn't certain.

'We both had check-ups and yes, my husband has something,' says Margaret. 'It was only detected because he had a particular blood test and it is a potentially serious illness if it isn't treated. So John is there waiting in the wings and getting the messages to us. I almost ignored the message because I didn't want to believe it. It's amazing.'

In late 2007, around the anniversary of her beloved brother's suicide, Deb Carr received a loving 'postcard' from him, but it, too, arrived by very circuitous means. 'I had toyed for years and years with the idea of getting a tattoo because I'm not a tattoo person, but I decided to get one – a feather, because I kept finding these green feathers all the time and I thought they were from Gary,' says Deb. 'Three weeks later, I had a psychic reading. The psychic said all this stuff to me and then he said, "You know your brother's here." I said, "What?" He said, "He's holding up the letter B. He's with a dog starting with the letter B."'

Deb was astounded. Her mum's dog, Bully, had just been put down. 'Then the psychic said, "He's with the other two dogs with the letter B."' And it was true that Deb's mum had previously had two other dogs, Blocker and Butch.

'He said, "Gary's jamming. He's playing the guitar." I said, "Gary left a suicide note on cassette tape, he was jamming his guitar." So by this time I'm thinking this has to be Gary, I mean this guy doesn't know any of this stuff! Then he said, "Your brother wants you to know he loves the tattoo of the feather," which was on my backside but no one could see it or knew about it!'

As if all of that wasn't baffling enough, there was more to come. The psychic informed Deb she'd be receiving a parcel in the post before Christmas, adding, 'Your brother was involved in sending that.' Deb remembers she thought, 'This is just ridiculous! Get out of here! It stretched the boundaries of possibility.' But when she next went to the post office, there was a parcel. 'It came from Queensland. I had no idea who it could be from. So I opened it up and there was a huge white feather with a golden bow around it and a poem.'

The parcel was from a woman who'd read about Deb's brother on her website. She, too, was grieving a monumental loss of her own, the accidental death of her five-year-old daughter, but something had propelled her to send a gift and words of support across the country, to a woman she'd never met but whose grief resonated with her own. After this, they'd strike up a friendship, but for now, it was just Deb in the post office with tears clouding her eyes as she read the poem, which said, in part: 'The other day I looked above and saw an angel near, I asked a favour for someone I love and hoped my message clear . . . the angel spoke and moved my way that's when the feather fell . . . This gift is yours to give her this day, it proves my promise well.'

The words couldn't have arrived at a better time, says Deb, who was in the midst of 'a really tough time' in her life and struggling financially. To her, it was clear that her brother was by her side throughout her troubles, and that his roundabout way of reassuring her of this was a clever trick to ensure she wouldn't second-guess herself. It was validation.

Validation plays a crucial part in the next story, too, in which Dee Gibson, a 67-year-old numerologist and psychic-medium from Melbourne received a specific and spontaneous message from a recently deceased friend via someone entirely unexpected. Communicating through a third party that he'd never known in life was the spirit's way of providing Dee with the 'absolute proof' she always demands in her exchanges with the spirit world.

It was the late summer of 1996 and Dee was in her kitchen chatting with a friend, Cheryl. The day before, Dee had attended the funeral of Kevin, her closest family friend, but Cheryl had never met Kevin, nor was she aware that Dee had been to his funeral. The next moment, a change came over Cheryl, who put down her cup. 'She went very still and just looked at me with eyes as wide as saucers,' recalls Dee.

'Who is Kevin? Do you know anyone called Kevin?' asked Cheryl. Her expression told Dee that she was just as surprised by what she was saying as Dee was to hear it.

'Why?' asked Dee.

'He said he is dead and that he wants to thank you.'

'Oh!'

'He's giving me the words *I am*,' said Cheryl.

Dee recalls when Cheryl said that, 'I went very cold from the top of my head to the bottom of my feet. I knew that it was spirit. My body reacts to truth and at that moment, I just stood there with tears in my eyes. I wasn't crying, I was just overcome. You know that visceral feeling when your eyes well up?'

Cheryl then pointed to some shelves in Dee's lounge room: 'It has to do with that bookcase over there,' she said. 'He is telling me to take out a book, and says you'll know which one to get.'

'Yes,' said Dee, understanding. As she made her way to the bookcase, Cheryl gave a perfect description of Kevin's appearance and accurately stated he'd died of cancer.

'It has something to do with "I Am,"' repeated Cheryl. 'It's in the book.'

Dee nodded and selected a book with a green cover entitled . . . *I Am*. 'Open it,' she told her friend.

Inside was a cloth bookmark handmade by Kevin's wife,

Lyn. In beautiful cross-stitch vertically down the centre were the words 'I am'. Before making the bookmark for Dee, Lyn had asked what she wanted embroidered on it: 'I said I wanted those words because my spiritual journey is all about "I am" – exploring where we come from.'

Two minuscule words, like a tiny door opening out onto a limitless landscape.

'At that moment, Cheryl just hugged me and hugged me,' says Dee. 'Then we sat down at the kitchen bench and I told her everything that had gone on the day before. She was totally amazed.'

While Cheryl knew she had these gifts, 'she didn't really work with it', explains Dee. 'It was something that came on now and then for her. It was there but she didn't use it every day.' The reluctant medium's wonder deepened as Dee went into detail.

Kevin, a friend of five decades, had been very sceptical about life after death. 'He was very much a practical man who worked with his hands and not given to anything fancy. He'd say, "Aah, Dee, all that bullshit."' But as he neared the end, he began to ask a lot more questions, recalls Dee. He became more curious about spirituality and Dee's mediumship. Now it seemed he'd found the answers he sought and wanted to share the epiphany with his old friend.

'In the end we were both crying,' says Dee. 'I was crying because I had absolute proof he had come through, and he was standing there smiling his heart out at me. And Cheryl was crying because she had brought through something that was so poignant for me. It was so truthful.'

Truth is at the heart of what Dee seeks to uncover in her work as a medium helping to connect grieving people with their late loved ones. The spontaneous and pointed communication from Kevin that unforgettable day almost two decades ago laid the foundation for her commitment to integrity in her work. 'What it taught me is that as I give readings, I must be able to push myself further to give people specific, tiny details only they know, to make them understand it is true. I never want to give someone something wishy-washy like, "He wore a green hat." I want to be able to be the best that I can be.'

And all of it is thanks to spirits like Kevin. 'He had made that journey and he was coming back just to laugh at me, with me,' ponders Dee. 'To say, "Ha ha Dee, you're bloody right after all."'

In Chapter Two, Rachel Larkins, a writer from Melbourne, described feeling comforted by the sight of her father's guardian spirit at her bedside a week after his passing in 1999. Eight years later, when her mother, who had emphysema, died, Rachel decided to consult a medium after her daughter began reporting nightly visits from her grandma.

'There were a few little bits and pieces where I thought, "That sounds like Mum," but the thing that really got me was when she said, "Your mother wants to know if you have the deck finished and if you have, she wants you to plant a rose, no she's *telling* you to plant a rose next to the deck to remember her." Before her death, Mum had been to visit and she'd seen our deck and said, "You've *got* to get that fixed." The deck was 35 years old and really quite dangerous and so she'd been very adamant about us having to get that deck sorted out,' remembers Rachel.

The tone of the reading also matched her mother's personality. 'It's not like she would say, "I'd like you to plant a rose for me," it would be absolutely her style to tell me, "You *have* to plant a rose."'

The medium's description of the rose Rachel's mum was

'showing' her was also uncannily accurate. 'She said it was a full-bloom red rose, and the thing is, Mum's name was Rosemary and so she used a red rose in full bloom as her symbol on all her stationery, that was her thing,' says Rachel. 'The kids called her Grandma Rosie. It was very much a personal symbol that she adopted for herself throughout her life.'

The reading left Rachel in no doubt that her mother's essence endured. 'I just thought, "Okay, yes, that's Mum, she's still bossing me around after her death." It seemed so clear.'

Soon after her appointment with the medium, Rachel was driving past a commercial rose garden and 'on impulse' decided to pull in and browse. 'Although Mum used the red rose as her personal symbol, she planted a lot of mauve roses in her garden, she really loved mauve roses,' says Rachel. 'I thought I'd just walk around and see if any rose felt right, and practically the first rose I saw was a mauve rose. I looked at the label and it was called Paradise, and I thought, "Yep, that's the one I've got to get." I've planted it right next to the deck and it's doing really well.'

Many of the mediums' messages carry a humble but powerful theme: the departed want their loved ones to know they're never far, that they share our extremes of happiness and heartbreak, as well as the tiny everyday moments – the meaningful minutiae – that in succession build a life.

Karen Davis, who in Chapter Two told of seeing her deceased grandmother, understood this following her meeting with a medium. 'Sometimes in the afternoons or early evening, I'm cooking dinner and my daughters will be sitting around the breakfast table talking to me and, you know, they'll put their music on, One Direction or whatever, and they'll crank it up. So I'll join in and they think that's really funny and so we have a bit of a dance and a sing-along. We just scream the lyrics and say, "How good are we?!" It sounds terrible,' says Karen, laughing, though perhaps not everyone agrees. 'The psychic said, "When you dance and sing in your kitchen with the kids, your mum's dancing and singing with you." No one else would know we did that . . .'

Rob Smith, a Melbourne funeral celebrant, doesn't like the term 'medium' but nonetheless considers himself 'a middle man', someone who can pass on those all-important messages from beyond. Rob, 66, is a former medical researcher, chaplain and medical laboratory technician. His methods differ from those we've explored so far: Rob records the voices of the 'supposed' dead. 'I see myself as a middle man for receiving anomalous messages from discarnate entities from unseen conscious realms and playing them for others to hear,' he says. 'These messages are clear and can be validated by others.'

He tells me about how he stumbled upon the field of EVP (electronic voice phenomena) in 2000. Working at his computer, which had a noisy whirring fan, Rob began to hear voices in the background of the fan, though it took him some time to pinpoint the source. 'Survival' was the first word he identified and recorded via the whirring fan. 'That made an incredible impact on me,' he says.

Soon, the 'human-like mutterings' began to turn up on mini tape-recorders he used for his work as a funeral celebrant. He initially dismissed the recordings as 'radio interference' until he began to hear his name spoken time and again. Then, 'I virtually fell off my chair when I heard the voices of my "deceased" mother, maternal grandmother and grandfather communicating with the same physical voice inflections, accents and intonations they used when physically alive.'

Hearing his mum say, 'Hello, Robert,' in her unmistakable English brogue, and his maternal grandfather letting him know he was thinking of him, 'imploded' the former Uniting Church minister's long-held scepticism about all things paranormal. 'My grandfather was an English Victorian gentleman and he said, "Hard luck, I say, Robert." It was his way of showing empathy,' says Rob, who was recovering from a mini-stroke and marriage breakdown at the time. 'It's extraordinary! That was the absolute same way he spoke in the physical, I could easily recognise it. It's very seldom that the spirits can create the identical timbre of voice, it's very hard for them, but that was him, no doubt, speaking to me many years after he passed on.'

The breakthroughs led Rob to investigate clairaudiency (the ability to hear sounds and voices of the dead) and EVP – today he has many hundreds of recordings on file, some of which you can listen to at his 'Continuity of Consciousness and Interdimensional Communication' Facebook page and on Sound Cloud. 'Many of my recordings provide an actual name with a comment. Many want to pass a message of survival of consciousness and provide comfort to a loved one,' says Rob. He relates the story of a woman who contacted him via his blog, 'Rising', requesting a message from her late husband. That night, he recorded a voice using the pet name the husband called her by, which no one else had known.

The experience was rewarding for Rob, who feels strongly that a 'message from beyond' can lighten the burden of someone in mourning. It's something he can relate to: his partner of sixteen years had breast cancer and 'transitioned', as he calls it, in 2010 – he has since smelt her perfume around him but has never recorded her voice. Through his work with EVP, Rob believes, 'I'm offering comfort in the sense that their loved one is still alive in some way, is still around, and can still relate to them – the base essence of their consciousness remains. That is so important. It makes life less fearful, more anxiety free, and encourages one to "live out the things" one wants to do, here in the physical world.'

Victorian medium Larna Bruzzese agrees that acknowledging the dead's indelible love can be a healing step, but she's hyper-conscious of her responsibilities in dealing with the bereaved and, since studying a course in grief and bereavement, feels better equipped to take her work beyond connecting people with their late loved ones. 'My job now is to support others and help them build up their own intuition,' says Larna, 42, who urges clients to turn their focus *inwards* to nurture their bond with their deceased loved one. Larna tells me she has had to 'ban' people from seeking multiple readings with her: 'It's a fallacy that people need a third party to continue their bond with their loved one. My philosophy is, to keep that bond going, it's you, only you. Your loved one doesn't stay with me, they need you!'

Mitchell Coombes agrees: 'You do not need a medium to help you experience these "reunions". People from all walks of life have experienced what I like to call "wonder moments" that defy logic. If you open your heart and mind you will find that the spirit world is closer than you realise – and our loved ones reach out to us from beyond. I often remind people, "We don't die, we simply change addresses." Talk to your loved ones in spirit more often because they are only a whisper away.'

It is, indeed, a two-way exchange, powered by a flame of love that can never be extinguished, like Tullia's Perpetual Lamp. Larna has published a book, *Life After*, co-written with five of her clients – all survivors of tragic losses, who 'never got to say goodbye' – and has no doubt the project was facilitated by their spirit loved ones. 'My job is to work for the other side, as it always has been, but I believe that by helping the living, I am truly honouring the dead. Those in spirit want only what's best for those they left behind and who now have to live on without them.'

As part of her ongoing commitment to supporting her clients and honouring their dead, Larna hopes to launch a national 'Remember Me' day, an annual occasion to remember and pay homage to those we've lost. The idea – as with her book – came to Larna in a vision, which in itself was a result of her experiences with one spirit in particular, an acquaintance called Mark, yet another beloved partner, father and son taken too soon. Mark's partner, Gill, who is now 36, the same age as her soulmate when he died in 2009, tells their story:

Mark and I were together for just on six years and the plan was to be together forever and grow old together. Mark had been in hospital for six weeks before he passed, the last three of which he was intubated and unable to talk and too weak to communicate. After he passed I had so many questions and things left unanswered.

We both had a curiosity with the spirit world – it's not as though we'd ever been to a psychic or anything – but we believed and loved hearing stories of proof of life.

The first few weeks were a blur, feeling nothing, just numb. The one thing I was looking for were signs that Mark was with me. It's hard to explain why, but I just felt him around me. I woke up one morning, sat straight up and knew I had to speak with Larna, a friend of a friend we had met on occasion – she was affectionately known as 'Spooky Larna' as she had the gift of being able to communicate with loved ones who had passed. I rang my friend and asked her for Larna's number. I explained how I woke up with her name in my head and knew she could help.

My friend said she had been wondering when I would ring about Larna. She went on to explain how Mark had been visiting Larna with messages he wanted her to pass on to me. I rang Larna and she explained to me, as she had explained to Mark, that she couldn't just ring me to tell me all these things, it wasn't how it worked. He had to get me to go to Larna, which I believe is why I woke up thinking of her.

I arranged a meeting with her and was blown away. I had written down questions I had to ask Mark, about him, the hospital and things I was worried about for my future without him. It was like he had read them over my shoulder word for word! He would tell Larna one of my questions, with his answer, things I had spoken to him about at the hospital when it was just the two of us and, of course, with him unable to communicate, just listening to me.

I definitely believe our loved ones are around looking after us through the hard times and feel so loved that Mark managed to find a way to get his messages through to me. Without them, I don't think I would have been able to work through my grief as well as I have, as there were so many unknowns.

Yet sometimes a message from the spirit world arrives entirely without warning, as unexpectedly as a letter in the mailbox from a friend you've long lost touch with, as Sydneysider Helen Sanderson reveals in her joyful – and spine-tingling – surprise encounter below. High-profile medium Charmaine Wilson also knows exactly how creative and opportunistic spirit loved ones can be when they have a message to deliver. Like Larna Bruzzese, whose gift returned Mark to Gill, albeit briefly, Charmaine is dedicated to helping her clients find a way to live through crushing loss. In her story, Charmaine also tells of the personal tragedy that sparked her journey to becoming one of the most famous psychics in Australia.

The tea-leaf reader

'The hairs stood up on the back of my neck.'

Helen Sanderson, 53, is a marketing executive from Sydney. In a rich and professional voice, tempered by warmth and a ready laugh, the accomplished career woman shares her tale about what happened in August 2012, when she decided to add a mystic twist to a high-tea party she was hosting at her home:

> My mother passed away at the beginning of March 2012. In her last few years we enjoyed a very close relationship. Throughout her life, she'd always had a sixth sense, she had premonitions about things, and her mother did, too. I think I've also got a little bit of that going on.
>
> My father died three years before my mother did so we moved her to Sydney and I spent a lot of time with her. I had said to her, 'Mum, if there's anything there when you go, you will come back and let me know, won't you?' and she said, 'Of course I will!'
>
> Five months after Mum died, it was my sister's birthday and she wanted to have a bunch of girlfriends over for afternoon tea at my house. I suggested booking a tea-leaf reader to make things a bit more interesting. I rang a few different friends and

one put me in touch with a woman called Sarah. We agreed on a price and that was it.

When Sarah arrived, she got there about fifteen minutes before we'd agreed and I was still rushing around getting the house ready and dressing myself, as you do. I showed her the spare bedroom I'd set up for her to do the tea-leaf reading and I walked back into my bedroom to put my shoes on. But then Sarah was standing at my bedroom door, there was something she wanted to say to me. I told her to come in and she said, 'Oh Helen, there are two old ladies here who want to speak to you.'

I shivered all over, the hairs stood up on the back of my neck! I said, 'What?' and she said, 'There are two old ladies here that want to talk to you. One's very excited and the other one's just standing back very patiently.' I knew immediately that the one standing back patiently was my mother, who never pushed herself forward, unlike me.

Sarah said, 'Let me talk to the lady who's very bubbly.' Then she asked me, 'Who's Barbara?' and I just looked at her and said, 'Barbara used to live here. She was in her early 70s when she was killed in a car accident.'

She said, 'Barbara's thrilled with what you've done to the house' – I'd renovated it all – 'she just loves that you both love orange.' Sarah laughed and said, 'Does she mean Orange in the [New South Wales] country?' I said, 'No, no, it's the colour. When I bought the apartment it had orange carpet and orange flock wallpaper and my favourite colour is orange.' It was just extraordinary!

Then Sarah said to me, 'Well, who's Lal?' and I just burst into tears because Lal was my mother's nickname, and no one knows that. Her brother gave her that nickname when he was very little and couldn't pronounce her name properly. I just burst into tears and she said, 'It's your mum, she wants you to know that you did the right thing putting her in the nursing home just before she died. She doesn't want you to worry about it anymore, you did the right thing given the condition she was in.'

My mother had been in hospital, and then they wouldn't keep her any longer but she couldn't go back to where she was living because she was so unwell, so I had to put her in a nursing home, which broke my heart. She died four days later and I've felt dreadful about that ever since. And that was the first thing Sarah said about my mother and no one, honest to God, no one would know that.

The second thing she said is, 'She wants to know if you found the watch?'

Well, I had given my parents matching watches, and when my father died we gave his to my sister but Mum still wore hers, until she lost it, because she used to misplace things all the time and I was exceptionally annoyed with her. I used to say, 'Mum, how could you?' and she'd say, 'I don't know, darling.' She lived in a retirement complex and things often got stolen, and I had made a big deal of it and when she died I finally found it. I said, 'Yes, I found the watch,' and laughed.

Sarah said, 'But did you find the wedding and engagement rings?' and I said, 'No, I didn't find those, they're gone.'

Then she said, 'She's very pleased with what you're doing in settling the estate and thinks you've done that very well and she also wants you to know' – and this was the cracker for me – 'that she and your dad are good friends again.' The last few years had been very difficult, my father had been chronically unwell, it had put a big strain on my mother and a big strain on their relationship, and so things hadn't been rosy between them. 'She wants you to know they're good friends again and everything's good.'

Sarah added, 'She wishes you were married but you're the organiser, you just organise everything, and everyone. She wishes you were married but understands you've had a very interesting life and you're busy.'

With that, the doorbell rang and the first guests arrived!

I had to say, 'I'm so sorry, I have to go,' and Sarah said, 'That's alright, obviously this is why I was meant to come here today.'

I was just in shock, you know, it was quite an amazing experience. You hear about these things and you think, 'Oh well, they've found it out online,' but no, these are the very things that were closest to my sense of loss for my mother, the private elements, how I wished it had been different for her at the end, and the fact that we had discussed that she would come back somehow and let me know.

I think this experience confirmed for me something I'd always known – that there was something else there. Even though it really shook me up, I also think it gave me some comfort, it made me feel that I'd be alright, that I'd be okay. Mum knew that I was very concerned about her relationship with my father, but the fact that she told me it was fine was quite remarkable.

It was an extraordinary set of circumstances. Some people go and seek that out, I had not sought that out, it happened accidentally. I told one of my friends who arrived soon after and she looked at me very sceptically, but I know it was real.

The long road to healing

'The gift is the life that they still have.'

'Mummy, Mummy, your life is in danger!' In a voice as pure as stars, Crystal, the little girl with the pigtails and the Cabbage Patch doll, threw her mother a lifeline that pierced the self-destructive shroud of drugs and alcohol she had drawn around herself. Eventually, Charmaine Wilson grabbed the lifeline, and began to haul herself out of oblivion, towards a new life of light and healing, guided by her baby's voice.

It was 1999 and being crowned Australia's most gifted psychic, via reality-TV show *The One*, was still almost a decade away for Charmaine, but hearing Crystal's voice thirteen years after her death proved the turning point in a long and harrowing spiritual awakening.

'I first started to wonder about the spirit world when I began to lose the people I loved,' says Charmaine, 48, who's documented her extraordinary life in the memoirs *Spirit Whispers* and *Spirit Children*. 'My journey with grief started when I was seventeen and my brother was killed in a motorcycle accident. Then four years later, my daughter was killed in a drunk-driving accident. Her father was the driver. She was four-and-a-half years old.'

Almost on the eve of Crystal's death, a prophetic dream signalled what, in retrospect, Charmaine believes was her first psychic experience. 'Two nights before she died, I had a dream that she was going to go missing and it was so real,' she recalls. 'I woke up and ran to her room and she wasn't there. I freaked out.'

There was a valid reason for Crystal's absence. She was with her father at his home in New South Wales; Charmaine lived in Brisbane and the couple, who'd split when their daughter was two, shared custody of her. But this knowledge did not diminish Charmaine's fears – fears which only swelled to monstrous proportions when Charmaine called Crystal the next night.

'She was frantic – "Mummy, I want you to come and get me now," she said. I was upset and said, "No, no, you're coming home next week." I was getting her the swing set she'd wanted and told her, "You've got a nice surprise when you come home." She never did come home, of course . . .'

Flayed by grief, Charmaine railed against a life without Crystal, empty of her tutus and sweetness and eyes of caramel. Only one thing helped her find acceptance: her dream.

'That dream made me understand that it was always going to happen, that she was meant to die on the 28th of June, 1986,' says Charmaine, whose story tumbles forth with her signature warmth, candour and sparks of irreverent humour. 'Because of this dream, I was able to visit Crystal's father in the hospital and say, "I forgive you for what's happened. It was meant to be." I was 22 and I didn't know what was to come, of course, but I knew that it was her time. It's what got me through.'

Yet self-discovery was still beyond reach. 'I was no different from any other parent that's lost a child, I didn't know I had a gift at that point. I wasn't looking for it. I think I had to get through life first.' Still, viewing Crystal's little body convinced Charmaine that the essence of Crystal had not died with her. 'She wasn't there, it was just a body. It was not my daughter, she was somewhere else.' For a time, Charmaine drew comfort from pretending Crystal was in Japan, but she soon turned to the spirit world for answers. 'I'd never really been interested in any of that stuff before Crystal died, before I had a reason to want to know where spirit was,' says Charmaine, who bought tarot cards and began to astound friends with the accuracy of her readings.

She had started on the path that would eventually lead to *The One*, to national tours and the grief retreats she runs for bereaved parents, but the journey was full of danger and detours. At her new partner's insistence – he didn't like anything 'witchy-poo' – she shelved the tarot cards, writing them off as a 'bit of fun' and plunged head-first instead into the darker world of drugs and alcohol abuse.

By the time of her father's death in February 1999, 'I was a full-blown speed addict,' says Charmaine, who lost custody of her two sons with her new partner that July. 'That was fair enough, I'd stuffed up. I had a nervous breakdown and that's when I started to hear voices. I thought, "Great, now I'm nuts! Yay, what else can go wrong?"' – she recalls this with a husky laugh – 'I never expected it to be the spirit world. The first voice I heard was my daughter's.'

The summer's day Crystal came back is tattooed onto Charmaine's heart, a private mirror of the ink she wears proudly on her body. 'I was in the hallway of my house. I was high, as usual, I'll be honest, and I just felt this coldness around me. I thought, "What the hell is that? Why is it so cold all of a sudden?" And then I heard it, crying, a child crying, and the words, "Mummy, Mummy, your life is in danger." It freaked me out.'

Charmaine concedes that if it weren't for the voices that soon joined Crystal's and the information they provided that could be validated time and again, it would be easy to write off these events as a drawn-out drug-induced episode, especially since it would take two years for her to heed Crystal's warning and clean up her act. In the interim, Charmaine says, 'I was having what could at worst be psychosis and at best be absolutely pure spirit communication. But where one ended and where the other started, I'll never be able to know for sure.'

By the time she turned her back on drugs for good in 2001 (on September 11), Charmaine was 'seeing spirits everywhere, I just didn't know what they were'. She put the visions, including the man she now identifies as her spirit guide, Peter, down to the drugs – 'So imagine my surprise when I finally gave up and these spirits are still bloody there!'

And they weren't planning to leave her side, as it soon became clear. They were also bossy. One day, the voice of her spirit guide said, 'Do you want a job?' and Charmaine, who was broke, replied that she did. 'He actually said, "Ring up the air force base, ask to be put through to the canteen and ask for Steve. He will give you a job and shortly afterwards, you will work for us."' With nothing to lose, Charmaine did as instructed, and was stunned when the manager of the canteen, Steve, asked how she knew there was a job going, when it had only become available 30 minutes earlier.

She started at the canteen, thinking that perhaps she was destined for a career in the military, but then her true calling intervened. Charmaine recounts: 'On the day I found out I was a medium, I was at the military police base, of all places, and they all identify themselves by their surnames. This fellow's name was O'Brien and a woman's voice said to me, "That's my son. His name's Ted." And I said, "G'day, Ted. How are you going?"'

Colour left the man's face like a wave receding. 'How do you know my name?' he asked and Charmaine answered, 'I just do,' all the while thinking 'how weird' this was. It would get weirder. She recalls the woman's voice said, 'He's born on the 14th of June; he's a Gemini, just like you, love,' so Charmaine told him that. Then the woman said, 'I'm his mother, I died of a heart attack.' Charmaine repeated her words and the man said, 'You can't know that,' then he turned and walked away.

The exchange with Ted was a revelation for Charmaine, but the true breakthrough arrived that evening. 'When I went home, I was still confused about it. I think there were seven voices in my head that day, seven different ones having conversations about me, while I was listening! *Big Brother* had nothing on me, I couldn't get away with a thing. All of a sudden, I heard this voice and it was so clear. I said, "You sound like my brother, Martin." And they all started to clap. They said, "*Finally*, you've got it."'

That night, the voices roused her from sleep. 'Wake up,' they said. 'Get out of bed and watch the television.' The American psychic-medium John Edward was on the screen. 'I'd seen him before but thought he was some type of scammer. They said, "Just watch him and don't judge him." And when I watched and I saw him giving validations to these people and I saw the relief in their eyes, I thought, "That's how I would have felt had I had that,"' says Charmaine, in a trembling voice. 'My guys said, "That is what you are, Charmaine, you are a medium." I said, "Can I do this to help people?" They said yes.'

Charmaine believes she made a choice that day. She could have gone on to be a life reader (also known as a future reader), giving people predictions, as opposed to a medium, where information arrives solely from communication with the dead. 'I chose to be a medium because a future reader can tell you anything and it can't be validated. But the validation is the most important thing. It's what leads to the road of healing.'

Since accepting her mediumship in 2002, this colourful, Harley-Davidson enthusiast, who once considered herself beyond redemption, has helped thousands of broken people spot a chink of light from the bottom of their well of grief. 'Once I started doing readings and found the amazing love that was coming through . . . Man, oh man!' says Charmaine, who takes joy in sharing some of the most powerful moments of validation she's facilitated.

During one platform event in Brisbane, she connected with the spirit of a little boy, Jack, who'd died in particularly tragic circumstances. Weeks later, and 1000 kilometres away, midway through a show in the New South Wales country town of Orange, Charmaine was speaking with a middle-aged man in the audience when little Jack showed up. 'I could see him so clearly! I said, "Hold on matey, this one is Jack." The poor man nearly fell off his freaking chair! I had absolutely no idea the family had relatives in Orange. Incredible stuff.'

Then there was this moment, which, Charmaine says, 'I will never forget for as long as I live.' And as she retells it, her reverence is as clear as her memory: 'I had a little fellow who was six when he passed away from cancer and his name was Elliott. To date, it was one of the most beautiful readings I've ever done. He gave me his name. It was as if that kid was sitting there solid and telling me stuff. But what was really incredible and what really clinched it for me, was at the end of the reading, he said, "Can you tell Mummy that she told me an angel was going to meet me at the gates of heaven?" I relayed that to her. She said, "Yes." He said, "You tell Mummy there was no angel." And I'm thinking, *Oh shit*. Then he said, "There was this old man. He had no teeth and he was wearing his jumper and he was in summer and his name was Rex. Tell Mummy that's who met me." She burst into tears. It ended up being her husband's grandfather who always wore a jumper, whether it was summer or winter. He had absolutely no teeth and his name was Rex.'

Signs from spirit are a gift of love, says Charmaine, who is passionate about helping bereaved parents. 'It's love saying, "I'm going to get back there and show my mother something," and that gives people hope, faith and belief again. That's what they need – and they need to be able to learn to love again.'

While the bond between spirit child and parent is, Charmaine believes, 'incredibly, incredibly, incredibly strong', grief can block the opportunity to receive an all-important sign. 'We grieve because we love, and that love's been lost. When you see your child in a coffin, it's the worst thing you can ever see in your life. In the early days after Crystal, I pushed away all the signs because I was in so much pain.

'So I can't even imagine what it would be like for a little soul on the other side seeing their parents in so much grief and pain. In these cases, if the kids feel they can go through a gifted medium to give them a little closure, they will do whatever it takes.

'There are far too many mothers who cry themselves to sleep every night. There are far too many fathers who close into a little ball and never talk about their child again. And that's not what it's about. It's about life and embracing all life has to give, whether it's good or bad. Spirit children know this – they want their parents to keep living again and that's why they want so much to come through. They don't want to see their parents stop living and loving simply because their own lives stopped.'

It's a refreshing perspective – that there's much to gain on both sides of the divide by recognising and accepting messages from spirit. As part of her 'Living with Spirit' workshops, which she launched in 2003 and runs twice a year in Brisbane,

Charmaine teaches bereaved people how to keep their hearts and minds open to 'the language of spirit' – signs their loved ones are reaching out. 'The first thing you have to do is learn to stay in the moment,' she advises. 'You can't always be in the moment of [their] death and you can't always be in the moment of the future. You have to learn to be present and notice things around you.'

Subtle signs may include numbers, letters, songs, animals, features of the natural world, and other people. 'It could be seeing that person from a distance who just for a second reminds you of them, or that person who turns around at the supermarket and just happens to say the same thing your old man used to say,' says Charmaine, who's lived through her fair share of losses. In 2006, her mum died, and two years later, shortly after her triumph on *The One*, a dear friend committed suicide.

As participants in her workshops appreciate, Charmaine has learnt (the hard way) how to grasp precious offerings of hope from her late loved ones. To give an example, 'Mum lived in Stanthorpe in Queensland. She was born in 1943 and always used 43 as her passcodes. I was having a bit of a down day about her, missing her, feeling sorry for myself, and a bus went past. It had an ad on it that said "Visit Stanthorpe" and the number plate was 043. Now, if I had ignored that bus, I would never have seen that hello from Mum. If I hadn't come out of that moment of gloom and into the present moment, I would have missed it.'

Whether they reach out spontaneously or during one of her readings, Charmaine believes every moment of communication from our spirit loved ones shares the same underlying truth. 'The main message is they just want their people who are left behind to keep on living. They want you to keep having a good time so they can vicariously go, "Yay, we're going on a cruise, dudes!" That's how I see it,' says this most down-to-earth of psychic-mediums. 'The gift is not what I have, as such, the gift is the life that they still have, you know? The spirits want the mediums to say, "Look, we're okay. Now we want you to be okay. Enjoy the gift of life you still have."'

*

I used to love watching the TV-series *Medium*, with Patricia Arquette playing real-life US psychic Allison DuBois. Then my husband began seeing full-figured apparitions in our little 1920s bungalow and the show lost some of its escapist appeal! That unexpected turn of events led to my first book, *Spirit Sisters*, part of which explored how people find out they are psychic-mediums – what awakens the gift? I learned that for some grief is a trigger, for others it could be pregnancy and childbirth or, as happened in my home, sometimes meditation is the key.

People who are mediums are said to shine, as if spotlit, to a spirit intent on sending a message to a loved one left behind – like the child who homed in on my elderly caller at the beginning of this chapter, or the little one who orchestrated the 'accidentally on purpose' meeting between Mitchell and the bereaved mother in the shopping centre. Then there's Helen, who'll never forget the 'tea-leaf reader' she booked for some light entertainment at her stylish drinks party. 'Obviously, this is why I was meant to come here today,' the psychic told the gobsmacked host.

Yet, as the professionals I've interviewed in this chapter told me, we don't have to be mediums to learn the language of the spirit world. It may be relatively rare to see the form of the one we've loved and lost (though it's certainly possible, as stories throughout this book demonstrate), but picking up on the clues and tokens of love they leave for us, like the tenderest treasure hunt, is something we can all learn to do. You'll be surprised, they promise, by what comes in once you start opening your heart. These cosmic love letters, from the sweet and subtle to spectacular show-stoppers, are all in the service of our healing, to help us embrace life again. 'They just want their people who are left behind to keep on living,' as Charmaine Wilson so succinctly put it.

To hear their plea, Mitchell Coombes says, 'Always listen to that still, small voice within.' He adds, 'I always like to quote the famous clairaudient medium Doris Stokes who once said, "You can't die for the life of you."'

Conclusion

∽

The path winds, and I follow

*'Somewhere, all the people we have loved and lost are still
among us, in the house that we call history.'*
—Graham Masterton

*O*ne night when I was eight years old, I saw a man in military
regalia standing in my bedroom doorway. In the dim light of
the hallway of our apartment in Sydney's Eastlakes, I could see his
medals gleaming and the broad bulk of his silhouette.

Those opening lines of my first book, *Spirit Sisters*, recalled a
moment that still ignites a spark inside me. My memories of
seeing the ghostly figure of 'the Colonel', as I came to call him,
are enmeshed with every recollection I have of growing up in
the 1970s; of *The Amityville Horror*, *Jaws* and *Puberty Blues*, of
illicit séances, *The Magic Faraway Tree* and my mother's own

enchanting stories about the faraway land of my birth. If I shut my eyes, I see the Colonel again, and am instantly transported to those vanished days when my fascination for the world of ghosts and spirits first took flight. All these years later, that fascination is intact, but now I believe some answers, long sought, are in my grasp.

They began to manifest, a ghost of an idea growing dense before my eyes, on the threshold of autumn 2013, one weekday beneath a skim-milk sky. Approaching the building where I work, I suddenly knew the ultimate destination of the road I've travelled since the Colonel, and the purpose of my enduring obsession with all he represented. It wasn't a thought I'd plucked from the air, so alive with the chill of the nascent season and the tang of urban rain; rather, it was as if it had been delivered to my mind like a precisely timed gift. Lessons, I realised, are being revealed to me slowly, layers being peeled back until the truth stands stark.

I stopped walking but my thoughts rushed on, alighting on the evolutionary nature of my lifelong passion. This book you're holding, this testament to the belief that love never dies, is where I was always supposed to arrive. It was meant to be.

Now, at the entrance to my office, I looked back into a past in which I stared, transfixed, at another threshold – the doorway to my childhood bedroom – trying to make sense of my midnight visitor. Today, from my vantage point atop the ladder of years, I see how aptly the mysterious Colonel encompasses the road I took after seeing him. Was this shadow figure inviting me to follow him through the door into a realm of mysteries it would take almost four decades to unravel? Did his opaque outline conceal the promise of substance behind the thrills?

For my early fascination with ghosts *was* very two-dimensional, it didn't delve into the deeper reasons for why a spirit might appear to a person still on this plane – in many cases, I now know, the answer is love.

My childhood hunger for spooky stories, my addiction to the visceral thrill of goosebumps sprouting, of my body alerting me to the possibility of extraordinary events, has matured into an understanding of what those stories signify, of what's *really* worth getting excited about. The ghost stories that enthralled me in childhood represented the first step on my path towards arriving at an understanding of a better way to live life.

Ultimately, that understanding is thanks to the people who shared their transformative experiences with me for this book. Across café tables or in long conversations over the phone with interviewees all over the country, stories of love surviving death found a home in me. Each had something to teach me, something for me to offer you today. Mary-Lou Stephens told me about how her father helped her kick a drug habit and turn her life around. Later, when she had to face the dismal reality of her mum's terminal cancer, it was only by acknowledging that death needn't mean the end *of* her mother, that she found some release from her mountainous grief.

'She'd always wanted to see the spring wildflowers in Western Australia. It was a dream of hers to see the colours and beauty of nature that she'd seen on television and in magazines, spread out around her in reality,' said Mary-Lou. 'Once the prognosis came through, I knew that she would never see that dream come true. Then I realised, who's to say she won't?

'Who's to say that she won't be a part of those very wildflowers? Who's to say she won't be in the warmth that causes them to blossom? Who's to say she won't be in the breeze that blows over them, the rain that falls on them, the very soil that nurtures them?'

I nodded at her lovely musing, which evoked the words of Victorian-era writer Vita Sackville-West: 'We are the day, the night, the light, the dark, the water drop, the stream, the meadow, the lark.' Yes, who's to say?

Accepting the possibility that her mother would go on, albeit in a different form, in a realm beyond the frames of our reality, proved the turning point for Mary-Lou in how she coped. The resolution she reached reminded me of when I was eight years old and troubled endlessly by a fact I'd learned: the sun would one day obliterate the earth, and there was nothing to be done for it. The idea of life after death delivered me from fear and worry. It offered hope.

For those who shared their stories in this book, their experiences changed everything; they don't just entertain a vague, tender wish that their loved one's spirit survives – for them it is a certainty.

'There is a lot more to life than what we can see and what is here,' as Ban Guo told me.

'He didn't want to leave me and he knows how hard it is for me now,' reflects Jenny Gersekowski, whose husband of 33 years died in 2008. 'Love never really dies, because I've still got that love for him and he's still got that love for me, no matter where he is.'

I felt so privileged to listen to these myriad experiences of reconnection and reunion. For hours they'd talk, so many different voices, each a tale within themselves – some crackling a history of cigarettes and red brick, some soft-edged, others raucous, and everything in between – all content to keep honouring and remembering their precious people with stories:

memorials built of words and hewn with love, not cold stone or marble.

Their voices were my companions over the past couple of years, murmuring to me in darkness when the sky wept all night long and my dreams overflowed with absent loved ones, only a few my own. They were with me as I rode the creaky old bus to the station, with me as a shower of golden leaves fell on a boy like a benediction as the bus pulled into his stop, with me as I thought how in parenthood, our hearts stretch to take in other children too. When the train crossed the Georges River on its way into the city, and a blast of heavenly blue – water and sky – filled my eyes, they were with me, too.

The working day would hush them, but later, walking the dog as the sun dipped over my leafy neighbourhood, they'd return. Watching fingers of cloud reach towards the waning light, I'd hear them again and consider anew the wisdom nestled inside each yarn spun of sorrow and joy and lessons hard learnt.

My dog, Remy, trotting beside me, my feet carrying me homeward along a meandering route, I realised the path winds, and I follow. The night I saw the Colonel was the beginning of a journey that brings me here today, writing the closing words of this book. And I travelled here on the wings of stories.

In *Love Never Dies*, those stories share one beating heart – tidings of transcendent love – but each of my interviewees travelled very different roads, often lonely and tearful, before reaching sanctuary, a place to rest, reflect and, finally, embrace the message. Many tell of newfound acceptance, of seeing, at last, that here is where they, too, are meant to be. After wading through bottomless and viscous despair, they've risen years later, lighter and gifted with a fresh perspective.

'None of this would ever have happened if Gary had never left me,' sums up Deb Carr. Though her brother's suicide almost destroyed her, she now accepts that all is as it should be in her world.

'I wouldn't change a thing,' concurs Marcus Lang, whose brother's death over 30 years ago also sent him on a remarkable spiritual odyssey. 'I've learned to appreciate so much that I didn't before. Being humbled was the greatest thing that happened to me.'

'I have no fear of death, I anticipate a transition or a transformation into something more than I am now,' added Rob Smith. 'It helps me live my life in a different way now, in that I live more openly and more courageously and less fearfully than I did before.'

In many respects, their conclusions echo the tranquil words of Julian of Norwich, the medieval Christian mystic who famously wrote of insights revealed to her on her deathbed: 'All shall be well, and all shall be well, and all manner of thing shall be well.'

Denise Mack understood this after her near-death experience, as she told me in Chapter Six. 'I feel that all humans have a purpose,' she said. 'And this purpose is to evolve through service and love. Whatever else we achieve in life, evolution through service and love is paramount.'

Of the millions of people who've experienced a near-death experience, most describe being swept up in emotions of indescribable joy, love and peace in a place so exquisite they comprehend for the first time the meaning of home. They don't want to return. Writing this book, I learned a new word and promptly pinned it up on the wall near my desk, since it so aptly defines a feeling I've long wrestled with, but put down to the melancholy of bearing the immigrant's curse – a heart in two places: 'Hiraeth' is a Welsh word meaning 'a homesickness for a home to which you cannot return, a home which maybe never was; the nostalgia, the yearning, the grief for the lost places of your past'.

Now I wonder if there isn't a little flame of Hiraeth inside us all? A yearning for that other home where there is no pain, fear or melancholy, only love? Is this the place where our beloved spirits dwell?

'There's no doubt in my mind that our loved ones survive death,' said Cathleen Ross, who told in Chapter Nine of helping Jess Tarn connect with her little brother.

Another medium, Charmaine Wilson, agrees: 'Love survives all,' she says. 'Love's what it's all about.'

Adds Mitchell Coombes, 'I know with absolute certainty that love, like life, can never really die. There is no death . . . death is an illusion. Our departed loved ones live on, not only in our hearts and minds, but also in the spirit world.'

As he and other mediums I spoke to never tire of pointing out, we can create a life bright with love and happiness right here, too. We can tame Hiraeth by building lives that brim with kindness, caring and love – it's what our late loved ones want for us. Shakespeare said 'All the world's a stage' and Charmaine Wilson sees it that way, too, though she adds that our spirit loved ones are our 'production crew', waiting in the wings, supporting us through every act. 'They are the makeup artists, the light guys, the sound guys, the directors,' she says. 'Behind the scenes, they're all working to make us shine.'

To feel the warmth of the light they cast, we have only to open our hearts. We have nothing to fear from welcoming them in, and everything to gain, say the people who've shared their stories with me. To Shayne Wallace, who described feeling her son's protection during a moment of danger in Chapter Eight, knowing that her boy 'is happy, he is healthy, he is *here*' is a fact as inarguable as her own name or her fierce love for her family. Yet, for Shayne and so many others I spoke to, the road towards this resolution was stalled by detours into pain, denial and self-doubt. 'Now, I am sharing my experiences in the hope that others will not have to go the long way around, like I did,' says Shayne. 'So that others will be able to move forward with hope.'

In sharing these accounts, that's my wish for my readers, too, but it's not the only one. Ablaze with the promise of love beyond death, these stories are potent harbingers of hope, yes, but each also carries a lesson about the way we *live* today. 'Do not keep the alabaster boxes of your love and tenderness sealed up until your friends are dead,' said the nineteenth-century clergyman and social reformer, Henry Ward Beecher. 'Fill their lives with sweetness. Speak approving, cheering words while their ears can hear them and while their hearts can be thrilled by them.'

Fugaz como la dicha
Te encuentro algunas noches
En tus cálidas manos
El paisaje de ayer
Tus ojos alumbrando
Cuan la luz de la luna
Las penumbras que inundan
Mi sendero apagado

Fleeting as joy
I find you some nights
Within the warmth of your hands
The landscape of yesterday
Your eyes illuminating
Like the light of the moon
The shadows crowding
My darkened path

—SILVIA MACHADO

Bibliography

Barbato M, *Reflections of a Setting Sun: Healing Experiences Around Death*, Copyright 2009 Michael Barbato.

Barrett W, *Deathbed Visions: How the Dead Talk to the Dying*, White Crow Books, USA and UK, 2011.

Bresciani, E, *The Raw Scent of Vanilla: A Memoir*, Australia, Macmillan, Australia, 2000.

Cobbe F, *The Peak in Darien*, George H. Ellis, USA, 1882.

Coombes M, *Sensing Psychic*, Simon & Schuster, Australia, 2012.

Coombes M, *Sensing Spirit*, Simon & Schuster, Australia, 2010.

Eaton B, *Afterlife: Uncovering the Secrets of Life After Death*, Inspired Living, Australia, 2011.

Guggenheim B and Guggenheim J, *Hello From Heaven!*, Bantam Books, USA and Canada, 1997.

Heneghan D, *Closer Than You Think: The Easy Guide to Connecting with Loved Ones on the Other Side*, Hampton Roads Publishing, Inc., Virginia, 2012.

Hopcke RH, *There Are No Accidents: Synchronicity and the Stories of Our Lives*, Macmillan General Books, Great Britain, 1997.

Jung CG, *Memories, Dreams, Reflections*, Fontana Press, UK, 1995.

Kessler D, *Visions, Trips and Crowded Rooms: Who and What You See Before You Die*, Hay House Inc., USA, 2010.

Kübler-Ross E, *On Life After Death*, Celestial Arts, USA, 1991.

Kübler-Ross E and Kessler D, *On Grief and Grieving: Finding the Meaning of Grief Through the Five Stages of Loss*, Scribner, USA, 2005.

LaGrand LE, *After-Death Communication: Final Farewells*, Llewellyn Publications, USA, 1997.

LaGrand LE, *Love Lives On: Learning from the Extraordinary Encounters of the Bereaved*, Berkley Publishing, USA, 2006.

Lawson L, *Visitations from the Afterlife: True Stories of Love and Healing*, HarperSanFrancisco, USA, 2000.

Lundahl CR and Widdison HA, *The Eternal Journey: How Near-Death Experiences Illuminate Our Earthly Lives*, Warner Books, USA, 1997.

Moody Jr R and Arcangel D, *Life After Loss: Conquering Grief and Finding Hope*, HarperCollins, USA, 2001.

Moody Jr RA with Perry P, *Glimpses of Eternity: An Investigation into Shared Death Experiences*, Rider, USA, 2010.

Moody Jr RA, *The Light Beyond: New Explorations by the author of Life after Life*, Bantam Books, USA and Canada, 1988.

Morse M with Perry P, *Parting Visions: Uses and Meanings of Pre-Death, Psychic, and Spiritual Experiences*, Villard Books, USA and Canada, 1994.

Shelby Spong J, *Eternal Life: A New Vision*, Fourth Estate, USA, 2009.

Thomas D, 'And Death Shall Have No Dominion', from *Twenty-Five Poems*, JM Dent and Sons, 1936.

Walker G, *Messages From Spirit: Breathtaking Insights Into Life and the Afterlife*, Inspired Living, Australia, 2013.

Ware B, *The Top Five Regrets of the Dying: A Life Transformed by the Dearly Departing*, Hay House, UK, 2011.

Wilson C, *Spirit Children*, Fontaine Press, Australia, 2009.

Acknowledgments

Once again, thanks first and foremost to all of my wonderful interviewees, whose gift of stories I treasure. I'm in awe of your strength and courage. I often felt like I had a dedicated team of your loved ones on the other side helping to make this happen, so a round of applause to them too! Special shout-out to Charmaine Wilson, who not only shared her life experiences with me but found time in her busy schedule to put me in touch with friends and clients including Vikki, Jenny, Kathy, Margaret and Deb, who in turn shared their inspirational stories.

Thanks, as ever, to my husband Anibal and our children Jasmin and Tabaré. I'll love you forever and beyond. To my mum, wordsmith extraordinaire Silvia, who generously shared her memories of Uruguay with me for this book: thank you, love you. To my sister and fellow author, Natalie, it's always a joy to share dreams, ideas (and bubbles!) with you. To my lovely 'spirit sisters' (you know who you are), the rest of my beautiful family – near and far – and all my wonderful friends, thanks for being there and caring. To *WHO* editor,

Nicky Briger, and all of my *WHO* family, I value your ongoing enthusiasm and support.

Bravo to the ever gracious Allison Langton, who designed and looks after my website, and to transcriber extraordinaire Carolyn Reynolds, who turned interviews around quickly and perfectly, all the way from South Africa – couldn't have done it without you! Thanks to Fraser, who helped out too. Heartfelt thanks to my agent, Selwa Anthony – am always uplifted after a chat with you. Special thanks to my publisher, Ingrid Ohlsson, for believing in this book – your clear and unwavering vision led the way. To editors Vanessa Pellatt and Emma Rafferty, and copy editor Susin Chow, I so appreciate your insights and guidance; huge thanks to Debra Billson, who designed the beautiful cover, and to Charlotte Ree and everyone in publicity, as well as the rest of the hardworking team at Pan Macmillan, I'm so grateful for all your efforts.

A big thank you to all the passionate booksellers out there, and lastly, to my readers: thank you so very much for spending time with me via the pages of my books. I'm privileged to tell you a story.

My mum and her cousin, Roberto,
c. early 1950s